Where to Take the Kids

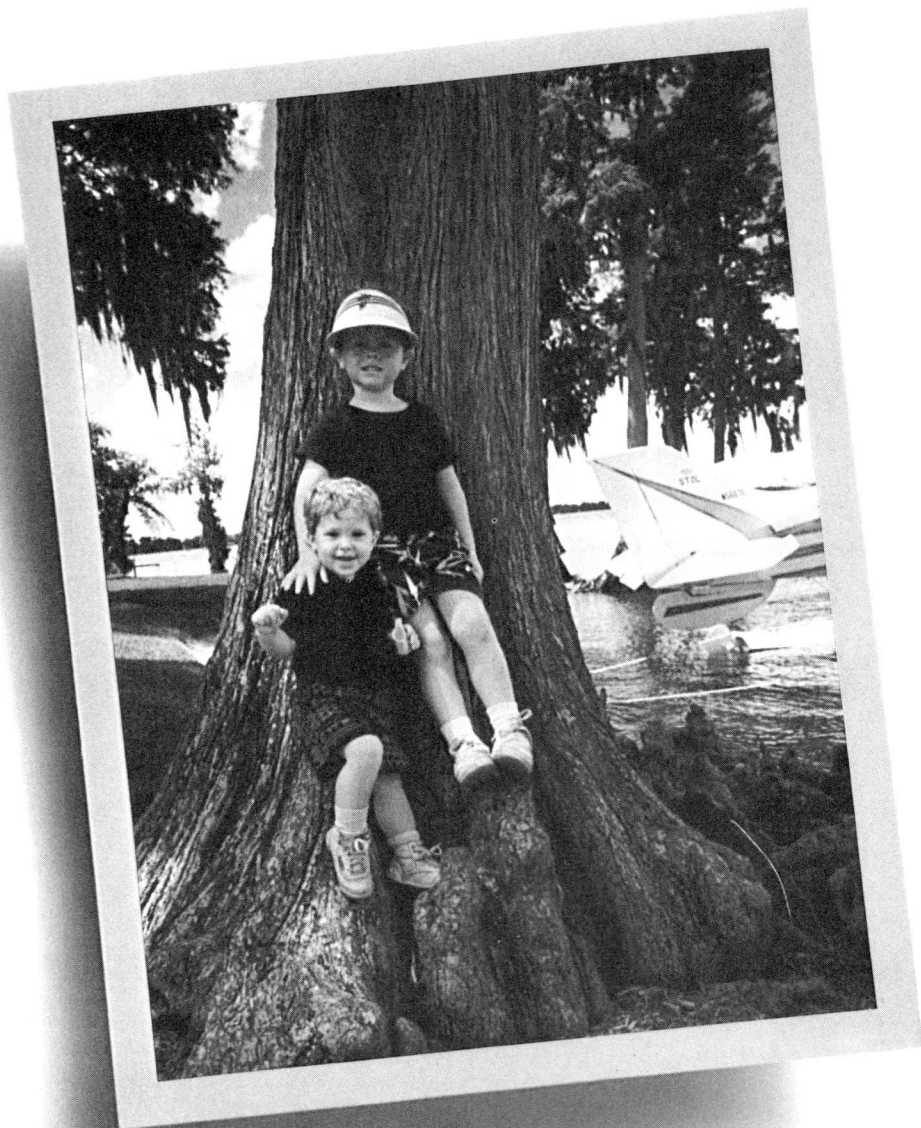

Jonathan and
Benjamin Clemmons
explore a bald cypress
at Cypress Gardens.

Where to Take the Kids

The parents' field guide to 500 Florida adventures

by LUANNE NAPOLI and contributors

Edited by POLLY SMITH

A publication of The Orlando Sentinel
Sentinel Communications Company
Orlando/1989

Copyright © 1989
Sentinel Communications Company
633 N. Orange Avenue, Orlando, Florida 32801

Edited by Polly Smith
Designed by Katie Pelisek

*Cover photo of Brittany Nicole Rinehart
on Cocoa Beach*

Printed in the United States by R.R. Donnelley

First Edition 1989

Library of Congress Cataloging-in-Publication Data

Napoli, Luanne, 1957 -
    Where to take the kids.

    Includes index.
    l. Florida — Description and travel —
1981- — Guide-books. 2. Family recreation —
Florida — Guide-books. I. Title.
F309.3.N37 1989 917.59'0463
ISBN 0-941263-06-1

About the Author

• • • • • • • • • • •

Luanne Napoli is an experienced writer, editor and an adventurous traveler. A graduate of the University of Wisconsin, she was a copy editor at the *Hartford Courant* and a magazine editor in Cairo before moving to Orlando two years ago. She explored the sights and countryside of Central Florida with her husband James, college students Jimmy and Christina, and a steady stream of houseguests.

Dedication

• • • • • • • •

For Jim, Nat, Bob, Jimmy, Christina, Jenifer and Kenton, fellow adventurers of the first order.

Acknowledgements

· · · · · · · · · · · ·

Many people deserve applause for their efforts toward making *Where to Take the Kids* a reality. First to Jim Napoli for inspiration, revelation and perspiration. Heaps of thanks to Polly Smith for her attentive, energetic editing. Also to Bethany Mott for patient handling of the author and all technical matters, and to Katie Pelisek for her designing eye. Thanks to Lynn Phillips and Michael for their time and special hints.

And thanks to Ed Malles, Joe Niekro and Tom Izor for their help on photos. The biggest round of thanks goes to the kids pictured in the book, their parents and those who helped the author with their opinions and suggestions. Their participation and cooperation in the project made it possible and fun along the way. Happy trails to them in years to come.

The Contributors

· · · · · · · · · ·

The following writers contributed articles from around the state: Bridget Balthrop-Morton, Jeff Babineau, Maya Bell, Max Branyon, Elena Mullar Garcia, Cheri Henderson, John Hicks, Brenda J. Lawrence, Ken Paskman, Denise Salvaggio, Edward Schmidt Jr., Gwen Stevenson, Nancy Taylor, Jan Walker and Russ White.

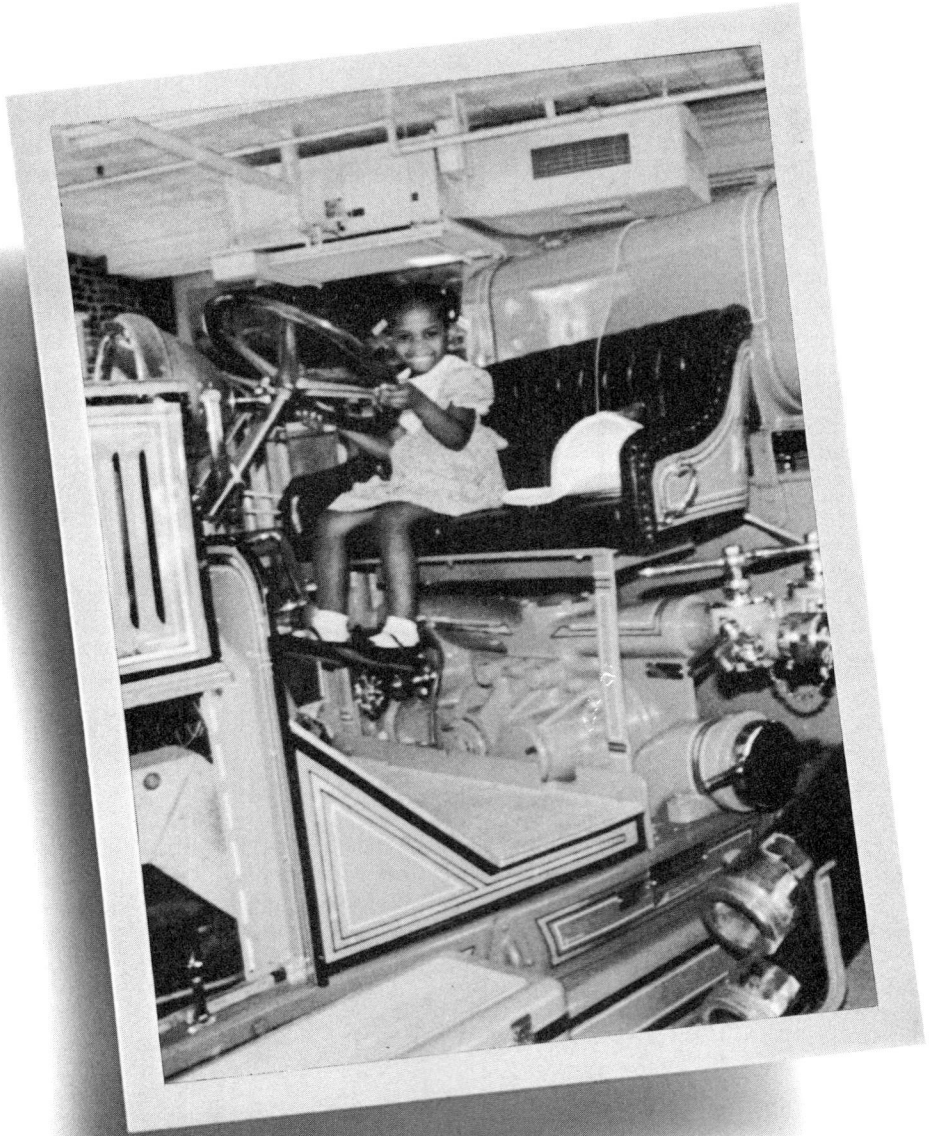

Firefighter Shayla
Scott at Fire Station
No.3

Contents

• • • • • • •

Contents

· · · · · · ·

The Photographs

· · · · · · · · · · · ·

Our thanks to all the children whose photographs helped make this book possible.

Brett Adams
Larry Adderly
Crystal Bandekow
Alisha Hannah Bates
Bryan and Lisa Beckner
Jessica Bell
Helena Belmonte
Christopher Blexrud
Sara Bogart
Nicole and Michelle Bolt
Dylan Brents
Michaile and Ryan Briggs
Daniel Caligiuri
Anna Metisse Carapellotti
Clint Carney
Shree Chauhan
Daniel Chavaroli III
Benjamin and Jonathan Clemmons
Chance Taylor Corbeil
Jaime Cousin
Brett Crager
Justin Lee Daughtry
Laura D'Allessio
Alexa and Jenny DeJean
Melissa Downing
Callie Rae Force
Terry Furbish
H. Cielo Gaitan
Laura Geier
Gianna Gibbs
Brant, Lindi, Keith and Craig Jaques
Anna Johnson
Jonathan Dean Johnston
Lindsay and Jennifer Kaiser
Beau Kelley
Emeri, Caleb and Jacob Keppeler
Takara Jacqleen Kershlis
Austin Hoover

Jennifer LaBrake
Adam Lineberry
Karen Nicole Llamas
Luis Marquez
Roger Martin
Shelby Martin
Kent Matthews
Karl Miller
John Moons
Lindsay Moore
Elijah Morse
Kevin and Cory Mulinare
Christopher Mullis
Jennifer and Laura Murchison
Kera Newkirk
Katrina and Brandon Nunes
Kathryn Jean Oberg
Amanda Perez
Jonathan Ezra Pittman
Shepherd and Hunter Pittman
Nicole Reinholt
Leigh Allison Rich
Brittany Nicole Rinehart
Moses Robinson
Heather and Luann Rundall
Christopher Douglas Scott
Shayla Shanese Scott
Michelle Short
Patrick Smith
Shonda Smith
Jan and Joe Spino
James William Thompson II
John Nathan Timmes
Jonathan Trapani
Lindsay, Benjamin and Callie Vinson
Tiffany Nicole and Lacey Desiree White
Christopher Williams

1

Jessica Bell at All
Children's
Playground, Turkey
Lake Park.

Introduction

· · · · · · · · ·

Where to Take the Kids is written so that parents can reach for a book instead of the panic button when their children are old enough to start exploring the outside world.

Florida is blessed with some of the state's finest natural and man-made wonders. The categories that follow were chosen as a representative sample of each, and the adventures emphasize fun and learning with an attempt to keep a child's perspective in mind. Many of the trips are well-known spots, but I hope there are some surprises, too.

The large attractions can be intimidating. The key is to remember that they were constructed to entertain, not strain, people of all ages. If parents enter the theme parks with a childlike curiosity, chances are a good time will be had by all.

Many beaches, parks, gardens, springs and zoos have play equipment and other facilities to help children explore nature and get some good kid-style exercise. The chapters covering these adventures will list what each has to offer in the way of programs, picnic grounds and recreation hardware.

The mention of museums and history may elicit a yawn from some youngsters (and many adults), but the state is rich with living history sites and "working" museums that can keep even the most skeptical kids interested. Concentrating on fun and activities at these sites can keep children busy and learning in spite of themselves. The chapter devoted to historical sites and museums will help families approach these adventures armed with information about special child-oriented features, events and programs.

Sometimes parents actually get to plan the family adventure calendar. For those lucky folks, the chapter on events will give them a place to start. Most events are scheduled far enough in advance that parents can put them in the family datebook under "Don't miss."

Many shops and restaurants like kids, too. On The Town lists some of these kid-friendly establishments for those times when nobody wants to stay home, or when grandma comes to visit.

The young athlete is not left out either. The chapter on sports includes entries on everything from sky diving to fishing.

Finally, though most of the adventures in this book were chosen with their convenience and closeness to Central Florida in mind, some in other parts of the state too good to miss were included. The back of the book, with road games and resources, will help fill the gaps of an adventure-filled day and amuse everybody on board. The list of resources includes books, bookstores, YMCAs, parent groups and other places that can help when you need a place to take the kids.

All admission prices and fees in the book are those that were available at the time of publication.

• • • • • • • • •

Chapter 1

COME ONE, COME ALL

Surviving the hassles of the world's No. 1 tourist attraction

Orlando area parents face the same dilemmas as all parents with one important difference — they are surrounded by some of the world's most famous theme parks. This is both good and bad news.

On the bright side, parents can always answer the question of "where to take the kids" with one of the parks. The variety and size of the parks can provide days of action for awestruck children. Some parks offer price breaks for Florida residents during certain times of the year. Moms and dads can have fun at the major attractions, too, and best of all, they are only a short drive from home.

But on the flip side, even a good day in one of the parks involves lots of walking, waiting in lines and crowds. Kids can run themselves ragged and still beg for one more ride on Space Mountain when their parents' feet, and patience, have given out.

None of these are life-threatening problems, however, and simple planning can eliminate some of the headaches.

1. Get to know tourist traffic patterns. Avoid major holidays, especially Thanksgiving, Christmas, New Year's, Easter, July Fourth and Labor Day. Worst tourist times: Just before Christmas through New Year's; February through Easter; and the hot summer peak, early June to mid-August. If

• Young Dan Chavaroli learns the official Mouse wave.

Tips

parents' blood pressures are low, they can take the kids any time, but if crowd avoidance is the goal, they should play it smart and stay out of the parks during these overloaded times.

2. Take advantage of lower rates for Florida residents (offered at various times of the year) and of multi-entry passes and family rates offered at some parks. That way you can save money on the ever-increasing gate prices and have more cash left over for souvenirs. Call the attractions in advance for special rates that may be offered during the time of your visit.

3. Call for exact hours of operation and prices before you go. The hours at the majors vary, sometimes day-to-day, but mostly season-to-season. Also, some attractions run late night special shows that might affect your touring plans. Entry fees at most parks are changed without notice.

4. Getting an early start is one point of theme park touring that cannot be stressed too strongly. If the ticket gates open at 9 a.m., plan to be there about an hour before that. Even on slow days, lines for tickets will get very long very early, and simply parking can be a chore.

5. Plan your day in the park by picking up all the maps and literature you can get your hands on in advance. Also, take full advantage of the information booths and staff provided by the attractions' management once you arrive. Kids will get exhausted enough during the day without a lot of backtracking to missed rides and shows.

Downing a hearty breakfast is always a good idea, but it is a must when you are planning to tour theme parks. There are plenty of watering holes and food stops at the parks, but most are expensive and eating can gobble up valuable touring time. With an early start, you will probably also want to beat the crowds by going to the busiest parts of the parks in the morning. Thus, any time spent chowing down means you'll pay for it by running into peak-hour crowds and longer waits. Food stops are best timed in the early afternoon when kids and parents need a break.

6. After you have done all your other planning, plan to have a good time and relax. Pace yourself and the kids, if possible. There is always a feeling in the parks that,"We've got to do it all or the kids won't have a good time." Not true. There is so much going on at the Central Florida attractions, nobody goes home feeling cheated. Just ask your kids.

Boardwalk and Baseball

Open daily from 9 a.m. to 10 p.m. Admission: around $20 for adults, and $15 for children less than 4 feet tall. Children age 2 and younger are admitted free.

Intersection of Interstate 4 and U.S. Highway 27, near Haines City.

(407) 648-5151 or (813) 424-2424

T he 135 acres of Boardwalk and Baseball combine two all-time great kid favorites: amusement park thrills and sports. The park is divided into three main areas — a midway, rides and a baseball stadium. All are connected by a beautiful mile-long boardwalk.

Dan Chavaroli gets in some batting practice at Boardwalk and Baseball.

Defying death at Boardwalk and Baseball, John Moons and friend.

The colorful midway features 20 games from ring toss and skee ball to the more high-tech pursuit of guessing the speed of your pitching or the goofy game of Whack-A-Mole. Most of the midway games are set up so that kids of all sizes can play them. As with any midway, monetary caution is advised. The price of tokens for games can push the cost of a day at the park beyond your planned budget.

The team of rides at Boardwalk and Baseball covers all the bases and then some. The tummy-tumbling Hurricane roller coaster is one of the largest in the South and the screams from its riders can be heard throughout the grounds. The 16-story Ferris wheel scores high with kids because they can see for miles when it stops at the top of its leisurely spin. The Grand Rapids log flume gets the title of MVP among rides, with a blend of slow cruising and splashy thrills along its half-mile run.

The bench of rides also includes a classic carrousel, bumper cars and spinning sensations like the Swiss Bob, the Monster and the popular Dizzy Dean.

The park distributes a list of height restrictions for all its rides. Guests more than 54 inches tall can ride them all and those less than 48 inches are allowed to ride some adult rides with a parent, and all the rides in Kiddie City.

The addition of Kiddie City to the park's activities

was a thoughtful one since it allows younger children to experience the terrific amusement park atmosphere of Boardwalk and Baseball on 12 rides just for them. Why shouldn't pint-sized people pilot their own dune buggy, airplane or spaceship? This is one of the park's big pluses for families.

The bat and ball midway games are only part of the baseball lineup. The Kansas City Royals began calling the park's 6,500-seat stadium home for spring training in 1988. And the Royals' Florida State League Class A team joins the other boys of summer on the six playing fields here, providing the genuine game for baseball fans who have finished touring the park. At other times, look for high school and college teams on the diamonds. Call the park for game times.

In the baseball-based games area adjacent to the stadium, the pitching alleys call balls and strikes and are calibrated for arms of all sizes. The alleys are a better bet for sports-hungry little athletes than the professional batting cages. These are for you, Mom and Dad. Your office softball team might

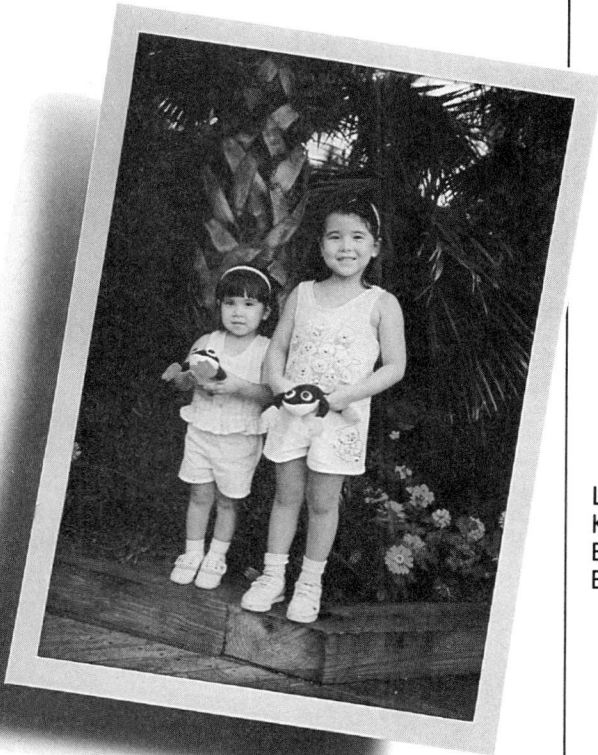

Lindsay and Jennifer Kaiser with frogs at Boardwalk and Baseball.

benefit if you practice your swings here. But younger children can step up to the plate in the softball or T-ball cages, which are designed for smaller folks. Helmets are required for all batters, and you'll probably be glad you have one as the 15 mechanically thrown pitches come zipping toward you.

Also appropriate for adults and older kids are the two fielding machines next to the batting cages. Many sports egos can get bruised as a machine records the time it takes a player to field a ball and throw it to first. Be sure to bring your "lucky glove" to the park to try this game of skill.

The park is filled with great souvenirs and naturally most are baseball oriented. Team jackets, T-shirts and hats are in plentiful supply and all come in children's sizes; but outfitting a team can be expensive. If you have a lot of little sluggers along on your trip, the best value in souvenirs is the park's Faceball Card. For $5, guests suit up in the uniform of their favorite team and get their picture on a baseball card. How could they top that? You guessed it. Visitors make up their own stats to complete the card. This is one souvenir kids will hang on to.

For a relaxing seventh inning stretch, try the IMAX film on the hidden secrets of the Grand Canyon, the half-hour film *The Eternal Game*, or the official National Baseball Hall of Fame museum exhibit, A Taste of Cooperstown. Younger children may get bored in the museum (though it is quite small) but parents might like a look at one of Babe Ruth's jerseys and the other artifacts from Cooperstown on display.

A good bet when you're ready for a taste of something else is the Grand Junction Station's Colorado Barbeque. Outdoor seating lets diners listen to the nearby country-western band as they chow down hickory-smoked ribs and chicken. Pizza, sandwiches and basic "park food" are found throughout the grounds, with full-service dining available at the Salerno Express. The restaurant's "dining car" overlooks the Grand Rapids Lagoon and is a relaxing spot around twilight. Kids can get ice cream at Barracini's Old Fashioned Ice Cream Shop or watch candy being made at Coffelt's Taffy & Fudge Company.

Recommended for age 3 and older.

Open 9:30 a.m. to 6 p.m. daily. Hours are extended in the summer and on holidays.

Admission for all is around $20. Children 2 and younger are admitted free. There is ample parking for a fee and a variety of foods from the exotic to homegrown American.

Florida seems to have everything in the way of adventures, including a taste of Africa at Busch Gardens, The Dark Continent. Young explorers can enjoy a safari into the sights and sounds of Africa mixed with some theme park classics during a visit here.

The park's seven sections cover 300 acres, with an overall theme of an African era gone by. More than 3,300 animals help make the park a wildlife showcase.

In Timbuktu, visitors enter an ancient trading center complete with craftsmen and a bazaar. From today's amusement high tech, they can sample the Phoenix boat swing ride, the Scorpion roller coaster, a carrousel, a Sandstorm thrill ride and a video arcade. To cool off during the journey, Timbuktu features the 1,200-seat Festhaus dining and entertainment complex.

Busch Gardens, The Dark Continent

Corner of Busch Boulevard and 40th Street, eight miles northeast of Tampa, two miles east of Interstate 275 and two miles west of Interstate 75.

(813) 977-6606

Nicole and Michelle Bolt get carried away at Busch Gardens.

Mystic sheiks and belly dancers haunt the streets of a walled city in Morocco. The colorful tilework and intricate architecture of the region give this section an authentic warmth. Three theatres (including the Moroccan Palace Theatre featuring the Kaleidoscope revue), craft demonstrations, restaurants, snake charmers and a big brass band complete the Moroccan canvas.

As in the real Dark Continent, the Serengeti Plain at Busch Gardens is the place to see animals. Nearly 500 head of African game can be viewed from the monorail, skyride, steam locomotive or the west promenade. Newcomers to the plain include Nile crocodiles, elephants and camels.

When your faithful guide has brought you back to civilization, the Nairobi Field Station is also a good spot to see animals. But don't expect to see the giants of Africa here, this refuge is just for

John Nathan Timmes among the pigs at Busch Gardens.

for babies. Infant animals from gazelles to chimps are on display at the station, with a petting zoo, elephant ride and the Nairobi Train Station nearby.

Over in the village of Stanleyville, a trained animal show and a cruise on the African Queen allow you to slow down the pace a bit; until the kids clamor to splash down the Stanley Falls log flume ride. The village also features a shopping bazaar and entertainment.

When everyone is ready for action, journey into The Congo for a white water raft trip, and the

1,200-foot spiraling Python ride. The Swinging Vines will feed any child's Tarzan fantasies while an exhibit of rare white Bengal tigers on Claw Island will fascinate all Africa fans. Also, a visit to Bird Gardens, with its 2,000 exotic feathered friends, is a must for animal lovers.

Each of the themed sections has live shows. Other entertainment includes The Wild Experience, a multimedia presentation in the Tangiers Theater, and a show at the Veldt Theater spotlighting the animals of Busch Gardens and their habitats. Equipment in the kid-size activity park, Dwarf Village, is off-limits to anyone more than 56 inches tall. (But parents are allowed to watch.)

Kids won't get to sample the product, but Anheuser-Busch Brewery offers a tour for visitors that shows how beer is made, including a peek inside an aging tank used during the fermenting process. The self-guided tour ends in the Bird Gardens near the Hospitality House.

Recommended for all ages.

Nearby Busch Gardens

Busch Travel Park: A campground is located just across from the theme park with campsites for recreational vehicles and tents. Camping is around $15 per night for RVs and a tent site is less than $10, including tax.

Adventure Island: For a separate entrance fee, visitors may cool off in a wide variety of thrill rides in this water-themed park just down the street from the gardens. Tube and flume rides are in a pleasant setting with many shade trees and grass for lounging and picnicking.

Church Street Station

129 Church St., Orlando.

(407) 422-2434

The nighttime charge to the complex is around $15 for adults and $9 for children ages 4-12, but there is no charge before 5 p.m. to the retail shops and eateries, which are open from 11 a.m. to 11 p.m. daily.

More for grownups at night, but during the day the cool marble walkways of this downtown Orlando attraction are a lively place to shop for real Wild West gear at the Buffalo Trading Company, look at "Old Duke," an antique train, and stop for a cool one at Le Chocolat Mousse ice cream parlour.

Dylan Brents at Church Street Station.

For more substantial fare, the Cheyenne Restaurant, Apple Annie's Courtyard, Lili Marlene's Aviator's Pub and Restaurant and the Morning Glory Bakery are open during the day. There is ample seating wherever you're eating, and restrooms off the main entrance. A variety of gift items are available at the Bumby Emporium and Apple Annie's Gift Shop.

New to the Church Street complex is The Exchange shopping area, which provides more shops and stops during a day here. There are some terrific stores for kids in this three-story enclosed complex. And, best of all, the third floor is a giant game room.

The first two floors wind easily around a center fountain, with shops and open or glass kiosks arranged to enhance the feel of an old-fashioned market. (Some visitors say that the tile floors, though beautiful, make The Exchange a little noisy for them.) The brass, glass and authentic antique interior and festive atmosphere are especially good for Christmas shopping, since kids can take a break on the third floor while parents slip into Santa & Company, the Exchange's Christmas shop, to pick out secret holiday goodies.

Stores that children will enjoy include: The Sport Shop, Mrs. Field's Cookies; Cards 'n Stuff, Sam Goody Records, Taxi, All Dolled Up, and The Fudgery. There are additional food outlets on the second level.

Recommended for age 5 and older.

Open daily from 9 a.m. to 7 p.m. with extended hours during peak season. Admission: adults, around $17, children 3 to 11, around $12. Children under 3 are admitted free.

Free parking. Wheelchairs, strollers, pedicoaches, lockers and kennels are available for a nominal charge. There is a picnic pavilion for large groups and restaurants and snack shops are scattered around the grounds.

Cypress Gardens

Forty-five minutes southwest of Sea World, off U.S. Highway 27 near Winter Haven.

(813) 324-2111, toll free in Florida 1-800-282-2123

Florida's history lives even in its theme parks, with Cypress Gardens being a prime example. This 223-acre family park was started in 1936 by Dick Pope, who some say coined the phrase "Florida: The Tourist Attraction."

Kids might not appreciate this bit of historical trivia, but they will find plenty to do at Cypress Gardens.

Start your day with a walk around Southern Crossroads. Restaurants, souvenir shops and a games walk are located on this Southern-flavored town square. The games walk features roller bowler, baseball throwing and hitting, skee ball and ball toss, all classics for children. Near the games is an area of rides for smaller kids, including a car track, parachute ride and the up-and-down Delta Dip.

The games can add to the cost of your stay so exercise some caution in how long children "stay at the fair." The rides are free with admission so you may want to steer youngsters toward this area after a short stay on the games walk. The souvenir shops carry a wide variety of keepsakes and Cypress Gardens has created a special shop for kids, Tots, Toys & Threads. It is the best bet for children, with stuffed gators, child-size clothing and Southern belle dolls. Another good choice is the House of Names, with personalized items from Abby to Zeke.

While you're rolling through Southern Crossroads, be sure to see the nationally famed Cypress Junction

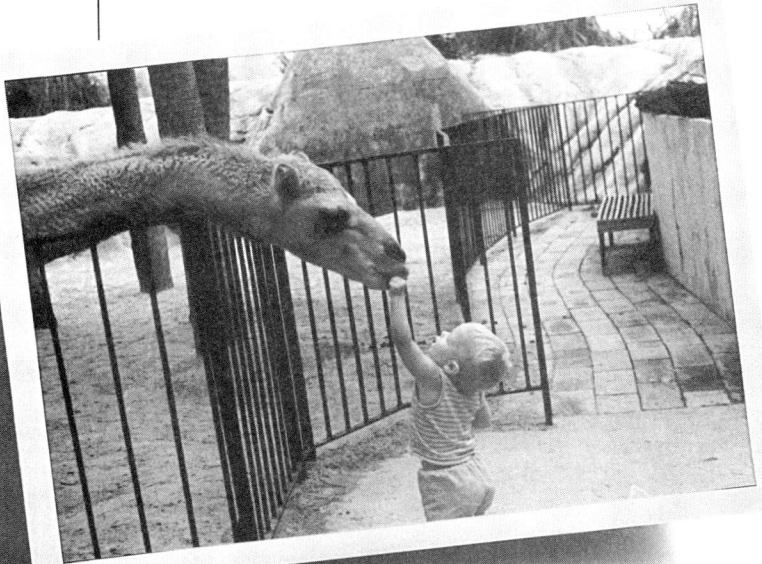

A petting session at Cypress Gardens with Adam Lineberry.

model railroad. This train runs through different areas of the country and shows each of the four seasons. Kids will be able to identify tiny ice skaters, animals, cars, a ski lift and a merry-go-round. The Cypress Gardens Model Railroad Society updates the exhibit and keeps the trains running on time. The Cypress Junction Gift Shop next door is stocked with model supplies if you have a model railroad or decide you want to create one.

The Crossroads is also the place to stop for food. The prime choice for families is Village Fare, with its carrousel of fast-food outlets. Children can find their favorites among burgers, subs, salads, chicken, pizza, Mexican and more. The food windows are lined up against one wall, and pleasant, open seating fills the rest of this spacious eatery. Prices at Village Fare are probably the best for families spending a day at the gardens. But if more formal dining is on your schedule, the Crossroads Restaurant is a full-service establishment featuring cocktails, appetizers and a fine list of entrees.

Consult the useful map and schedule available at the gate for show times and for planning your day at Cypress Gardens. When you are ready to see the water ski show, be sure to get to one of the stadiums about 15 minutes before showtime if you want to get seats in the shade.

The park maintains its title of "water ski capital of the world" with The Greatest American Ski Show, a must during any visit. The show on Lake Eloise is a medley of thrills and grace, mixing the daring of the ramp jumpers and the beauty of the Aquamaids' ballet moves on skis. Children will enjoy the antics of Corky the Clown and his assistant Corkette as they recreate great moments in history, such as Columbus discovering America. Well, sort of. Barefooters zip over the water without skis, and tow gliders go aloft then land right in front of the stadiums to help round out this well-paced ski extravaganza. After seeing this terrific show, nobody will question the prominent place in water skiing history given to Cypress Gardens. It doesn't get better than this.

Another show that offers special wonders for kids is Southern Ice. Jackie Frost, your wisecracking guide through this winter wonderland, begins by making it "snow" in the Ice Palace theater. After she's cooled down the stage, she welcomes a troupe of Southern belles, alligators in Santa suits and others in a funny, well-choreographed skating presentation. Bright costumes, lots of slapstick and the visual treat of gliding skaters earns this show five stars from young viewers.

Some of the animals perform at Cypress Gardens, too, in the gator handling demonstration and the bird show. Both are excellent, with handlers playing to the audience and giving lots of information about the animals on stage. The gator handling offers the most thrills because in a live performance you never know whether a gator will cooperate or not. The show also introduces pythons and boa constrictors, which coil around the handler with an eerie ease. If you want to see more birds after the performance, visit the Fly Free Aviary with its huge winged creatures, including toucans and scarlet ibises.

Other animals live in Animal Forest and at Critter Encounters. The camel and the deer are curious enough to come up to visitors for a pat on the nose.

Machines throughout the area dispense food so kids can feed the giant Aldabra tortoise or the lemurs. Hug Haven is the park's baby animal outpost and the tiny creatures are visible through windows. Tapping on the glass is not allowed, but visitors get good views of dwarf lemurs, cotton-top tamarinds and, sometimes, baby Bengal tigers.

Seeing the spectacular gardens of Cypress Gardens is most fun for children if done by boat. Botanical boat cruises leave at regular intervals from The Landings area. The staff is always improving the gardens and the results are impressive. The state's general climate and several "micro-climates" allow brilliant color and growth of plants in a natural setting all year. Thousands of plant species, from the familiar bougainvillea to the Brazilian jacobinia, are carefully maintained. This is the spot for pictures, and the hard part is picking which settings you want to photograph among all this greenery. The mansion lawn and the rose garden also offer eye-pleasing stops for kids and picture enthusiasts.

To give children an overview of the garden and lakes at day's end, take a ride on the Island in the Sky, back in the Crossroads area. From hundreds of feet in the air, the revolving island gives riders picture-perfect panoramas of the entire area. The ride is short, one trip up and then down on a giant arm. Island in the Sky makes a happy ending to a stay at the gardens.

Recommended for all ages.

Jonathan Trapani with Baby Shamu.

Open 8:30 a.m. to 9:30 p.m. daily, hours extended during summers and holidays. Gates will close one hour before the park. Admission is less than $25 for adults, and around $20 for ages 3-11. Children 2 and younger are admitted free.

Sea World

Florida kids are probably more at home in the water than on dry land. If the family doesn't own a pool, they have access to one or make regular trips to the beaches, which are within a few hours drive from anywhere in the state.

Sea World packs a hefty learning punch for water babies and landlubbers alike. Nobody leaves without learning something about sea life and having a thoroughly good time.

7007 Sea World Drive, off Bee Line Expressway at Interstate 4, southwest of Orlando.

(407) 351-3600

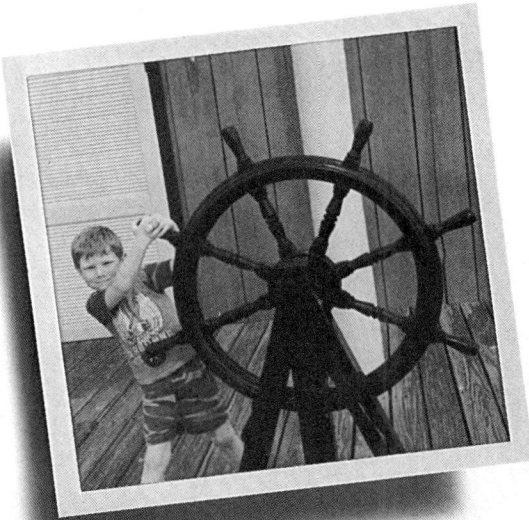

Christopher Williams at the helm at Sea World.

But then, what's not to like about the penguins at the finely designed Penguin Encounter? They seem to be funny even when they are just standing around. And kids get to see real, not animated, seals, whales, dolphins and walruses perform some pretty unbelievable tricks.

A word to the water wise: When viewing the shows, except the water ski show, which is performed by humans, sit in the back if you don't want the kids (and yourself) to get a thorough soaking. Shamu, Kandu and their frolicsome killer whale family and, in fact, the animals at all the shows displace an amazing amount of water and most of it lands on the first 10 rows of spectators.

Keith and Craig Jaques go for a ride at Sea World.

These well-paced shows, however, will capture every child's attention. The narration is easy for kids to understand, and the animals spin, jump and swim through the water at dizzying speeds.

Cap'n Kids World playground is a good place to burn off some excess energy before heading to the petting tanks with stingerless stingrays and frolicsome dolphins that the kids can touch if they can catch them.

Sharks! is a fascinating, if slightly unnerving, meeting with one of nature's eating machines. The

Christopher Mullis among the balls at Cap'n Kids World, Sea World.

exhibit includes sharks swimming in pools outside the exhibit hall, and the "encounter" itself is a long, plexiglass tunnel that allows viewers to actually walk through the shark's environment. Kids who grew up with fears induced by *Jaws* will get to see the creatures up close and personal while learning about their physiology and history. A chilling, informative half hour.

No description of Sea World would be complete without a mention of the penguin-themed gift shop. Perhaps you don't need to buy a set of crystal shot glasses with engraved penguins, but the variety and quality of the gifts is remarkable. Be prepared to part with some cash when kids catch sight of a penguin-festooned hat or mug. After all, kids know the penguin is a very classy bird.

Karen Nicole Llamas in front of the seals at Sea World.

Sea World also offers classes for kindergarten through college-age students. Structured programs are available for scouts, clubs, teachers and Spanish-speaking students. Topics include sharks, coral reef ecosystems, tropical fish, exotic birds, marine ecology and animal training. The Interworlds-on-the-Road program brings students from kindergarten to third grade face-to-face with the ocean right in their classrooms. Puppet shows and hands-on activities teach the fundamentals of marine ecology in this learning program.

Recommended for all ages.

Walt Disney World

From Interstate 4, exit at U.S. Highway 192 and follow the signs to Walt Disney World.

(407) 824-4321

Hours vary, call for hours of operation on the day you plan to visit.

Admission: one day only to either Epcot or Magic Kingdom is less than $30 for adults, and around $22 for children ages 3 - 9. Children age 3 and younger are admitted free. Three-day passes good any three days of the year are available. Call for full schedule of prices and price breaks for Florida residents, which are given during certain times of the year. Prices are subject to change.

It is unlikely that any parents reading this have **not** already been to Walt Disney World with their children. It is the single biggest attraction in the country, and kids the world over clamor to visit the park.

The facilities at both the Magic Kingdom and Epcot were designed with kids and families in mind. They are arranged for maximum convenience and ease of touring. Strollers are available for a nominal rental fee and deposit. Baby care items and changing tables are available. Benches and water fountains can be found all over the park.

If you would like a sane game plan for having a good day at either area, here are some rules to keep in mind and a schedule that will maximize your fun during a one-day tour.

Lindi Jaques on the carousel at the Magic Kingdom.

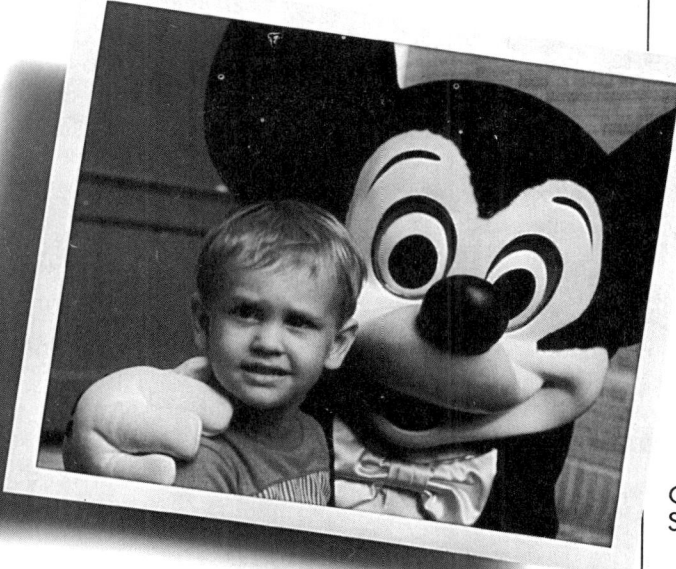

Christopher Douglas
Scott with Mickey.

Below is an outline of the rides and shows in order of how they ought to be done in a single day to keep your waits in line as short as possible. The outline was drawn up after talks with Disney regulars and several visits. This schedule assumes an early arrival at the park, about an hour before the gates open.

These are only suggestions for rides that are most popular with kids and that are "must dos" during a single day trip. Keep in mind that for maximum enjoyment of the Disney complex, you need a full guide to the park, such as *The Unofficial Guide to Walt Disney World & Epcot,* $6.95, Prentice-Hall.

Take the monorail from the Transportation and Ticket Center to the Magic Kingdom. It's faster than the ferry.

Stop at City Hall on Main Street and pick up a schedule of special events and shows slated for that day. These may come in handy when you want to take a break from the rides and stop and look.

Head out for Adventureland and ride the Jungle Cruise, then go to Frontierland and catch the Big Thunder Mountain Railroad roller coaster. These are among the most popular rides in the park, and it is best to get your wait in line over early.

Next ride 20,000 Leagues Under the Sea in Fantasyland. While in this "land" take your pick of the follow-

Magic Kingdom

ing rides as they are also busy ones: Snow White's Scary Adventures, Peter Pan's Flight, Cinderella's Golden Carrousel, Dumbo the Flying Elephant, Mr. Toad's Wild Ride. Check the lines at It's a Small World, and Fantasy Follies and do them if the lines are short. Otherwise, backtrack later in the afternoon.

Go to Tomorrowland and ride the Grand Prix Raceway then take your pick of the following: Space Mountain (a must for the stout of heart), WEDway People Mover, Carrousel of Progress and Mission to Mars.

Next, and not to be missed for kids, go to Liberty Square and visit the Haunted Mansion. When your fright has passed, try cheering up at the Country Bear Jamboree and then explore Tom Sawyer Island in Frontierland.

James William Thompson II, pirate, at the Magic Kingdom.

Pirates of the Caribbean in Adventureland is next, though you might want to try this one very early in the day. It seems to be jammed all the time.

Recommended for all ages.

While You're There

Mickey's Birthdayland is recommended for ages 2-10. Take the steam train; Birthdayland has its own station.

Young and old alike have wondered where Mickey Mouse lives. Welcome to Duckburg, with its designs from vintage 1950s Disney comics. The town features

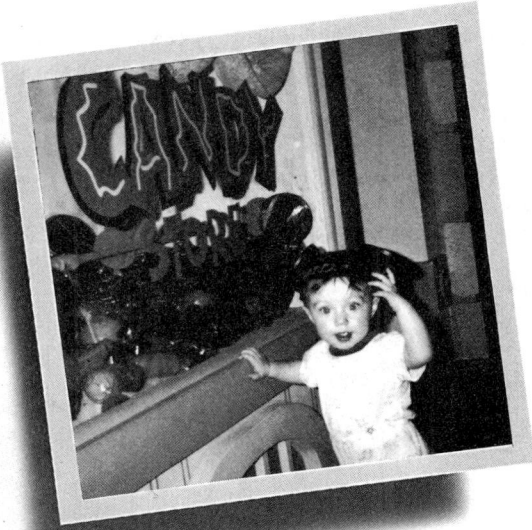

Chance Taylor
Corbeil explores
Mickey's Birthdayland.

Walt Street, Daisy's Cafe, Minnie's Dress Shop and the Duckburg News, all kid-size and perfect for picture taking.

Big people may find the Birthdayland area gives them claustrophobia, with its toy town layout. The maze, buildings, playground and Grandma Duck's Farm animal petting area are packed tightly into a small area. There are few places to sit while children play on the playground equipment so the best bet in Birthdayland is to see the show and then "get out of town."

Just off the train, Mickey's house comes up on your right. Just walk right in, through the mouse's living room, study and kitchen and see all the souvenirs of his life from his earliest days to mega-stardom. The house is charming, but may take some explaining for very young children, who may not know that friendly-looking man in the framed photo on the wall is Walt Disney.

When you enter the house you also enter the show area. In the first waiting area, visitors are shown old Disney cartoons. After that, the show begins and everybody sees Pluto, Minnie, Chip 'n' Dale, Goofy and Donald make a party for the unsuspecting birthday mouse. The next phase lets the audience help Mickey blow out his candles, after which those who are willing to wait get to go backstage and see Mickey in his dressing room. Take children's autograph books if you visit Birthdayland and plan to go backstage. Mickey is happy to sign his name between shows and this is a terrific souvenir.

Food is available in many forms at the Magic Kingdom, but the Tomorrowland Terrace is perhaps the easiest place to eat. Seating is ample and the food is reasonably priced. The compulsion when touring with kids is to "do it all" in a day. Plan snacks and rest stops that are short but numerous enough so that you and the children aren't totally wrecked when the sun goes down.

The Disney characters will probably show up for a photo opportunity or two during your visit. But if you have younger children (ages 3 - 6) call the park and ask about Disney Character Breakfasts. Kids get to share a glass of Florida orange juice with Mickey, Goofy and the whole gang during these scheduled events.

Epcot Center

Start your day with a ride on Spaceship Earth, if the lines are short. This is an educational ride through the famed dome of Epcot, depicting progress in communications from cave painting to the computer age. If you complete the ride early in the day, go to the Guest Relations desk in Earth Station (behind Spaceship Earth) and get a schedule of live shows and special events for the day.

Next take in the Living Seas with its underwater ride and exhibits about oceanography and sea life. The ride under the 200-foot wide aquatic tank is short, but a movie and an elevator ride to the bottom of the tank help round out the journey. Visitors can stay as long as they like at the Living Seas, to watch dolphins being trained, see short films, and view other exhibits on marine life.

Move on to The Land pavilion and take the Listen to the Land boat trip. The ride is all about agriculture, moving visitors through different environments and past some working greenhouses that use the most modern techniques.

The Land, sponsored by Kraft, is the best place to stop for lunch during your visit. There is a ring of food outlets surrounding an open seating area, and the prices are reasonable. Other attractions in The Land are the Kitchen Kabaret (animated food stuffs singing about nutrition) and the Harvest Theater's 70mm film on symbiosis and man's relation to the environment.

The Journey Into Imagination features a whimsical ride with Figment, the dragon, and Dreamfinder, the mind traveler. They guide people through the avenues of ideas and creativity on this AudioAnimatronic adventure.

Next stop is the Image Works, with its hands-on creative devices for the eye and ear. The Works is not a must during a one-day trip and can be saved for another trip, unlike Captain EO at the pavilion's Magic Eye Theater. This is Michael Jackson and the art of three-dimensional moviemaking at their finest. It is a rock and roll trip into space with Jackson's music providing the driving backbeat. You've got to see it no matter how tight your schedule.

Other pavilions at Epcot are The World of Motion with its AudioAnimatronic history of transportation; The Universe of Energy, with a theatre that moves past dinosaurs and volcanoes to tell the story of fossil fuels; and Horizons, which features a ride through our changing visions of the future. These last three exhibits can be scheduled for your next trip if you are only spending a day, but all are musts (especially the dinosaurs in the Universe of Energy) at some point.

Recommended for all ages.

Dan Chavaroli among the bubbles at Epcot Center.

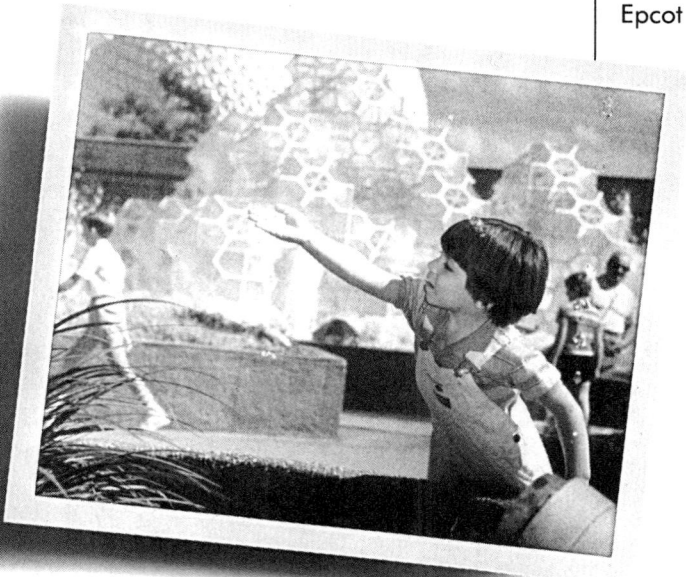

World Showcase

The non-stop world's fair of Disney, the World Showcase, may keep families walking to exhaustion but each of the 11 countries represented here has something unique for visitors and can't be missed. Overall, World Showcase is oriented toward adults with its realistic streets, wonderful films and shops. Don't let that stop you from taking children here. The rides, engaging performers and color of the pavilions enhance this setting and make it easy for kids to learn about other cultures.

Each pavilion in the World Showcase, as well as The Land and the Living Seas in Future World, includes a restaurant. Reservations for lunch or dinner must be made the day of your visit, very early in the day. Upon your arrival at Epcot Center, go immediately to Earth Station at the base of the dome to make reservations on a video display terminal. Have one or two "back up" restaurants in mind if the one you want is fully booked. The eating establishments at Epcot are, for the most part, a true enhancement to any visit. Especially in the World Showcase, local flavor can only improve an already exciting adventure into another country.

The items in the World Showcase area will all seem pretty exotic and inviting, but restraint is the rule here. Unless you think you absolutely, positively can't get it anywhere else, put off purchasing it. Choose carefully when children clamor for keepsakes. The Japan and Moroccan pavilions probably have the best buys, but there are interesting, inexpensive items in each country if you hunt for them.

Mexico: The Mexico pavilion features a boat ride down the River of Time, El Rio del Tiempo. The country's history, from the Aztecs to the present, is depicted in delightful AudioAnimatronic scenes on this ride. The interior setting of the pavilion is extremely well done and a joy for the eye. The exterior is marked by a pair of imposing pre-Colombian pyramids.

Norway: The rowdy Maelstrom ride gets squeals from children at this newest member of the World Showcase family. Viking boats take sailors on an exciting Nordic voyage, and visitors "disembark" for a short film about Norway. This ride, with its splashy dips and dark passages, is the most exciting thus far at World Showcase. Other countries have rides in the planning stages. The Norwegian village street offers shops with wooden toys, sweaters and other crafts and authentic dishes at the Akershus Restaurant. Visitors can also tour a stave kirche (stave church), which holds a museum exhibit.

People's Republic of China: Perhaps the most ornate and beautiful pavilion, China features a Circle-Vision 360 film, *Wonders of China*. This movie is breath taking. The audience stands and is surrounded by the sights and sounds of this stunning country. A replica of the Temple of Heaven in Beijing, gardens and reflecting pools, and an art gallery help complete the exhibit. This is not a rock 'em, sock 'em pavilion, but some children may enjoy for its sheer beauty.

Germany: The main attraction at this pavilion is the Biergarten, a reservations-only restaurant with German food and beer. Folk dancing, singing and music are scheduled during evening meals. But walk about anytime in the pleasant outdoor plaza with its clock tower and fountain depicting St. George finishing off the dragon.

Melissa Downing dressing up at Epcot Center.

Italy: Like Germany, Italy offers more atmosphere than thrills, but the street found in this pavilion is the most relaxing in the World Showcase. A bell tower, a replica of a 14th century Venetian palace, a central plaza, and striped-pole moorings on Showcase Lagoon help set the exterior mood of this stop in Italy. The art of pasta making is on view at the L'Originale Alfredo di Roma Ristorante, which requires reservations.

United States: AudioAnimatronic Mark Twain and Ben Franklin narrate The American Adventure, the stage production at this pavilion. The theatre is a replica of Philadelphia's Liberty Hall and the characters move along with an enormous rear-projection motion picture depicting the history of the U.S.A. This moving production is the high point of any visit to the World Showcase. The food is (what else?) good old American fast food at The Liberty Inn.

Japan: Beneath a five-story roofed pagoda, visitors will find the simple charm of the Japan pavilion. In the courtyard, kids should be on the lookout for a street magician who likes to have youngsters help him demonstrate his art. The huge building on the right of this pavilion houses a restaurant and a terrific retail store with a marvelous array of Japanese goods. This wins as the hot spot for browsing and shopping in the Showcase.

Morocco: Richly detailed and exotic, the Morocco pavilion features lively musicians and dancers who stroll about and invite visitors to join their performance. The narrow streets, graceful minarets and noisy market heighten the authentic flavor of this pavilion. And the Marrakech Restaurant provides North African delicacies and belly dancers to spice up a visit. The restaurant takes walk-in reservations and is usually a good bet for last-minute dinner plans.

France: The film *Impressions de France*, an 18-minute excursion into the natural beauty and urban chic of France, is exceptionally well-crafted. Visitors get to sit down for this movie, so you may want to schedule a visit at a time when your feet are tired. The streets in France are very narrow, which can lead to crowding when the pavilion is busy. The croissants from the pastry shop are wonderful and, true to French style, it's no surprise that the sidewalk cafe is one of the most popular hangouts at World Showcase. (Keep in mind that reservations are required here, too, even for hanging out.)

United Kingdom: There are no rides or films in the UK, but kids might find some of the toys (some old-fashioned ones are made of wood) in the shops fun. The quaint streets depict different periods of city and country life, and parents will enjoy a walk through the shops or a sit in the garden. The Rose and Crown Pub makes for realistic quaffing (listen for a lot of British accents in here), and the dining room puts diners on the lagoon side of the promenade.

Canada: An enchanting film, *O Canada!*, is the centerpiece of the Canada exhibit. The film covers the ethnic diversity and amazing natural beauty of our neighbor to the north. Canada also features the LeCellier restaurant, a cafeteria that serves real food (not fast food) and does not require reservations. Giant totem poles, an Indian village and a replica of a landmark stone building help complete the grounds of this so-near, yet so-different country's pavilion.

While You're There

The Disney characters have started doing greetings and photo stops at Epcot in the national costumes of various countries in the World Showcase. Now that the Norway pavilion is open, the kids can pose next to Goofy in his Norse helmet.

Keep in mind that Epcot is nearly twice the size of the Magic Kingdom. You'll have to cover a lot of territory. Be ready to carry the kids by late afternoon. You may want to schedule a midafternoon break if you're planning to stay into the evening.

Around Walt Disney World

Discovery Island: This lush tropical isle in Bay Lake is an 11-acre sanctuary for more than 100 species of animals and 250 species of plants. Exotic animals, reptiles and birds, some threatened with extinction, thrive on this tropical haven. Designated as a zoological park, Discovery Island is home to disabled native Florida birds such as the brown pelican, sandhill crane, hawks and eagles. There is also a colony of Capuchin monkeys being trained to aid physically disabled person. Visitors may view a bird show and tour the island by purchasing tickets at Disney World. Admission: adults, around $8, children ages 3 to 9, half price.

River Country and Fort Wilderness Campground Resort: Whatever your pleasure on the water, you'll probably find it at River Country. Let kids splash down a 260-foot slide, play on a sandy beach, or take an inner tube trip through the rapids. Admission: adults, around $12, and around $10 for children ages 3 - 9. River Country and Discovery Island combination tickets are available.

Make camp overnight at the campground if kids want to stay longer. You don't even have to have a tent. Mobile homes are available for rental complete with air-conditioning, carpeting, color TV, radio, cookware and housekeeping services. Campsites are available for between $25 and $30. As a Fort Wilderness Resort guest, you are entitled to use the transportation system to reach the Magic Kingdom, Epcot and the rest of the resort.

Leigh Allison Rich and Lindsay Moore get wet at River Country.

There is also entertainment right in the campground. Pioneer Hall is home for the Hoop-Dee-Doo Musical Revue, (reservations required) and you can wake up with Chip 'n' Dale at the Melvin the Moose Breakfast Show.

Resort hotels: If you are a Disney regular and want to do something different during one visit, try getting on the monorail for a trip to the Grand Floridian resort hotel. The breathtaking main building features a stunning, open lobby full of pastel light and period decoration. The entire complex, done in white wood, was designed to recall the Florida of yesteryear and no expense was spared in the undertaking.

The pool and other facilities are for resort guests only, but the casual visitor can stroll on the white sand beach (on the lake) or sit in a patio chair and get some sun. After touring the lobby shops and restaurants, walk around the main building's porch to Gasparilla Grill & Games for lunch. This eatery is the place for light meals, which can be taken to an outdoor seating area or eaten inside. The winning point for kids here is the attached video game room, which beeps, rings and buzzes right next to the indoor seating area.

The monorail will also transport you to the other resort hotels — the Polynesian with exotic birds and waterfalls, and the Contemporary, which houses an entire floor of video games on its lowest level.

Wonders of Walt Disney World seminars: Classes in the areas of art, nature and entertainment have been created just for youngsters ages 10 - 15. Costs are between $50 and $55. The six and a half hour seminars have been approved by educators nationwide, and some schools award credit for completion of one or more of the programs. Cost covers lunch, use of a camera, and books for kids to keep. For reservations, call (407) 345-5860, or write: Seminar Production Department, Walt Disney World, P.O. Box 10100, Lake Buena Vista, Fla. 32830-0100.

Hours of operation vary but usually open 10 a.m. to 5 p.m. during spring and fall and 9 a.m. to 9 p.m. during summer. Admission: about $12 for adults and $10 for children. Group rates available for 20 or more. Children 9 and younger must be accompanied in the park by an adult.

Water Mania

6073 West U.S. Highway 192, Kissimmee

(407) 239-8448

There's water, water everywhere in Florida and hydro-attractions make a big splash with all youngsters.

Water Mania boasts Florida's largest wave pool yet, The White Caps, for an easy start to a day here. The pool has lots of chairs and tables along its shores and graduated levels for swimmers of every size. When the "waves" roll in, the sound will remind you of the beach. And if it's sand you want, The Banana Boat Beach area has that and volleyball nets and palm-umbrella tables. This is the place to throw down a towel for some quality tanning time.

But this is a water park and the rides are where the action is. The Mad Skipper puts riders on surfboggins for a wet plunge down one of two flumes. The Looney Flume looks like the work of a mad scientist, with its three twisting flumes and is probably the most fun for the kids who meet its height requirement of 44 inches. The Double Berserker giant twin flume lets riders go solo or challenge a friend to ride alongside for a big splashy finish.

As for the grand daddy of the flume rides, they call

it The Screamer. There's a good reason for that. If you don't scream as you practically free fall down the 72-foot flume then you're not human. This daunting ride carries the same height requirement as the Looney Flume and the Double Berserker but it's doubtful that any child less than 44 inches tall (or most adults over that height) would want to try The Screamer.

Kids under 12 get special attention at The Squirt Pond and have a playground area all their own. Tommy Turtle spouts water into the pool, which has kid-size slides and colorful tubes. (A sign here says parents are allowed if accompanied by a child, so be advised.) As with most of the theme parks, the area designated for little visitors is a big plus for parents, especially in a park like Water Mania where safety requires restrictions on who can ride the flumes.

There is one dry area at Water Mania where families can unwind after their water thrills. The Great American Picnic area lets picnickers lounge in the shade, break bread together or swing in a hammock. Florida pines and oaks provide a place out of the sun, and a nearby playing field is just the ticket for touch football, softball or any sport played on grass. This eye-pleasing picnic area comprises three acres with plenty of room to stroll.

For those who would rather travel light, The Wave Pool Walkside Eatery features the Maniac Burger, pizza and barbecue pork sandwiches. Tubes and rafts and even volleyballs are for rent, and lockers are available. Lifeguards are on duty at all pools and rides, and the gift shop sells tanning supplies, swimsuits, sunglasses and beach covers.

Recommended for all ages.

Wet 'n Wild

Ten miles northeast of Disney World off Interstate 4 in Florida Center. From Orlando, head west on Interstate 4 to International Drive.

(407) 351-3200

Summer hours: 9 a.m. to 9 p.m., other months roughly 10 a.m. to 6 p.m. Call for exact hours.

Admission: adults around $15, and children ages 3-12, around $13; children 3 and younger admitted free. Admission is half price starting at 5 p.m. when closing is 9 p.m., and 3 p.m. on shorter days.

Ample free parking on site, shuttle bus service available from most hotels for nominal charge. Picnic lunches allowed but no glass bottles or alcohol.

It's not hard to describe Orlando's Wet 'n Wild. Just say, "It's everything you could possibly think of to do in and around water and then some." This water theme park is small, 25 acres, by theme park standards but a recent expansion has packed in even more aquatic pursuits at the 11-year-old attraction.

Be a Pepper Park is just for kids, with mini-flumes, forts, water cannons and a playground all set in just a few inches of water.

To start slow, water bugs can use the float of their choice to meander down The Lazy River, a quarter-mile long gentle stream. Next step or stroke up to Surf Lagoon for ocean-sized waves in water from 8 feet to 2 inches deep. The lagoon covers 17,000 square feet for wave riders of all ages and sizes. A cable operated tow gives visitors a lift to the Knee Ski, a half-mile hexagonal course for kneeboarding at speeds up to 15 mph.

Things start to get interesting as swimmers hang on to their goggles and go for bigger thrills on the following water rides: the Kamikaze, Mach 5, Hydra-Maniac, Der Stuka, Corkscrew, Raging Rapids, Blue Niagra and the Bubble Up.

Swimwear, film, souvenirs and suntan products are for sale at the Beach Connection gift shop. Beverages and food, including burgers, chicken and pizza, are available.

There are locker rooms and showers for visitors, and raft/tube/towel rentals. Lifeguards and a full-time registered nurse are on duty.

Recommended for all ages.

Daredevils Clint Carney and Jaime Cousin at Wet 'n Wild.

OTHER ATTRACTIONS

• • • • • •

Citrus Tower

U.S. Highway 27, Clermont.

(904) 394-8585

• *Open from 8 a.m. to 6 p.m. daily.*
Admission to tower's observation deck: around $2 for adults and children age 9 and older. Children under 9 are admitted free when accompanied by an adult. The tram tour costs the same and combination tickets are available.

Just 30 minutes from Disney's land of make-believe is a real-life attraction built around Florida's citrus industry.

The 226-foot high Citrus Tower offers visitors a panoramic view of Central Florida's citrus country from a comfortable observation deck.

Down below, a leisurely tram tour takes visitors on an educational horticultural excursion through the attraction's specially maintained groves, home to more than 30 varieties of citrus trees.

The inside look at the history of the citrus industry in Lake County and the Citrus Tower's packing plant and candy-making operation give youngsters a tangible understanding of one the state's major economic industries.

Recommended for age 8 and older.

Disney-MGM Studios Florida

Southwest of Epcot Center at Walt Disney World.

Guests will be able to see working sound stages and participate in the TV show (past or present) of their choice in the television studio area. Disney will also offer a special inside look at their famous animators at work. Stunt demonstrations will include some audience participation for the stout of heart. An elaborate adventure ride, Star Tours, is scheduled to open in 1990. Visitors will fly through the sets of *Star Wars* with the films' characters, including R2D2.

Fun 'n Wheels

6739 Sand Lake Road at International Drive, Orlando.

36 **(407) 351-5651**

Open 10 a.m. to midnight daily. No general admission charge.

Anything on wheels is the theme here. Park has three go-kart tracks, cars, a Ferris wheel, kiddie rides, bumper boats and an arcade.

Recommended for age 4 and older.

Nicole Reinholt at
Fun and Wheels.

Open daily from 9 a.m. to 5:30 p.m.

*Admission to the privately-owned park: around $7
for adults, and $4 for children ages 3-11. Senior citi-
zens 62 and older get a 20 percent discount.*

Homosassa Springs

*One mile west of
Homosassa on U.S.
Highway 19.*

(904) 628-2311

A walk around Nature's Giant Fish Bowl lets kids
look down into the water to see a manatee and
feed the fish. But they can also get a fish's eye view of
more than 10,000 species of aquatic creatures from
the inside by walking down into a glass-walled
observatory.

And every day, Lucifer the hippo and the alligators
are fed before crowds of visitors during daily reptile
shows at the nature park. The petting zoo is home to
deer, goats and burros. Birds and squirrels are
everywhere and are eager for visitors' handouts.

Boats tour the waterways and nature trails provide
glimpses of the environment on dry land. Other
amusements at Homosassa include a historical
museum, snack bar, gift shop, reptile show, orchid
collection and the spring, which gushes 185 million
gallons of water each day.

Also at Homosassa is the **Yulee Sugar Mill Ruins
State Historical Site**, on State Road 490, west of
U.S. Highway 19. The mill was once the heart of a
sugar plantation owned by David Levy Yulee. His
5,100-acre plantation on the Homosassa River began
production about 1851.

The mill, made of native limestone, has been

Roger Martin in front of Homosassa Springs' Fish Bowl.

partially restored. It consists of a large chimney about 9-feet square, with a 40-foot-long structure that houses the boiler. Interpretive signs guide visitors through the complex. Phone: (904) 795-3817.

Recommended for all ages.

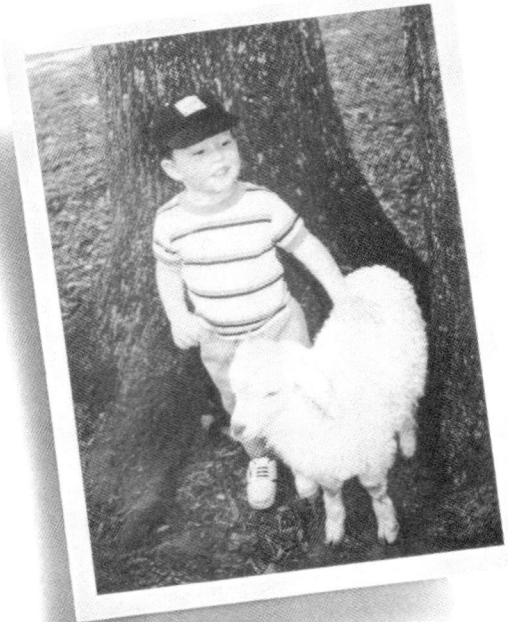

Brant Jaques and a furry friend at Silver Springs.

Open from 9 a.m. to 6 p.m. with admission less than $15 for adults, and less than $9 for children ages 3 to 11. Wild Waters is open from 10 a.m. to 5 p.m. with admission around $8 for adults and $7 for children ages 3 to 11.

Silver Springs and Florida's Wild Waters

One mile east of Ocala on State Road 40.

(904) 236-2121

A family water-themed park, Wild Waters features flumes that wind around old oak trees, picnic areas, children's play area, a mega-wave pool and snack bars. Silver Springs features glass-bottomed boats for viewing the underwater life in the deep, crys-

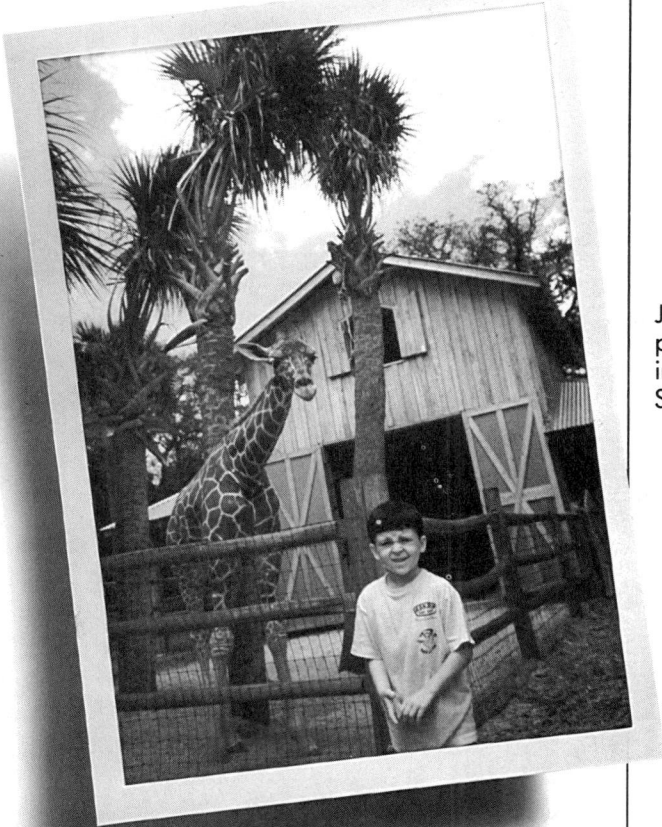

Justin Lee Daughtry practices giraffe impressions at Silver Springs.

tal-clear waters of Silver Springs, photo sub boats, swimming, picnic areas and restaurants.

There is also a petting zoo called Deer Park with sheep, deer, goats and a giraffe.

Recommended for all ages.

39

Universal Studios, Florida

Offices at 5750 Major Blvd., Suite 500, Orlando.

(407) 351-7600

Everyone is talking about the movie industry coming to town and one of the best ways to see it all will be through a classic studio tour. These lively tours have been a hit in Hollywood for years, with visitors seeing how scenes were shot, and sets from famous movies. The tour at MCA/Universal opens in late 1989.

Weeki Wachee and Buccaneer Bay

U.S. Highway 19 at State Road 50, about 12 miles southeast of Brooksville.

(904) 596-4829

Weeki Wachee is open 9 a.m. to 6 p.m. daily with admission for adults around $10 and children ages 3 to 11 around $8. Combination tickets to both attractions are available. Buccaneer Bay is open 10 a.m. to 5 p.m. daily with admission for adults around $6 and children ages 3 to 11 around $5.

Weeki Wachee features mermaids in an underwater theater, bird shows and jungle cruises. Adjacent Buccaneer Bay has a beach for swimming in the Weeki Wachee River, children's water play area, rope swings and flume rides.

AROUND THE STATE

• • • • • • •

Lion Country Safari

Southern Boulevard (State Road 80) West in West Palm Beach. Fifteen miles west of Interstate 95.

(407) 793-1084

• *Open every day from 9:30 a.m. to 5:30 p.m. Entrance gates close at 4:30 p.m. Admission: adults, around $12; children 3 to 11, around $10; under 3 admitted free.*

Throughout the ages children have been fascinated by animal stories.

Lion Country Safari offers them the opportunity to see real elephants, lions, deer, tortoises, chimps, llamas, and birds like those that have inspired the classic tales. Bring your children and drive with them through hundreds of acres of natural African, Asian and North American settings where the animals are allowed to roam freely.

Some younger children might need reassurance from their parents that the large animals approaching the cars, be they ostriches, rhinos, elephants, or giraffes, will not harm them.

After completing the safari in your car, stop at Safari World Amusement Park where children and adults will be able to pet and feed the animals in the Great American Farm Yard, take a safari boat cruise, ride paddle boats and a carrousel, play mini-golf and see many other animal exhibits. All this is included in the admission charge, except the special animal feed available at vending machines throughout the park.

You may purchase hot dogs, ice cream, popcorn and soft drinks at several snack stands, and hamburgers, pizza or chicken at the Safari World Snack Bar. There are tables in different areas for those who bring their own picnic baskets.

Several gift shops offer inexpensive toy animals and books, mugs, T-shirts and plush animals, and more costly items.

Plan to stay at least three hours but there are enough activities and exhibits to spend the whole day. You may take the safari ride as many times as you wish during the day. Car windows must remain up through the drive. If you do not have an air conditioned car you may rent one at the park office, for an added fee.

Recommended for all ages.

Hours vary according to the season. In the summer it is open from 10 a.m. to 10 p.m. every day; in spring and fall it is usually open only on weekends, from 11 a.m. to 8 p.m. Atlantis is closed after Labor Day weekend and reopens in March. Admission: adults, around $12; children 3 to 11, around $10; under 3, free.

Six Flags Atlantis

Interstate 95 and Stirling Road, Hollywood. Take I-95 to Stirling Road (exit 25) and follow the signs.

(305) 926-1000, recorded message; (305) 926-1001, receptionist

Six Flags Atlantis, a 65-acre water theme park, has more than 80 rides, slides, shows and attractions.

The Slidewinder, the gigantic slide complex seen from Interstate 95, consists of more than one mile of slides. It features the Thunderball, a straight drop, and the Triple Drop, a roller coaster of water slides. The Wave Pool, with more than a half million gallons of water, is activated for 10-minute periods throughout the day. At the Raging Rampage riders splash down a 50-foot slide.

Tots can splash around in the Kiddie Karwash, located at the Kiddie Cove activity pool. The Daffy Duck Romp-A-Round is fun for youngsters up to 48 inches tall, with its ball crawls, punching bags and rope walks.

The Looney Tunes Land is a playground especially for young children. Older children and adults can ride the Enterprise and the Matterhorn.

Six food stands offer a variety of fast foods, including pizza, hot dogs and hamburgers. Long lines requiring long waits may form on peak attendance days. There is a large picnic area outside the park for those who prefer to bring their own lunch.

The gift shop offers a variety of souvenirs and sun tan and sun block products. Visitors should protect themselves from the sun. Small children and weak swimmers are advised to wear life preservers, available at no extra charge.

Plan to stay the whole day.

Recommended for all ages.

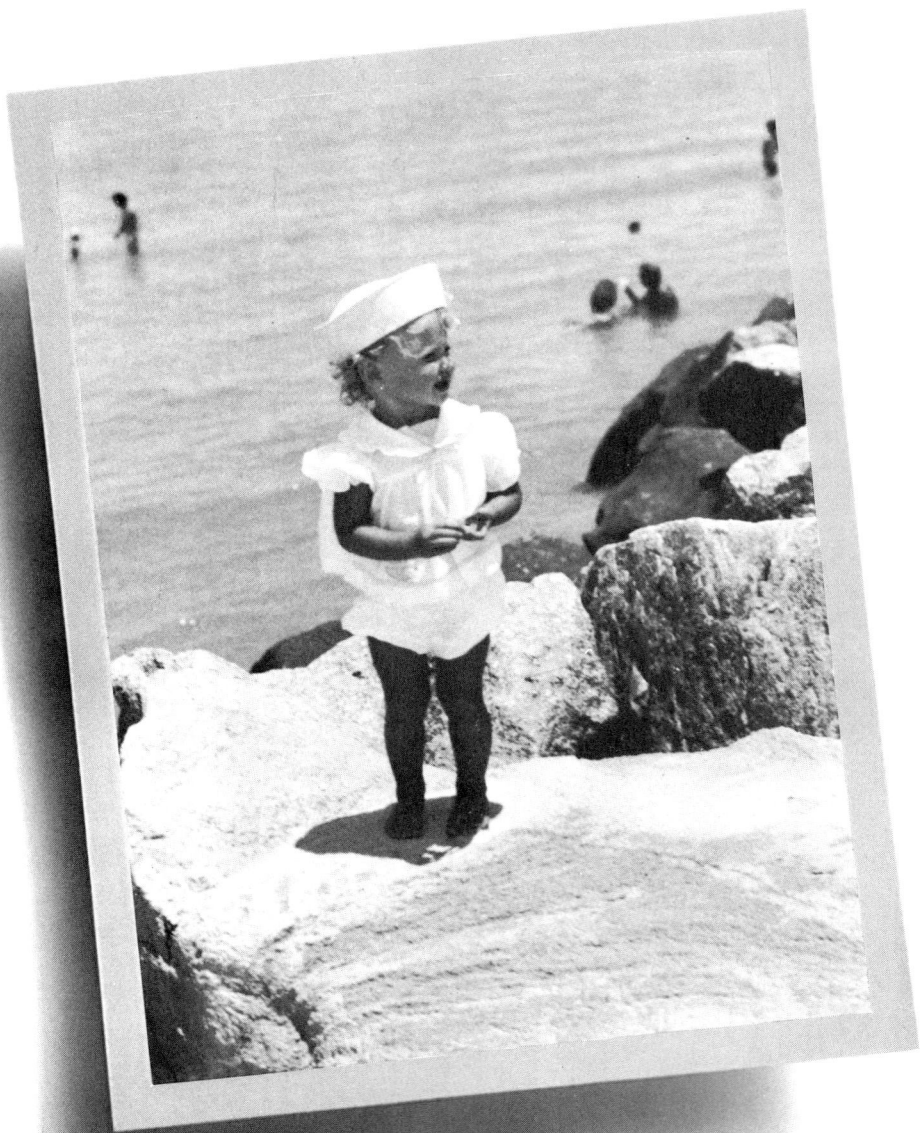

• • • • • • •

Chapter 2

PERMANENT WAVES

Florida's coastline is the ultimate child's sandbox

This isn't going to be easy. Trying to squeeze in a complete rundown on all the beaches in the area would take a book the size of *War and Peace*. Florida has hundreds of miles of beaches, some more picturesque than others.

Following is an enhanced listing of beaches with information on where they are, when the lifeguards are around, costs and other basics. Every family loves the beach and the point of visiting one is to let kids swim or surf or build sand castles. Children have no problem amusing themselves on a beach, and parents usually find keeping watch and playing with the kids a little more relaxing with the sand and surf for background.

• On the jetty at Jetty Park, Lisa Beckner.

Open daily from 8 a.m. to sunset. Admission: $1 per driver and 50 cents per passenger. Kids age 5 and younger are admitted free.

Boulder Beach might be called a sculpture gallery with a sandy floor. The coquina formations here form the largest protected area of the stone in the world. The outcroppings are a rocky-road mixture of shells, coral and sand, and can provide hours of oceanside discovery.

A museum on the natural and cultural history of the area can give you a break from the beach, and tidal marshes and hiking trails allow for some legwork after getting a tan. There is also a picnic area.

Recommended for age 8 and older since the footing on the rocks can be tricky.

Boulder Beach

At Washington Oaks Gardens State Park on State Road A1A south of Marineland.

45

H. Cielo Gaitan chases waves.

Only access is by private boat or ferry that departs from Honeymoon Island State Recreation Area every half hour from 10 a.m. to 6 p.m. on weekends and holidays, and 10 a.m. to 5 p.m. on weekdays. The schedule is subject to change and service is reduced during December, January, and February. Ferry tickets are almost $4 for adults and around $2 for children age 12 and older. Maximum time allowed on the island is four hours. The park is for day use only, however, a limited number of boaters may stay overnight.

Caladesi Island

West end of State Road 586 near Dunedin.

(813) 443-5903

Caladesi Island is one of the few remaining undisturbed barrier islands in Florida. Even today, no roads or bridges lead there, adding the adventure of a ferry trip to a day at the beach. It takes about 20 minutes on the 70-passenger ferries to reach the island just north of Clearwater.

More than two miles of white sand beach front the Gulf of Mexico, and the bay side of Caladesi is a mangrove swamp. Much of the interior of the island is dominated by virgin pine flatwoods.

Besides swimming, snorkeling and other water sports, one of the island's more popular activities is hiking the three-mile nature trail that leads to the interior. Along the trail, visitors can view coastal strand

2

plants, virgin south Florida slash pine flatwoods, and a mangrove swamp. Park rangers conduct guided walks on the beach according to seasonal demand and upon request.

Recommended for all ages.

Parking fees around the shore area are in the $2 range.

With Ron Jon's right in the neighborhood, surfing is the order of any day spent on this pretty, but usually crowded, beach. No pets, glass containers or alcohol other than beer are allowed on the beach; no driving, either.

Recommended for all ages.

Cocoa Beach

Take State Road 520 to State Road A1A south of Cape Canaveral.

Surfer baby, Lisa Beckner at Jetty Park.   47

Daytona Beach

Follow the signs from Interstate 4 or 95 to this famous beach.

A $3 toll is charged between Feb. 1 and Labor Day. No toll is charged before 8 a.m. and after 5 p.m. Season passes are available.

Man's drive to the seas never has been better illustrated than at Daytona Beach. If you're nervous about keeping track of the kids amid all the vehicles allowed on the sand here, perhaps you should consider a quiet day by your pool. Cars, sand bikes and wheeled boards of all types are all allowed on the beach, helping to maintain Daytona's dedication to the world of wheels.

It is also a vortex of the spring break madness when the universities let students loose for a week or two. A fishing pier and boardwalk, concession stands, restrooms, game parlors and lifeguards are in place to serve the crowds. If kids enjoy other amusements

Sara Bogart sand constructing at Daytona.

along with their swimming, Daytona is the place for them.

Recommended for age 10 and older.

New Smyrna Beach

A $3 toll is charged between Feb. 1 and Labor Day. No toll is charged before 8 a.m. and after 5 p.m. Season passes are available.

Some ruins of the British colony founded by Dr. Andrew Turnbull in 1768 may still be found in the New Smyrna area. The remains of the coquina giant called Turnbull Palace are located on Riverside Drive across from the municipal yacht basin. Off State Road 44 are the ruins of the colony's sugar mill.

Smyrna Dunes Park is about 2½ miles north of Flagler Avenue on Peninsula Avenue. Lifeguards are on duty in summer, and surfing is allowed.

Canaveral National Seashore, which is free to the public but has no lifeguards, is about 10 miles south of New Smyrna Beach on State Road A1A. Pamphlets on the seashore's wildlife are available from the ranger station at the park's entrance.

Recommended for age 5 and older.

Take State Road 44 exit from Interstate 4 and follow the signs.

(904) 428-2449

Pine Island Beach

Open sunrise to sunset. Alcoholic beverages are prohibited.

This charming, pocket-sized park is the only gulf coast beach located less than an hour and a half from metropolitan Orlando.

A favorite park with local families, this beach is particularly suitable for children and timid swimmers of all ages. The gulf waters are warm 12 months a year,and you will need to walk 100 yards or more to encounter water above your waist. Sandy beach space is limited on this two-acre island, but families traditionally set up folding chairs, card tables and floats out in the cooling water. A quiet, old-fashioned beach for families who seek the basics of sun, sand and clean, warm water.

After the beach, it is worth exploring some of the tiny, coastal roads south of Pine Island and Bayport. The old, overgrown lanes and sometimes ramshackle houses evoke a rural, timeless Florida hard to find among our superhighways and condominiums.

Recommended for all ages.

Alfred A. McKethan County Park, Hernando County. To reach Pine Island, take State Road 50 west, past U.S. Highway 19 to State Road 595 North (toward Bayport). Take the right hand fork where the road splits and in two miles you will reach the park.

(904) 754-4031

49

Playalinda

*Take State Road 50 east
to U.S. Highway 1 north,
then State Road 406
east to the shore.*

Playalinda is one of the loveliest protected jewels in Florida's coastline. High dunes frame this picture-perfect setting. There is no driving allowed so families can relax and enjoy the ocean, wildlife and plentiful vegetation on the dunes. Parking is available.
Recommended for all ages.

Ponce DeLeon Inlet

*Between Daytona
Beach and New Symrna
Beach on State Road
A1A.*

A $3 toll is charged between Feb. 1 and Labor Day. No toll is charged before 8 a.m. and after 5 p.m. Season passes are available.

Historians say Ponce de Leon sought refuge on this beach before being driven back to his ship by attacking Indians. Early New Smyrna Beach settlers called it "The Mosquitos" for the obvious reason, but the name officially was changed to Ponce de Leon Inlet in 1926.

To enhance your enjoyment of the beach, there are lifeguards, fewer mosquitos, concessions and surfing. Driving on the beach is allowed from sunrise to sunset. Dogs are permitted on no more than a 7-foot leash. Alcohol and glass containers are prohibited.
Recommended for age 5 and older.

Satellite Beach

*Located between
Cocoa Beach and
Melbourne on State
Road A1A.*

Parking is 75 cents and pets, alcohol and driving are prohibited on the beach.

This is better as a quick beach stop during a day on the space coast, rather than a place to spend a whole day with the kids. There are no guards, no driving on the beach, no pets, and no alcohol. Surfing is allowed and parking is available.

On State Road A1A in Satellite Beach, Pelican Beach State Park is a nice, low-key place to bring a picnic and let the kids surf or take a dip.
Recommended for all ages.

Sebastian Inlet

*South of Melbourne
Beach on State Road
A1A.*

A good place for Dad to fish while the rest of the family plays in the surf. Some of the best surfers in the state come here to ply the waves created by a man-made jetty.

Lifeguards work Memorial Day through Labor Day. There are concessions and restrooms, and parking. Pets are welcome on a 6-foot leash. No driving or alcohol is permitted on the beach.
Recommended for age 5 and older.

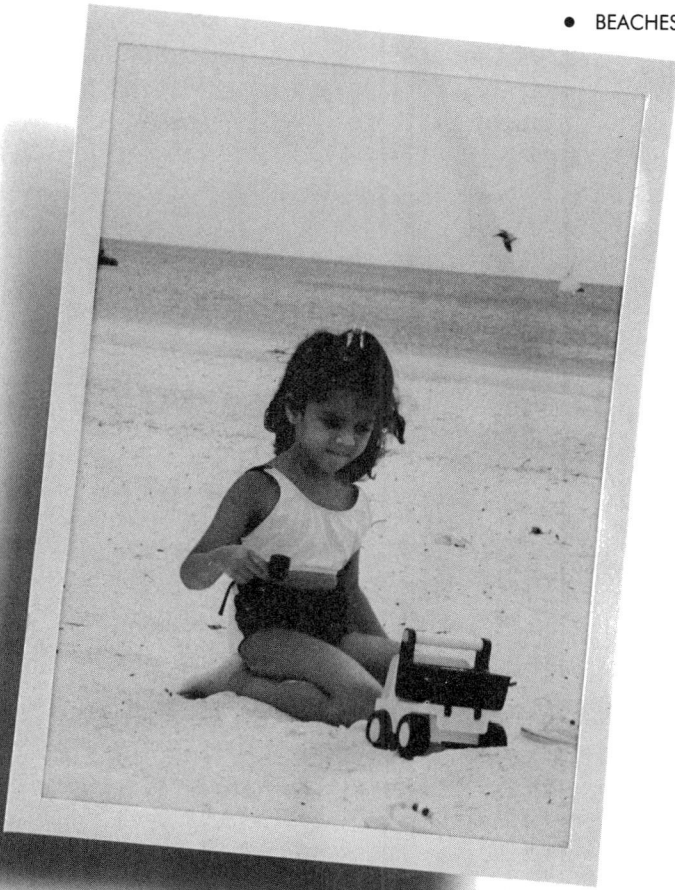

AROUND THE STATE

Shree Chauhan exploring West Coast sands.

Admission to Carl Johnson Park: around $2 for adults and half that for children.

I t's recognized by many as the ideal family beach. Because there are no riptides or steep dropoffs, Fort Myers Beach on Estero Island enjoys a reputation as one of the world's safest beaches.

Carl E. Johnson County Park is located at the southern tip of Estero Island. A tractor-driven tram transports visitors along a rustic boardwalk, crossing over picturesque Oyster Bay and several mangrove islets to a public, yet somewhat secluded beach, Lover's Key.

Claim a section of unspoiled beach, cast a line into

• Fort Myers Beach

Estero Island, off the southwest coast of the state near Fort Myers.

(800) 533-7433

51

the surf, picnic, explore nature paths or spend some time searching for shells along the shoreline. The park also has showers, a pavilion, concession stand, and canoe rentals.

Recommended for all ages.

Grayton Beach

Some 17 miles east of Destin in the Panhandle.

(904) 213-4210

Open 8 a.m. to sundown daily. Camping fee is around $8 per day, plus an electric charge, if needed.

Grayton Beach is a wonderful example of the pristine white sand beaches and emerald waters of Florida's Panhandle beaches. Uncrowded and secluded, the beaches are highlighted by rolling, white sand dunes dotted with clumps of sea oats.

The park's attractions include picnic areas, fishing, boating, diving and nature trails winding through barrier dunes and piney woods. It also has sheltered campsites with water, electric hookups, and dumping stations for recreational vehicle campers.

Recommended for all ages.

Gulf Islands National Seashore

Fort Pickens and Naval Live Oaks are two areas included in Gulf Island National Seashore. Fort Pickens is on Santa Rosa Island just west of Pensacola Beach. Naval Live Oaks is about 10 minutes away on U.S. Highway 98, one mile east of Gulf Breeze.

(904) 932-9994
Fort Pickens
Visitor Center
(904) 934-2600
52 *Naval Live Oaks*

Fort Pickens is open 9:30 a.m. to 4 p.m. or dusk daily year-round. Admission: $3 per car, for seven days. Live Oaks, same hours, free.

These two unspoiled beaches are unique in that they also offer history lessons and examples of plant and animal life from centuries ago.

Fort Pickens originally was constructed to secure the approaches to Pensacola Bay and the U.S. Navy Yard from foreign invasion in the early 1800s, and was occupied by a force of 50 U.S. Regulars during the Civil War.

While they're exploring the imagination-filled Fort Pickens and battery, children will find a small tucked-away museum free of charge. It has a sandbox, aquariums with sea life native to the area, and taxidermy of birds and small animals, including abandoned reptile skins. There is also a small Indian exhibit featuring Geronimo, and a cutaway display of Indian relics showing at what point they were found underground.

A full-scale model of a section of the U.S.S. Constitution, built out of the live oaks, is inside the Naval Oaks Visitor Center. At both Fort Pickens and here, there are lectures, tours, slide shows and movies available, as well as a selection of books.

2

Many children dream of becoming a park ranger, and they can almost do that at Fort Pickens. Three ranger-led classes, a test booklet, a map and a lesson about litter will make a young person eligible for a Junior Ranger badge and certificate.

Various interpretive programs are scheduled from June to mid-August, such as short talks about acid rain and eagles, as well as snorkeling lessons complete with equipment, and ghostly stories around the campfire. Call ahead for programs scheduled, because they are subject to change.

Recommended for all ages.

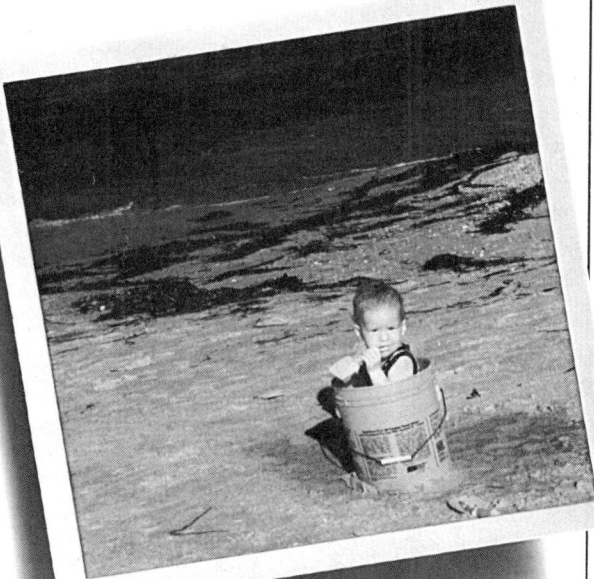

A big enough bucket for Brant Jaques.

There is a $3 toll per passenger car for the bridge connecting the islands to the mainland.

Some Florida beaches are just too good to leave out. Trips to Sanibel and Captiva will have children talking for weeks about their adventures on these islands.

Residents have fought long and hard to save these islands from the horrors of development and their efforts have paid off. Sanibel's J.N. "Ding" Darling National Wildlife Refuge and the Sanibel-Captiva Conservation Foundation are the best

Sanibel and Captiva Islands

Off the southwest coast of the state near Fort Myers.

places to see the natural fruits of their labors. There are nominal fees at both places.

Bird watching here will hold even a child's interest since the antics of the roseate spoonbills and anhinga are more Cathy Rigby-like than birdlike. The spoonbills fly about in squadrons and dip into the shallow waters for what seems like 10-course meals with their spatulate bills.

Pamphlets to identify shells are available all over the islands. These will allow kids to indulge in the most famous exercise on the islands — The Sanibel Stoop. Sanibel ranks among the top places in the world for shelling, and there is no end to what kids can pick up on the beach in the way of shells and information about sea life.

The beaches on both islands are made for walking, with no cars allowed but parking available. Sanibel has designated public and resident beaches with special decals required to park at resident beaches. There is a $2 fee at Bowman's Beach and pets are allowed here on leashes. There are also public restrooms, a fishing pier and picnic sites. Parking spaces fill up quickly on Sanibel, so an early morning start is recommended.

Captiva does not allow pets or alcoholic beverages. The only public restrooms and picnic facilities on Captiva are at Turner Beach just beyond the Sanibel-Captiva bridge.

There's no question about where to take the kids for dinner on Captiva. The original Bubble Room (smaller than Orlando's and the "real" Bubble experience according to purists) is the choice of natives and visitors alike.

Recommended for all ages.

Chapter 3

• • • • • • • • •

SWINGS AND THINGS

Parks and campgrounds provide 'back to nature' experiences

T he state parks department likes to say that it is the keeper and protector of the "real" Florida. No assertion could be more accurate.

As development booms all around Florida, the area's natural resources and cultural heritage face a daily battle for survival, but state parks provide an escape "back to nature" or to a quieter time of yesteryear. The diversity of activities, inland and coastal diving and boating, island camping, biking and hiking, reflect the variety of Florida's landscape, from white dunes to subtropical coastlines. All these elements combine to create a symphony of outdoor life.

With so much from which to choose, families will find it easy to tailor their nature activities to a child's interests. There are more than 100 parks statewide, with many just a short drive from home. You can find animals in the wild, crystal-clear springs, meandering canoe trails and a full menu of activities for outdoor adventures.

Camping reservations are taken in some parks, though only half the campsites are allowed to be reserved. Reservations will not be accepted more than 60 days in advance of the check-in date. Guests may camp for up to 14 days, and reservations will be held until 5 p.m. on check-in day. Children must be accompanied by an adult at least 18 years of age. Check out time is 2 p.m. Fees are $6 plus tax for inland parks and $10 plus tax for coastal areas.

There are also group camping areas with special facilities in many parks.

For more information and a complete listing of all

• Daniel Barret Caligiuri steering through the Community Park Playground in Winter Park.

Florida state parks and recreation areas, write Department of Natural Resources, Division of Recreation and Parks, Marjory Stoneman Douglas Building, 3900 Commonwealth Blvd., Tallahassee, Fla., 32399. Telephone: (904) 488-7327.

Blue Spring

Two miles west of Orange City, off Interstate 4 and U.S. Highway 17

(904) 755-3663

Sharing refreshments at the Blue Spring Manatee Festival, Terri Furbish and Crystal Bandekow.

Open daily from 8 a.m. to sunset.
Admission: $1 for driver and 50 cents for each passenger 6 years and older.

B lue Spring is a very special place; just ask any manatee. These gentle giants spend their winters here and children can not only see these endangered animals during a visit, they can adopt one. Call the park for details about the Adopt-A-Manatee program. Park rangers provide "manatee facts" during a series of scheduled talks.

Thursdays through Sundays you also can tour the 100-year-old Thursby House and learn about the steamboat era on the St. Johns River. The tour costs an additional 50 cents, but kids 6 and younger are admitted free with an adult.

Other activities here include a beach, camping and

cabins, boating, canoeing, picnicking and nature trails. There is also a refreshment stand in the park.

Recommended for all ages.

Open 8 a.m. to sundown daily.

Admission: $1 for driver and 50 cents for each passenger. For reservations at the Old Spanish Sugar Mill Restaurant, call (904) 985-5644. Restaurant hours: weekdays 9 a.m. to 5 p.m. and weekends 8 a.m. to 5 p.m. Serving ends at 4 p.m.

Kids who are eager to grow up might not understand the legend of Ponce de Leon and his search for a fountain of youth. A visit to DeLeon Springs, supposed site of that fabled font, offers some insights into the explorer and a full day of outdoor recreation.

The manageable 55-acre park offers an all-day outing with swimming, an Indian mound, and a boat ramp close at hand.

A highlight of your visit here could be a cooking lesson for youngsters. Before you groan and say that "Billy will never learn to cook" consider this: The Old Spanish Sugar Mill Restaurant makes pancake flipping a family affair, with grill-equipped tables and an all-you-can-eat menu. You buy the batter, then everybody fries their own cakes on the tabletop grill. The restaurant is in a replica of the original 19th century mill, with the first mill's equipment on display inside.

An egg breakfast with your choice of meat and bread costs around $2 per person. Side orders of extra meat are between 60 and 90 cents each. For $2 you also can order the all-you-can-eat pancake-only meal, with apple slices, bananas, apple sauce and blueberries available for toppings at 60 cents per serving.

Recommended for all ages.

No vehicles are allowed on this island in the St. Johns River, but a ferry will transport you across to swim, fish, see a Timucuan Indian ceremonial mound and walk the nature trails of the 1,060-acre park. You also may tie up your own boat at the park's marina and go ashore for a picnic. Park rangers lead regular observation tours of the plant and animal life.

Recommended for age 5 and older.

DeLeon Springs Recreation Area

Ponce DeLeon Boulevard, off U.S. Highway 17 near De Land. For information: DeLeon Springs State Recreation Area, P.O. Box 1338, DeLeon Springs, Fla., 32028.

(904) 985-4212

Hontoon Island State Park

Six miles west of DeLand off State Road 44.

(904) 736-5309

Ocala National Forest

East of Ocala between the St. Johns and Oklawaha rivers. For information: Lake George Ranger District, Route 2, Box 701, Silver Springs, Fla., 32688.

(904) 625-2520

Visitors' Center at State Road 40 and County Road 314 in Silver Springs is open daily from 9 a.m. to 5 p.m. Admission: $1.25. Reservations are accepted and recommended.

You might say that Ocala is a full-service national forest, with all the trimmings. The 430,000-acre forest is dotted with springs, campsites and wildlife and combines many recreation areas into one. Some of the land surrounded by the forest is privately owned, and part of that, like Juniper Run, is included in the list of recreation sites here.

Tubing, canoeing and cave diving are draws at Juniper Springs. Alexander Springs offers tubing and canoeing in 72-degree water all year, as well as picnicking and camping. Three popular spots for families with swimmers are the Mill Dam lake, Salt Springs and the Juniper Run lake.

Wildlife is abundant in the forest with species from the striped newt to the black bear. The foliage includes cypress, longleaf and slash pine, and hardwoods. Your junior rangers can enter nature's classroom in the Ocala Forest and come away with a semester's worth of learning about natural Florida.

For now, humans are allowed to roam free in most areas of the forest. Conservation of the land and animals, however, may one day mean closing parts of the forest to visitors, so see it while you still have the opportunity.

Families may cut their own Christmas trees in the forest if they obtain a permit from the park service. Permits are issued beginning in November and the cost is $5 per tree, though this is subject to change each season. For information, call (904) 625-7470.

Recommended for all ages.

Paynes Prairie State Preserve

Off U.S. Highway 441, one mile north of Micanopy.

(904) 466-3397

Open 8 a.m. until sundown every day; visitor center is open Wednesday through Sunday. Admission: $1 for driver and 50 cents per passenger.

Upon entering, you will encounter trees, trees, trees and a Florida as it was centuries ago.

The naturalness is part of the Florida parks plan — to have the land appear as it did when the first Europeans arrived. The 18,000-acre preserve is one of the more significant historical areas in the state. Indian artifacts found here have been dated to 10,000 B.C. During the late 1600s, the largest cattle ranch in Spanish Florida was in operation in the area, and naturalist William Bartram paid a visit in 1774.

The basin is covered by marsh and wet prairie vegetation with areas of open water. And what water it is! Lake Wauberg, part of which is used by the University of Florida, offers bass fishing and boat ramps for sailing, canoeing and floating things that use electric motors. No gasoline power here; it is prohibited. There is swimming at a beach shaded by live oaks and sabal palms, and lifeguards are on duty weekends and holidays from May through Labor Day.

You can even bring the family horse, provided you have proof it has had a negative Coggins test. There are several miles of trails available, and a ranger will tell you where and how to find them. Markers along the way help, too.

In addition, there is rustic playground equipment, including a slide and swing; restrooms and picnic tables, barbecue grills, 37 recreational vehicle sites, 20 tent sites, two bathhouses and a dumping station. Most facilities are equipped for the handicapped. There are additional fees for some of these activities.

Recommended for everyone, including the family horse(s).

Shepherd and Hunter Pittman swing at Whiting Park.

Open 8 a.m. to 10 p.m. for campers; 24 hours for fishing. Free.

A man-made jetty stretches out into the Atlantic here, providing fishermen access to deep ocean waters. Sebastian is also one of Florida's best surfing spots because of the waves created by the jetty. Lifeguards are on duty in the swimming area from Memorial Day through Labor Day.

A bait store, gift shop and concession stand do

Sebastian Inlet State Recreation Area

On State Road A1A in Sebastian Inlet.

(407) 727-1752

Wekiwa Springs State Park

Five miles southeast of Apopka on Wekiwa Springs Road, off either State Road 434 or 436.

(407) 889-3140

business on the grounds. There are restrooms and 90 campsites available. Pets are allowed on six-foot, hand-held leashes in all areas except the beach. No driving is permitted on the beach, but parking is available.

Recommended for age 5 and older.

Open 8 a.m. to sunset daily.
Admission: $1 for driver and 50 cents for each passenger 6 years old and older. Camping fees vary but park staff can provide the information by phone or at the park entrance.

Everyone has childhood memories of picnics and the old swimming hole. Nature's beauty is never lost on kids, no matter how oblivious they may seem during an outing. Wekiwa Springs State Park, with its stunning spring, hiking trails, canoes and fishing, is full of settings sure to keep the family camera clicking.

Kids who swim will enjoy the paved-edge spring, with its dramatic setting, nearby playground and bubbling source (also the main source of the Wekiva River.) Signs warn that there is no diving, because the swimming area is very shallow. There is also an even shallower area for younger swimmers and splashers.

Older children will enjoy all or part of the 13-mile hiking trail. The path winds through several types of vegetation, with glimpses of the upland wildlife providing a natural sideshow. Hikers can get the feeling of truly being "away from it all" in more remote parts of the trail.

Huge palms and pines shade the path as you cross easy bridges and follow the blue or white blaze marks. Overnight stays are possible at two backpack campsites with park staff's permission. A concession stand will keep kids and parents fueled up for the walk, in case they forget their granola bars.

The horse trail crosses the hiking trail at several points. Families who are at home on horseback can bring their own mounts and tour the park. There is a fenced site for horse trailers.

If you want to get the kids out for a weekend away from the citified environment, a family camping area is available for those with tents or trailers. The campsites are located in the park's sandhill community, one of the many ecological areas explained in the park's literature.

Water sports don't stop at the spring. The

youngsters can get their first fishing lesson at several points along the Wekiva River or Rock Springs Run. Swampy shorelines and thick vegetation make boats or canoes necessary to reach the best fishing holes, but canoes can be rented in the park for this purpose, or for a leisurely paddle along the Wekiva.

The park staff is working with members of the Orange County School Board to develop special programs for children to educate them about taking care of the fragile resources of our environment. Give the rangers a call in advance to see what's available and arrange for a guided tour for the family or a school or recreation group.

Recommended for age 4 and older.

Brett Crager, Kera Newkirk, and Heather and Luann Rundall picnic at Wekiva State Park.

3

Maybe one of the simplest pleasures left to kids is going to the park. From the time they are in a stroller until they become "sophisticated," children can take full advantage of their "kid" instincts to swing, run, jump, play in the sandbox or go fishing with grandpa. It's a classic pursuit and an easy, inexpensive one for parents.

Central Florida is rich in green spaces, planned and wild. Tot lots, designed especially for kids' recreational

Parks Just Around The Corner

needs, are plentiful in cities, and the lakes provide a lovely setting for a picnic or a place to cool off on hot summer days. The selective listing below includes facilities and fees, if they exist, for Central Florida parks.

Orlando

(407) 849-2285
Department
of Parks
and Recreation

Ben White Recreation Center: Corner of Lee Road and U.S. Highway 441. Trotting horses train next door during winter at the Ben White Raceway. Park includes restrooms and activity room.

College Park Playground: Westmoreland Drive and New Hampshire Street. Facilities: tot lot, fitness trail and playground.

Delaney Park: Corner of Delaney Avenue and Delaney Park Drive. More than seven acres hold a playground, tot lot, recreation complex, tennis and basketball courts, softball field, picnic tables, a shelter and restrooms.

Dover Shores Playground: Gaston Foster Road and Curry Ford Road. Facilities: junior Olympic pool, tot lot, playground, lawn bowling, activity room and restrooms.

Englewood Neighborhood Center: 6123 La Costa Drive. Facilities: tot lot, tennis and basketball courts, softball field, weight room, gymnasium, open play area, locker rooms and showers. A library, kitchen and meeting rooms for community functions.

Lindsay, Callie and Benjamin Vinson out for a swan boat ride on Lake Eola.

Anna Metisse Carapellotti running through Lake Eola Park.

Eola Park: Downtown Orlando at Rosalind Avenue and Robinson Street. A pretty urban park features a one-mile scenic walk around Lake Eola. Facilities include picnic tables, tot lot, restrooms, fountains, forum, plant displays, swan paddle boats, gardens and a Chinese-style gazebo. Paddle boat rental is $4 for 30 minutes.

Fern Creek Playground: Northeast corner of Fern Creek Drive and Lake Highland Drive. Facilities: junior Olympic pool, grills, picnic tables and tot lot.

Hankins Park: Lake Park Court and Columbia. For a change in your park adventures, this site offers boardwalks and nature trails. Facilities include a pool, softball field, tot lot, tennis courts, open play area, activity room, weight room, shelter and restrooms.

Lake Fairview Recreation Complex: Lee Road and U.S. Highway 441. This is a large seasonal park with lifeguards on duty from May through August. Facilities: boat ramp, dock, picnic tables, grills, ball fields and concessions during summer. Admission for swimming is $1 for adults, 50 cents for children 17 and younger and seniors over 62.

Lorna Doone Park and Beach: 1519 W. Church St. A scenic lake is the setting here for swimming, fishing, picnic tables, tot lot, softball field, tennis and basketball courts.

Orlando Loch Haven Park: Corner of Mills Avenue and Princeton Street. An enormous park that is also a cultural mecca for Orlandoans. The museum of art and civic theater are on the grounds. For a park outing, take a blanket and picnic lunch, or fishing gear for nearby lakes. It is also the perfect place to go fly a kite in the April breezes.

Turkey Lake Park: 3401 Hiawassee Road. A 300-acre favorite with area families, this park has something for every child. They can even camp overnight for $1 per head, age 2 and younger free. Facilities include swimming, picnic tables, shelters, pool, nature trails, ecology study area, concession stand, boating, canoeing, tot lot, fishing pier and a petting farm. Park is 97 percent accessible to the handicapped. Admission is $1 per person 2 years and older.

Emeri, Caleb, Jacob Keppeler share a towel at Turkey Lake Park.

Lake Adair: Edgewater Drive and Lake Adair Boulevard.

Lake Como Park: Bumby Street south of Anderson Street.

Lake Davis: South Summerlin Street and Lake Davis Drive.

Lake Emerald: Lake Emerald Drive, south of East Gore Street.

Lake Estelle: Corner of North Mills Avenue and Rollins Street.

Central Park: On Park Avenue in downtown Winter Park. Whether you are cruising the annual art festival or just meandering through this delightful shopping area, you can rest on the benches in Central Park. Fountains, a rose garden, the train station and walkways complete the "old country" atmosphere.

Cady Way Recreation: Cady Way east of Ward Park. Kids should bring their racquets for this outing. Facilities include four lighted tennis and raquetball courts, playground, softball field and fitness trail. Court fees vary. Open 9 a.m. to 9 p.m.

Dinky Dock: At Ollie Avenue and Lake Virginia. This park offers the chance for a real canoe adventure, for a $2 per hour rental charge. There also is swimming and a public boat ramp. Lifeguards are on duty during operating hours from 8 a.m. to 8 p.m. in summer and 7 a.m. to 6 p.m in winter.

Lake Baldwin Park: South Lakemont Avenue and Glenridge Way. Walk in the woods in the middle of town on one of the nature trails here. Also, fishing dock, boat ramps, picnic tables, grills, playground equipment. Open 8 a.m. to dusk.

Lake Island Park: Denning Drive. This park is 75 percent accessible for the handicapped. Facilities include playground equipment, pavilion, grills, softball field and shuffleboard.

Mead Gardens: Denning Drive. A green getaway with botanical gardens, walkways, bridges, greenhouse, picnic tables. Open 8 a.m. to dusk.

Azalea Lane Recreation Center: 1045 Azalea Lane. Tennis is for everyone here on 10 lighted courts. Also, tot lot, playground, softball field. Hourly court fee. Open 9 a.m. to 9 p.m.

Just For Fishing

Winter Park

(407) 623-3334
Department of Parks and Recreation

Jan and Joe Spino, Jennifer LaBrake and Callie Rae Force at Lake Eola.

Brevard County

(407) 269-1870
Department
of Parks
and Recreation

Brothers Park Community Center: Lime Street in Melbourne. (407) 723-8340. Open noon to 9 p.m. Monday, Wednesday and Thursday; noon to 8 p.m. Friday; 9 a.m. to 9 p.m. Tuesday; 1 to 5 p.m. Saturday. Facilities: pool, playground, basketball courts, restrooms and recreation hall with kitchen.

Jetty Park: At the end of the causeway in Cape Canaveral. (407) 783-7222. Lifeguards are on duty on weekends from April through May, full time from June to September. No pets, alcohol or driving is allowed on the beach. Cape regulars say Jetty Park is a prime spot for watching rocket launches from Kennedy Space Center. Facilities: concession stand, picnic and camping areas.

Lipscomb Street Park Community Center: Monroe Street in Melbourne. (407) 724-6962. Open 8:30 a.m. to 5 p.m. daily. Call for court hours. Facilities: weight room, four lighted basketball courts, soccer and softball fields, playground, jogging and fitness trail, picnic pavilion, two lighted tennis courts.

Wells Park: Adjacent to Melbourne Auditorium on Hibiscus Avenue. (407) 727-0511. A bell tower, botanical garden and lake highlight this park.

Orange County

Barnett Park: Pine Hills Road. Picnic area, dirt bike track, tennis and basketball courts, baseball and softball fields, fishing dock and exercise track. Fee is 50 cents per car.

Christmas Park: State Road 420 in Christmas. This park centers on the Fort Christmas museum, but there are also tennis, basketball and volleyball courts, a playground and softball field.

Kelly Park: Five miles north of Apopka off State Road 435. Tubing the Rock Springs Run is the highlight of this 200-acre park. The three-quarter mile natural spring run can be tubed many times in a day and a boardwalk guides tubers back to the start of the run. An outlet near the park entrance rents tubes for $2, with a $1 deposit. Picnic tables and pavilions line the swimming hole and tube run. Hours are 9 a.m. to 7 p.m. Plan to get there early for a good spot on the weekends because it fills up rapidly in the summer. Admission to the park is 50 cents for everyone over 12 years of age. A campground is available for extended stays.

(407) 420-4290
Department of Parks and Recreation

3

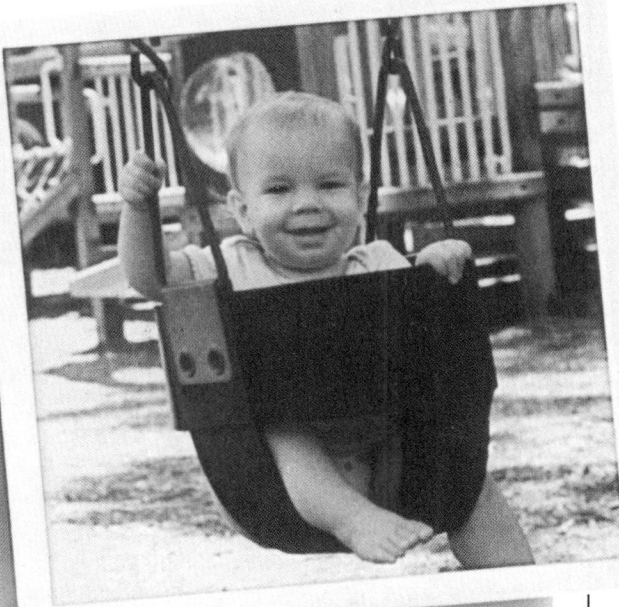

Swinging Christopher Blexrud at Community Park Playground, Winter Park.

Lake Cane-Marsha Park: Corner of Conroy and Turkey Lake roads. Facilities: two ball fields, picnic tables, two tennis courts, fishing and playground equipment.

Moss Park: Off State Road 15 at Moss Park Road. It seems nothing has been forgotten at Moss Park. There's a horseshoe pitching area, two boat ramps, tennis courts, playground, four pavilions, nature trails, fishing, swimming, camping and picnic grills.

Orlo Vista Park: Nowell Avenue. Facilities: shuffleboard, playground, two multipurpose courts, ball fields, swimming, two tennis courts and community center.

Warren Park: Swimming is available at this park on the Conway Chain of Lakes. Open 9 a.m. to 7 p.m. daily. There are also tennis courts and a picnic area.

Osceola County

(407) 892-7488
Department
of Parks
and Recreation

These Osceola County parks are open from 8 a.m. to sunset.

Alligator Lake: In St. Cloud off Hickory Tree Road. Facilities: grills, picnic tables and boat ramp.

Hopkins Park: In St. Cloud at 17th Street and Crawford. Facilities: Pavilion, picnic tables, playground equipment and baseball field.

Oren Brown Park: In Kissimmee at Old Tampa Highway and Airport Road. Facilities: grills, restrooms, playground equipment, baseball and soccer fields, pavilion and horseshoe pit.

Partin's Triangle Park: On Neptune Road in Kissimmee. Facilities: grills, picnic tables, restrooms, handball courts, pavilion.

Smith's Landing: On Lake Gentry in St. Cloud off Hickory Tree Road on County Road 535. Facilities: grills, picnic tables and boat ramp.

Whaley's Landing: On Lake Tohopekaliga off Kissimmee Park Road. Facilities: grills, picnic tables and boat ramp.

Lacey and Tiffany White up a tree in Kissimmee.

Big Tree Park: One mile west of U.S. Highway 17-92 on General Hutchinson Parkway. This seven-acre park includes the 250-year-old oak tree, The Senator, believed to be the largest in the state.

Mullet Lake Park: Eight miles east of U.S. Highway 17-92 on State Road 46 North on Mullet Lake Road. Open 9 a.m to dusk. Facilities: picnicking, primitive camping (permit required), fishing, boat ramp and restrooms.

Sylvan Lake Park: Three miles west of Interstate 4 on State Road 46, then one mile south on Lake Markham Road. Facilities: picnicking, playground, fishing, boating, restrooms, soccer field and a boardwalk.

Red Bug Lake Park: Two miles east of State Road 436 on Red Bug Lake Road. Open from 8 a.m. to 10 p.m. Facilities: picnicking, pavilion, soccer and softball fields, playground, shuffleboard, basketball, racquetball and tennis courts, restrooms, boating and fishing. Recreation programs. Fee and reservations required

Seminole County

(407) 323-2500
Department
of Parks
and Recreation

71

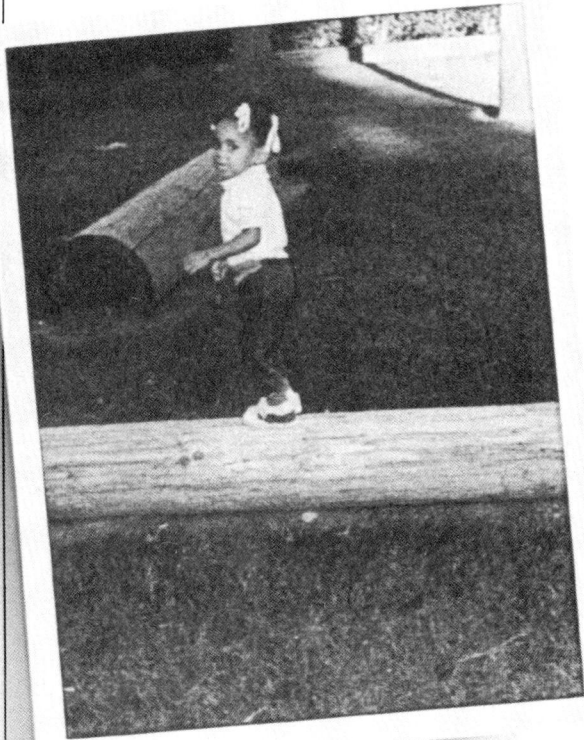

Gianna Gibbs learning to balance at Cherry Tree Park.

for tennis and raquetball. Reservations are taken starting at 9:30 a.m. for play that day or the next. Fees Monday through Friday are $2 per hour for games played from 8 a.m. to 6 p.m., $4 per hour for games from 6 p.m. to 10 p.m. Saturday and Sunday fee is $2 per hour for play anytime. (407) 695-7113.

Sanlando Park: One mile north of State Road 436 on Douglas Road. Facilities: playground, picnicking, restrooms, 25 hard-surface tennis, racquetball, and basketball courts, and pavilion rental. Reservations and fee required for tennis. Fees are $2 per hour from 8 a.m. to 6 p.m., $4 per hour from 6 p.m. to 10 p.m. Saturday and Sunday fees are $2 per hour anytime. (407) 869-5966.

Seminole County Environmental Center: At U.S. Highway 17-92 and State Road 419 across from the soccer field. This free educational center features nature trails and programs set up with kids in mind. The center's staff also does environmental awareness classes through the county's schools. No reservations are required for visits. The center is open from 8 a.m. to 3 p.m. Monday through Friday during the school year. In summer, grades 10 through 12 can earn science credit through Youth Conservation Corps jobs arranged by the center. For information, call Bettie Spratt at (407) 321-0452.

Sunland Park: One half mile south of Lake Mary Boulevard on U.S. Highway 17-92. Facilities: playground, tennis and basketball courts, picnicking, softball field.

Westmonte Park: 624 Bills Lane, Altamonte Springs, (407) 869-2516. A new heated pool with access for the handicapped is provided here, also programs for the handicapped including bowling, square dancing, and wheelchair tennis.

AROUND THE STATE

● ● ● ● ● ● ●

Open year-round from 8 a.m. until sunset daily. Guided tours are provided daily for $3 per adult, and $1.50 for children ages 3-12.

N ot all of Florida's attractions are located above ground. Below the 1,783 acres that are contained in Florida Caverns State Park lies an intriguing network of caves. Droplets of mineral-laden water, dripping through the ages, have formed these underground passages into a scenic array of formations.

The formations include sodastraws, stalactities, stalagmites, columns, rimstone, flowstone and draperies. The caverns have been compared in beauty, though on a smaller scale, to such famous ones as Mammoth Cave in Kentucky, and Carlsbad Caverns in New Mexico.

The caves are believed to have been used by the Indians as a refuge from Gen. Andrew Jackson's forces during his expeditions into Spanish Florida in 1818. In addition to the caverns, an extensive trail system meanders along the Chipola River flood plain, through hardwood hammocks and limestone outcroppings.

Other park activities include camping, fishing, canoeing and picnicking.

Recommended for all ages.

Florida State Caverns Park

2701 Caverns Road, Marianna. About 20 minutes off Interstate 10 on State Road 167.

(904) 482-3632

Ichetucknee Springs State Park

Five and a half miles north of Fort White, off State Roads 47 and 238.

(904) 497-2511

The park is open from 8 a.m. to sunset daily. Park admission is $1 per vehicle and 50 cents per passenger. Tubers are charged an entrance fee at each entrance. Tubes are rented by private companies and prices start at $1. Children and non-swimmers should wear life jackets.

You can pretty much do whatever strikes your fancy at Itchetucknee Springs — snorkel, swim, fish or hike. But the most popular pursuit is tubing down the lazy Itchetucknee.

Children get a "boat" (tube) of their own for gliding down the river. They may not take in much of the natural beauty since the simple act of tubing is so much fun.

The Department of Natural Resources asks that tubers float the lower stretch of the river to preserve the environment. This allows use of the free in-park shuttle that runs from May through September. Float time: 1 to 1½ hours on this stretch.

Tubers may also use the south entrance, walk to Dampier's Landing, and float to the last take-out point. They can return to the south parking area via park tram. Float time: 1 hour.

If starting your float at the north entrance, leave the river at Dampier's Landing and a concession shuttle will return you to the north entrance for a fee. Float time: 2 hours.

Groups are asked to stay together on the river. Climbing on or jumping from the river banks, trees or docks is prohibited.

Recommended for children who know how to swim.

John Pennekamp State Park

Follow the signs off the Overseas Highway on Key Largo.

(800) 432-2871

Open daily from 8 a.m. to 5 p.m. Admission: $1.50 for driver, $1 per passenger; children age 6 and younger admitted free. Boat launch is $2.

If you're a diver or snorkeler, John Pennekamp Coral Reef State Park, which covers 178 nautical square miles of coral reefs, seagrass beds and mangrove swamps, is a marvel not to be missed.

But even if you're not an underwater sport enthusiast, you can see the undersea wonders by glass-bottom boat. The glass-bottom boat tours over the coral reef are available daily, weather permitting. The boat departs at 9 a.m., noon and 3 p.m. and costs around $11 per adult, $6 for children age 12 and younger.

The park is the first underwater state park in the United States. It offers a swimming area, natural history exhibits, a 30,000 gallon, saltwater aquarium, nature trails, marina, boats, camping and picknicking facilities.

A nine-foot bronze statue, Christ of the Deep, is a special feature of John Pennekamp Park. Located in 20 feet of water beneath the Atlantic, the statue symbolizes peace for mankind and may be seen by divers and snorkelers.

Park rangers provide special snorkeling programs to familiarize visitors with the most desirable method of observing the coral reefs.

Recommended for all ages.

Open daily from 8:30 a.m. to 6 p.m. Admission: $3 per vehicle or $1 per walk-in.

Shark Valley

On Tamiami Trail, U.S. Highway 41, about 25 miles west of Florida's Turnpike extension.

(305) 221-8776 or 221-8455 for tram reservations.

Don't be fooled by the name. Visitors to Shark Valley in Everglades National Park outside Miami won't see any sharks.

They will, however, see the heart of a fragile ecosystem unlike any other on earth. They'll also understand why environmentalist Marjory Stoneman Douglas calls the 1.4 million-acre national park the river of grass. The sawgrass prairie at Shark Valley extends for miles, seemingly forever.

It's also a haven for a variety of Everglades residents. White-tail deer roam the plains while bald eagles, osprey and hawks circle above. Herons, wood storks, ibis and spoonbills wade in the water while turtles and every species of freshwater fish found in South Florida swim below.

And, stay alert. There are plenty of alligators. Their bumpy lumps move swiftly through the water or rest dead-like on the banks. They even lay by the road, sometimes with their mouths open, catching some rays.

Though there are no sharks in the valley itself, the name is not without significance. Shark Valley rests on the edge of the Shark River Slough, the broad, shallow body of water that starts at Lake Okeechobee and sweeps to the southwest, emptying into the Gulf of Mexico. Sharks find the rich mangrove forests of the coastal part of the river a perfect place to breed.

A 15-mile paved road loops through Shark Valley, giving visitors a comfortable route to commune with nature. There is an observation tower at the midpoint.

Two-hour tram tours, at $5 for adults, $4.50 for seniors and $2.50 for children, are available. Reservations for the tram are suggested. Hikers, joggers and bicyclists are welcome. Rental bikes are available for $1.50 an hour.

It is advisable to call ahead for a mosquito report.

Recommended for all ages.

Water baby, Kent Matthews, at Lake Fairview.

Wakulla Springs State Park

From Tallahassee, take County Road 319 south to the junction of State Roads 267 and 61, following the signs for the park. For information: call (904) 222-7279 or write Wakulla Springs Lodge, 1 Springs Road, Wakulla Springs, Fla., 32305.

Park is open from 8 a.m. to sunset daily. Park admission is $1 per driver and 50 cents for each passenger.

This adventure is a must if you're in the Panhandle. Parents will never hear, "Are we there yet?" aboard one of the glass-bottomed boat rides at Wakulla Springs. Children get to see where they're going, where they've been and right into the water on this unusual cruise. Glass-bottom boats run only when the water is clear.

The park also offers three-mile tours with lively commentary and animal spotting by the rangers along the Wakulla River, a registered national landmark. A floating theater makes the most of the park's aquatic setting and, of course, swimming ranks high with young visitors here.

What's the perfect way to end an afternoon of

boating and swimming? What about ice cream from the old soda fountain at Wakulla Springs Lodge? For a stay, management at the 1937 Spanish-style lodge recommends making reservations about two months in advance. All rooms look out on either the park area or the springs. Dining room opens at 7 a.m.

Boat rides start at 9:30 a.m. and cost $4 for adults and $2 for children ages 6 to 12 years. The floating theater (a 20-minute movie about the underwater caverns of the spring) costs $1 for adults and 75 cents for children.

3

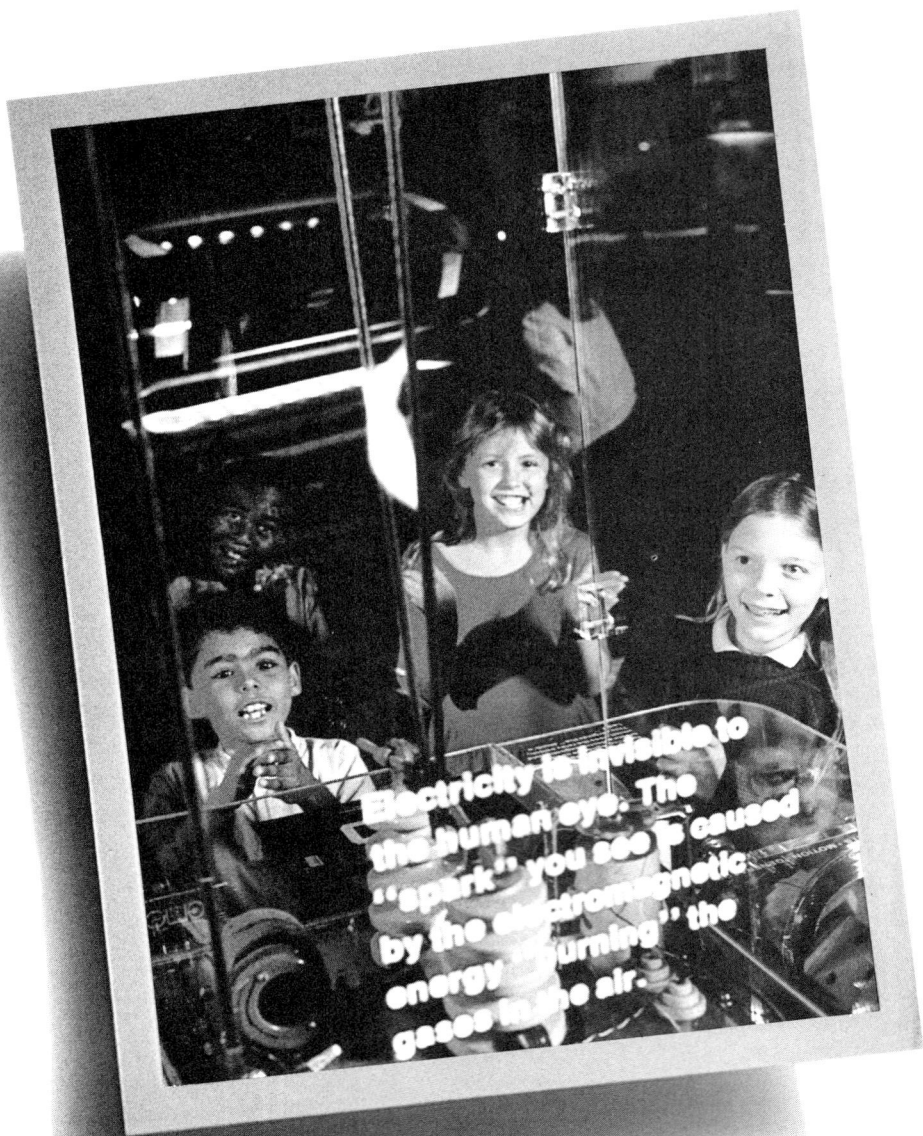

Electricity is invisible to the human eye. The "spark" you see is caused by the electromagnetic energy "burning" the gases in the air.

• • • • • • • •

HISTORY, SCIENCE LESSONS

4

Visit the past and explore the future

There's no doubt about it — Florida holds an important place in the history of the United States. And the state's past is filled with a rich cast of rogues and heroes, eccentrics and geniuses.

Historical sites and museums come in all shapes and hues here. The traditional museum smells of old wood and stone mix with the fresh smells of the outdoors and the rich aromas of preserved gardens to give the region's history a distinct twist.

Hands-on exhibits in some museums convey scientific information without the kids even realizing it.

The historical drama of Florida is also accessible and entertaining at many sites. These characteristics help dust off Florida's history and let it shine in a special way for children.

• Luis Marquez, Amanda Perez, Moses Robinson and Michelle Short in front of the Orlando Utility Commission exhibit on electricity at the Orlando Science Center.

Open 10 a.m. to noon and 1 p.m. to 4:30 p.m. daily except Tuesday and Wednesday. Guided home tours held every half hour. Admission for all 6 years and up: $1.

History is always a little easier for kids (and grownups) to take when they are learning it in a beautiful, natural setting. Enter the Marjorie Kinnan Rawlings home and Cross Creek.

Rawlings dropped out of New York to pursue serious writing in the steamy backwoods of Florida. She drew on nature and the lives of local residents to

Cross Creek

Marjorie Kinnan Rawlings Historic Site, 21 miles south of Gainesville. From Orlando, take U.S. Highway 44 north to

Ocala, then U.S. 301 to Route 3 and follow the signs.

(904) 466-3672

Daytona Museum of Arts and Sciences

1040 Museum Blvd., Daytona Beach, off South Nova Road.

(904) 255-0285

Florida State Museum

Museum Road on University of Florida campus off U.S. Highway 441 in Gainesville.

(904) 392-1721

fill her volumes with the rural magic that so many have read and remembered.

The author's book, *The Yearling*, made Cross Creek famous, but her restored home and the privately owned Yearling restaurant nearby keep the spirit she wrote about alive today. The restaurant serves dishes from Rawlings' book *Cross Creek Cookery* (Scribner's $12.95). The home tour, a meal at the Yearling and the rich, green beauty that surrounds the site will give children plenty to see and enjoy during a day trip here.

Recommended for age 4 and older.

Open from 9 a.m. to 4 p.m. Tuesday through Friday; noon to 5 p.m. Saturday and Sunday. Closed Monday. Admission: adults, around $2; children, 50 cents. Free Wednesday and Sunday afternoons.

The only complete giant ground sloth in North America is on display here. The fossil is 20 feet high, 130,000 years old, and weighed in at five tons. Pre-history rooms hold a nine-foot nearsighted armadillo whose shell weighs a thousand pounds, and dinosaur skulls and elephant bones from the Daytona bone pits. You'll also be able to feel 1 million-year-old elephant teeth and other relics in the touching room.

This is only one of five sections in the complex. There is also an art and science gallery, planetarium and pre-Castro Cuban arts exhibit with pearl, emerald and topaz jewelry. In addition, a coastal hammock trail offers about a 20-minute adventure outside.

Recommended for age 4 and older.

Open 9 a.m. to 5 p.m., Monday through Saturday; 1 p.m. to 5 p.m., Sundays and holidays. Closed Christmas Day. Free.

Although it is on the campus of the University of Florida, all the gators are stuffed at Florida State Museum, a sister institution to the Museum of Florida History in Tallahassee.

A simulated Florida cave and natural habitat exhibit have been among the most inviting displays at the museum in the past, but were recently under renovation.

There is an intriguing display of Spanish Florida, a diorama of life around a pioneer trading post and a good collection of artifacts from the 1800s and early 1900s. This is housed in the hall outside a room displaying biological and fossil collections, and live snake exhibits.

There are restrooms and a gift shop in the main lobby. For food, count on the prolific number of fast food places inhabiting a college town. This would be a good place to take the family before or after an outing at Paynes Prairie State Preserve, 10 miles south of Gainesville. (See entry in Swings and Things.)

Recommended for age 8 and older, though tours are available for younger school groups, too.

Hours for the park are 9 a.m. to 7 p.m. daily. The fort is open from 10 a.m. to 5 p.m. Tuesday through Saturday, and from 1 p.m. to 5 p.m. Sunday. Free.

Fort Christmas Museum

4

County Road 420, two miles north of State Road 50, Christmas.

(407) 568-4149

Florida kids don't get to build snow forts, and building leaf forts is out unless they have the right kind of trees in their yard. But the state has loads of forts for them to explore and there is none better than Fort Christmas.

The name sounds like the title of a children's story, and the tale of Fort Christmas is a quirky one in the state's history.

As the Seminole War whirled around them, 2,000 U.S. soldiers began construction of a supply depot in the Florida wild on Christmas Day, 1837. The structure, built to protect supplies and ammunition, was finished three days later. The only attacks on the fort, however, have been by Florida's bugs and a forest fire that later destroyed the structure. The fort has been rebuilt, but historians still are arguing about its original location.

A powder magazine, historical exhibits, a storehouse and replicas of the fort's two-story blockhouses are featured in the museum.

Recommended for age 4 and older.

Open 9 a.m. until 4 p.m. Saturday and Sunday and holidays. Admission: adults, $1.50; children ages 6-12, 75 cents; plus admission to Hillsborough River State Park: Florida residents, $1 for driver, 50 cents for passenger 6 or older; out-of-state cars, $2 for driver, $1 per passenger.

Fort Foster

Hillsborough River State Park, six miles south of Zephyrhills on U.S. Highway 301.

(813) 986-1020

History comes alive here. Rangers dressed as soldiers during the Second Seminole War will tell you what their life is like at the fort — all staged

81

as though it is indeed the 1830s — and, as you start down the quarter-mile trail soldiers will warn you of dangers ahead.

The original Fort Foster was a battle post and supply depot, abandoned and destroyed in 1835, rebuilt a year later and finally closed down in 1838 because of disease and generally damp conditions. It had a brief revival in 1849.

The state Division of Recreation and Parks operates the fort, rebuilt in 1979, as a "living history" program. Inside the stockade are a couple of two-story blockhouses, a commissary and an ammunition warehouse open for tours.

Visitors to the Hillsborough River State Park, where there are numerous recreational activities as well as campgrounds and a few concessions, are transported by van from a welcome station to Fort Foster. It can take some time, but it's worth the visit. Tours are on the hour 9 to 11 a.m., and again 1 to 4 p.m.

The state park also has a large spring-fed swimming pool and bathhouse for changing clothes if you want to take a dip.

Recommended for all ages.

Great Explorations

1120 Fourth St. S., St. Petersburg. From Interstate 275 take exit No. 9 to Fourth Street South. Turn right and travel a few blocks to 11th Avenue South.

(813) 821-8885

Open 10 a.m. to 5 p.m. Monday through Saturday, and 1 to 5 p.m. Sunday. Admission: around $4, slight reduction for senior citizens; children age 2 and under are admitted free.

S ome museums can be boring for kids if there's nothing to do but walk around slowly, and look at things. Well, Great Explorations is devoted to "hands on" exploring where, for the most part, you don't just look, you touch, move and play with the displays. Exhibits encompass the arts, science and some that can't be categorized.

As you enter the museum, you are greeted by Phenomenal Arts: make music by the pressing of a bar; touch a glass globe and see color dance at your fingertips; move your hands across or down a neon sculpture and it magically lights up — driven by the electricity in your body; use prisms and mirrors to create a masterpiece with the help of the sun. Kids will be enchanted before they've taken five steps.

Then comes the Think Tank, designed to stretch "mental muscles." The puzzles range from easy to more complex and there is always plenty of watchful staff on hand to make sure you understand what you're doing.

For children 6 and under, there's Explore Galore with slides and tunnels in a maze, complete with checkpoints, for an educational and fun experience.

The Body Shop helps determine how fit you are, how good your lunch time nutrition is, and what your real age is. Kids will have a good time testing the strength of their grip or their endurance, as they hang from a bar above a computerized platform.

The Mirror Rooms turn normal faces and bodies into something else through the creative use of reflective glass.

Finally the touch tunnel. This is designed for children 7 years and older — and whether your 7-year-old is ready for it is a judgment call only a parent can make. The 100-foot tunnel is totally dark and you are forced to rely solely on the sense of touch to guide you through the inky black as you wind up and down and around. It is not for anyone with claustrophobic tendencies or for children who have a strong fear of the dark. But it is an experience. It is open only on the half hour and participants go through the tunnel one at a time.

To refresh those little minds after all this activity, the Museum Deli is open during museum hours and there is a gift shop to browse through.

Recommended for age 5 and older.

Open from 9:30 a.m. to 4:30 p.m. Saturday and Sunday and legal holidays.

Kissimmee Cow Camp

Twenty miles east of Lake Wales, on State Road 60.

(813) 696-1112

Introduce your child to the Florida counterpart of the Western cowboy at Kissimmee Cow Camp. The camp is an authentic re-creation of those used by cow hunters, as they were called, on the South Florida frontier cattle trail of the late 19th century.

Everything in the camp — guns, saddles, whips — is an authentic replica of that used in the era, even down to the hand-carved wooden buttons on the cow hunter's shirt. He can be questioned about his life and work, but his lauguage and thoughts are all based on the knowledge of that time.

A herd of small scrub cows of the Andalusia breed, first brought into this country by the Spanish, wanders around the compound surrounded by a wooden fence. The cow hunter may be standing over a fire in front of a crude shelter, but he'll be glad to tell you about cattle drives to Punta Rassa near Fort Myers. About 300 cows would be rounded up at a time and sold at an average of $16.80 a head paid in Spanish doubloons.

The terrain of the country made the lariat used by the Western cowboy impractical, so the cow hunter used whips and dogs to drive cattle. The "crack" of the whips is believed to have lead to the use of the term Florida "cracker."

The cow camp is contained in Lake Kissimmee State Park where camping and other facilities are available.

Recommended for age 4 and older.

Museum of Science and Industry

4801 E. Fowler Ave., Tampa. Take Fowler Avenue Exit 34 from Interstate 275, three miles east; or Fowler Exit 54 from Interstate 75, two miles west. The museum is one mile northeast of Busch Gardens, directly across from the University of South Florida.

(813) 985-5531

Open daily from 10 a.m. to 4:30 p.m. except holidays. Admission: adults, around $2; children ages 5-15, $1. Free parking, fully accessible to the handicapped.

Survive a hurricane in Tampa's kid-friendly Museum of Science and Industry. A wind tunnel that blows 75 mph currents is one of the most popular exhibits in the three-story, award-winning complex.

The energy efficient building of durable concrete block with exposed color-coded pipes, has an open-air feeling with ramps open to the outside climbing from the atrium to the third floor. It's possible to take a quick look down three flights to check for any missing members of your party.

It's probably best to follow the kid's lead here to whatever interests them, from fiber optic technology to how a power plant works. Or, join Dr. Thunder for a thunderstorm, excite your impulses in the Electric Plaza, feel a fossil and learn about geology, and see what's blooming in the greenhouse.

Try to steer them away from the computer center until last, since there is so much to see you don't want to get plugged in before you have seen everything else.

Special shows and demonstrations are given throughout the day in the Wizard's Workshop or museum theatre. The Starlab Planetarium is portable and quite an adventure for kids. You crawl through a tunnel to an air-filled cavity, actually inside a black balloon, where different star configurations are projected on the walls of the sphere. You can almost reach out and touch the stars. There is also a special hands-on room for the under-7 set. A schedule of shows is posted at the museum entrance.

Traveling exhibits from all over the country make each visit to the museum different. If you want to make a day of it, bring sandwiches for a picnic on the tables out front. There is a snack bar, but the only food available is from vending machines. The Science Store provides appropriate souvenirs of your visit.

Recommended for age 3 and older.

Kevin Mulinare and friends build a dinosaur at the Orlando Science Center.

4

Open 9 a.m. to 5 p.m. Monday through Thursday; 9 a.m. to 9 p.m. Fridays; noon to 9 p.m. Saturdays, and noon to 5 p.m. Sundays.

Admission: adults, around $4; senior citizens and children under 18 years old, around $3; families $10. Snack bar on grounds.

Orlando Science Center

810 E. Rollins St., Orlando, in Loch Haven Park.

(407) 896-7151

S cience projects are part of any child's education and the city's science center has been earning A's from parents and kids alike for 25 years.

The see-and-do activities at the center take children into a black hole, the human body, the mysteries of sound, electricity and more. Whether they are blowing a giant soap bubble or pumping up the hydropower exhibit, kids get a science lesson along with a dash of magic. Each exhibit is an invitation to participate and ask why. And with parents on hand to help, the answers are provided in kid-sized words that would win even Albert Einstein's approval.

Daily schedules provided at the ticket counter list special events, such as physics, reptile or chemistry demonstrations, and what's on at the John Young Planetarium. Shows there include "Orlando By Night" and "The Seven Wonders of the Universe." Special exhibits are scheduled throughout the year.

If kids want to dig a little deeper into the mysteries of nature after their visit, the center runs a full schedule of workshops and trips for children ages 4 to 17. During the school year, workshops run from 11 a.m. to 1 p.m. on the second and third Saturdays of each month. Content and costs vary.

Summer activities include weeklong classes, camp-ins and teen trips. Call the center for more information on all programs.

Recommended for age 3 and older; ages for Science Center programs vary.

Orange County Historical Museum

812 E. Rollins St., Orlando. In Loch Haven Park.

(407) 898-8320

Open 10 a.m. to 4 p.m. Tuesday through Friday, 2 p.m. to 5 p.m Saturday and Sunday. Closed Mondays.

Free. Large group guided tours may be booked in advance.

While you're in Loch Haven Park, why not teach the kids what the word "Cracker" means? That's easy enough with a trip to the Orange County Historical Museum.

A thousand-year-old Timucuan Indian canoe is one of the older relics at the museum, linking the county to ancient times. The implements used by settlers to work the land look almost as crude as stone-age tools, and they provide a clear picture of what early Floridians had to cope with in civilizing the region.

A pioneer kitchen and village blacksmith shop represent the next rung on the ladder of the county's evolution, and visitors can even browse in a country store. A 16-foot Cracker whip (eat your heart out, Indiana Jones) is part of the informative exhibit on the Crackers and their place in Florida lore.

Children also get a look at a bygone parlor scene, Victorian hotel lobby, and a newspaper in the days of hot lead composition. The museum exhibits are accessible and, for the most part, easy to understand. This is a history lesson youngsters can enjoy.

Fire Station No. 3

The free museum is open from 10 a.m. to 4 p.m. Wednesday through Friday.

Just behind the museum is Fire Station No. 3, Orlando's oldest standing firehouse and the region's only fire museum.

The station was built in 1926 and served Orlando for more than 40 years from its Dade Street location in College Park. It was moved to Loch Haven and restored in 1978.

The main attractions here for children are the old hose cart (from the city's volunteer firefighting days), a 1908 horse-drawn steamer, and the 1915 American La France, the city's first motorized truck.

In the displays, visitors can see old toys, helmets, patches, nozzles, axes and uniforms. Photographs tell the stories of Orlando's worst fires, and a pot-bellied stove authentically sets the scene of firehouse life when No. 3 was in service.

Recommended for age 4 and older.

Open 1-5 p.m. Tuesday through Saturday; 2-5 p.m. Sunday; closed Mondays and holidays. Admission: around $2 for adults and $1 for children ages 6-18; under 6 years free.

This is old Florida on a small scale. Exhibits in the main building recall the basic liftestyle of earlier days, and a history lesson sort of sneaks up on the kids.

There are tools to show how the pioneer Floridian lived every phase of life — built a house, made furniture, plowed land, harvested crops, did leather work, attended school, traveled and even engaged in blacksmithing. Small children may find it tedious, but it can be a hands-on experience for older ones since the items are there for close inspection.

An exception is a collection of dolls, each wearing a replica of the inauguration gown of Florida's first ladies. These are protected behind glass, as — for the pleasure of adults — is an

Pioneer Florida Museum

East of U.S. Highway 301 on Pioneer Museum Road, one and a quarter mile north of Dade City.

(904) 567-0262

impressive collection of Roseville pottery donated by a Pasco County collector.

On the grounds are the 19th century Lacoochee one-room schoolhouse, the John Overstreet House built in Dade City around 1864 and the 100-year-old Enterprise Methodist Church, all furnished with period pieces.

The kids, however, could be more fascinated by the Old No. 3 engine that in the 19th century pulled logging trains for Cummer Sons Cypress Co. It sits on a track at the old depot moved to the 16-acre museum grounds from nearby Trilby.

No refreshments are available on the grounds, other than soft drinks.

Recommended for age 6 and older.

Ponce de Leon Lighthouse

4931 S. Peninsula Drive, Ponce Inlet. From Daytona Beach, go south on State Road A1A, right on Beach Street and left on Peninsula Avenue.

(904) 761-1821

Open from 10 a.m.-4 p.m. daily, summer hours 10 a.m. to 7 p.m. Admission: around $3 for adults and $1 for children under 11.

Structures like water towers, fire towers and lighthouses beg to be climbed and children can really make the trek up in the Ponce de Leon Lighthouse. The 203 steps lead up to a sweeping view of the Atlantic, Volusia County and Ponce Inlet.

A sense of history and adventure awaits you on the lighthouse's circular balcony, perched almost 170 feet above the ground. From a point less than 10 feet above the balcony, lighthouse keepers would light a lamp that flashed a brilliant signal to mariners nearing the treacherous Mosquito Inlet. There is plenty else to see on the lighthouse grounds, including the buildings where the keepers of the light lived with their families (one of which now houses the original lighthouse lens) and the 46-foot F.D. Russell tug boat.

But the true sight to behold at Ponce Inlet is the lighthouse itself, built of sturdy brick and completed in 1887. The spiralling stairs that lead to the top may be too much for younger children, and parents themselves will even find the climb a bit tough on the legs, though there are several good resting points along the way. The last 20 or so stairs are especially steep.

Once outside a hatch door that leads to the fenced-in balcony, the trip proves well worth every step. The warm winds gently blow salt air from the

Atlantic, and one gets a scenic 360-degree view — across the narrow waterways to New Smyrna, and below to the many boats coming in and out of the marinas. It's a sight you won't soon leave: A panoramic perspective leaves one looking to the far-away horizon where the sea meets the sky, fostering a fond respect for the sea and its glorious past, and for those who kept the light.

Recommended for age 8 and up.

Open daily from 10 a.m. to 6 p.m. Admission to the museum is free. The movie costs $1 for adults and 75 cents for children. The Diving Exhibition leaves from the Golden Docks Family Restaurant every half hour from 10 a.m. to 5 p.m. and costs around $4 for adults and half that for children.

Tarpon Springs Spongerama

4

Tarpon Springs Sponge Docks, Dodecanese Boulevard, Tarpon Springs.

(813) 942-3771

Take a walk through history in the sponge village on the docks of Tarpon Springs. As you wind your way down a narrow alley inside the "village" at Spongerama, various storefronts depict the scenes that were familiar to sponge divers as they plied their trade at the turn of the century.

Inside the museum, behind a shop arrayed with every kind of sponge imaginable, tableaux show how divers used to gather the sponge: some hung over sides of rowboats and raked them from the deep, others dived nude, with only a rope in one hand to link them to the boat and a bag in the other to gather sponges; others dived with only a light helmet.

There are illustrations showing how a sponge grows and how sponges eventually are sold at auction on the sponge exchange. For an underwater glimpse at how the sponges are gathered, a film runs every 15 minutes throughout the day.

To get out on the water and see the diver actually go overboard and bring up a live sponge, take the half-hour boat trip from the Golden Docks Family Restaurant. A narrator explains the history of diving in Tarpon Springs, and a diver is suited up like divers in the past, using an air hose connected to an on-board compressor (no scuba gear here) for the demonstration.

Large shrimp boats can be seen along the docks, as well as deep sea fishing boats, since Tarpon Springs is still a bustling port.

If all this sponging work makes you hungry, Spongerama has some great treats — fresh salt-water taffy and fudge to name two. If you really wish to get into the swing of things and eat authentic Greek food, there are a variety of restaurants from which to choose, most with menus posted on the door. These restaurants can also whistle up a hamburger or fried chicken in case younger tummies aren't yet ready for souvlaki.

Recommended for age 4 and older.

Ybor City State Museum

1818 Ninth Ave., Tampa. Exit 21 off Interstate 4.

(813) 247-6323

Open 9 a.m. to noon, and 1 to 5 p.m. Tuesday through Saturday. Admission 50 cents, except children under 6 years are free.

Non-smoking parents might not care to get into the evils of stogies with their kids during an outing, but a pleasant day can be spent in and around this historic site in the cigar city.

Some historic photographs show a huge room full of workers, carefully wrapping cigars at the Ybor City cigar factory, started by Vincente Martinez Ybor in 1886. The work was tedious. A "reader" used to sit on a platform above the workers, reading selections from poetry books, newspapers and books to keep spirits up in the workroom.

Ybor City today is somewhat less lively than it was in its Cuban heyday. But you can still buy Cuban coffee and other items on the street and, though automation put most of the cigar factories out of business, you can look for some perfectionists who still hand wrap cigars.

Many restaurants and shops are cigar "themed" with history in mind. Teddy Roosevelt, his dog Cuba, and the Rough Riders galloped into town on their way to San Juan HIll and today visitors can grab a bite at the Rough Riders restaurant. Teddy and his men even show up in old photos on the restaurant walls.

The Ferlita Bakery museum is located about 5 blocks east of Ybor Square. It holds some remembrances of the 1930s, when the town was known as the "Cigar Capital of the World." The museum portion of the bakery holds exhibits depicting the city's rowdy history and also contains the bakery's original oven from 1896.

A visit to Ybor City isn't complete without a stop at the Columbia Restaurant at 2117 Seventh Ave., if for nothing more than a look at the tilework brought over from Spain. The Columbia is famous for its traditional Spanish dishes, seafood and chicken. For lunch, one of its Cuban sandwiches easily would fill the bill.

Recommended for age 6 and older.

Dan Chavaroli on a cannon in St. Augustine.

4

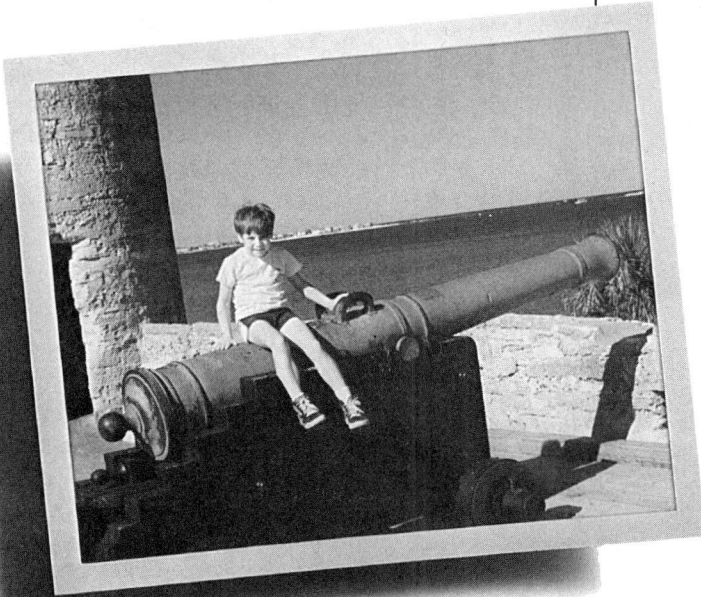

ST. AUGUSTINE AND AREA

• • • • • •

St. Augustine might be called the epicenter of Florida history. It is the country's oldest city. The operative word here is "oldest," with many of the city's sites being the first of their kind in the United States.

A brief rundown of the oldies in the city includes the oldest store, the oldest house and the oldest wooden schoolhouse. And the massive Castillo de San Marcos holds the title of oldest fortified structure in North America. More about these later.

St. Augustine is a patchwork of oddities and antiquities set amid the greenery of Matanzas Bay. The Spanish architecture of the area reflects the heritage of the early inhabitants. There are many ways to see the city — on foot, by tram, horse-drawn carriage or even a 75-minute cruise along the bay. Kids might enjoy the latter two touring methods best. The commercial historic district is quite contained and accessible, but parking spaces are at a premium. Plan to park and walk or take the trams.

Parents will want to be careful choosing places to take younger children, under 8 years of age. Some of the museums are only mildly interesting for adults and some kids interviewed in these places said they were bored. But don't worry, there is so much to see and do in St. Augustine there won't be a problem filling a one-day tour.

Any visit should begin at the Visitor Information Center, on the corner of Castillo Drive and San Marco Avenue. Free brochures and maps can get you started and the informed, friendly staff can help fill in the gaps. Several package tours combining transportation and admission are available.

The sights and delights in St. Augustine can't all be seen in one day. But children can hear street musicians, see plays and movies, tour a real castle and experience the magic of history that is preserved so well in this remarkable city. Choose from the sites listed below for a single-day trip.

Castillo De San Marcos

(904) 829-6506

Open from 9 a.m. to 5:45 p.m. daily in summer, and 8:30 to 5 p.m. during the winter. Fee is 50 cents for adults. Children under 16 and U.S. senior citizens are admitted free.

Work on the majestic coquina structure of the Castillo San Marcos began in 1672, after nearly a hundred years of ruined wooden forts and political haggling. Admiral Pedro Menendez de Aviles had founded St. Augustine and established its worth as a strategic military post, but nobody in Madrid or Mexico City would listen to his pleas for a stone fort on the site.

In 1668, an English privateer and his crew during a surprise attack seriously damaged the garrison, and the Spanish government finally ordered it increased and reconstructed in stone. After an energetic start, the project slowed and wasn't completed until 1695.

A park brochure quotes Freeman Tilden's book *The National Parks*, saying that the Castillo stands "grim, vital, defiant of time..." Kids can get the feel of being in a real castle at San Marcos; the moat and drawbridge might have been designed by a fairy-tale inspired child. The ranger tours provided by the National Park Service are lively and easy to understand. Rangers stop often during their talk and discuss points in the fort's history with young visitors.

The fort's second level allows a full view of picturesque Matanzas Bay. Be sure children get a glimpse of the huge cannons and pose for snapshots in the sentinel turret here. The cannons are fired each day at 1 and 3 p.m.

4

Runs from mid-June to mid-August at 8:30 p.m. nightly except Sunday. Tickets are in the $6 range for adults, $4 range for children under 12. Reserved seats are slightly higher. Group rates are available.

Cross and Sword

Amphitheatre is on Anastasia Island off State Road A1A.

(904) 471-1965

T he official state play, Cross and Sword, was written by Pulitzer prize winner Paul Green. Children can see a spirited dramatic presentation about the founding of St. Augustine.

Open 9 a.m. to 5 p.m. daily. Ticket office closes at 4:45 p.m. Admission: adults, around $3; children ages 6-12, $2; and age 6 and younger admitted free. Free parking.

Fountain Of Youth Archeological Park

Williams Street, off State Road A1A South.

(904) 829-3168

P once de Leon came ashore here, at the Indian town Seloy, to make his own bit of history in 1513 — the discovery of North America. The spring called his fountain of youth and his landmark cross are preserved at this archeological mecca. Other points of interest on the site include a planetarium, Indian burial site, train station and several significant archeological discoveries.

Open 9 a.m. to 5 p.m. daily. Admission: adults, around $4; children ages 6-12, around $2; senior citizens, $3, and kids age 6 and younger admitted free. Free parking.

Gonzalez Alvarez House

14 Saint Francis St.

(904) 824-2872

T he Oldest House, as it is known, is one of the country's best documented historic sites. Remnants of its many occupants span hundreds of years in time. The kitchens, dining and living areas recall the rough-hewn elegance available during Florida settlement times. It is an open book for kids, brimming with history and worth a couple of hours of your time.

Lightner Museum

City Hall Complex, King Street.

(904) 824-2874

Open 9 a.m. to 5 p.m. daily. Admissions desk closes at 4 p.m. Closed Christmas Day. Tickets in $3 range, children 12 years and older half price, under 12 years free when accompanied by an adult.

Like Flagler College, the Lightner Museum is housed in what was originally a hotel built by Henry Flagler. The Alcazar Hotel, which also contains city hall offices, is an enchanting blend of 19th century resort architecture and Florida landscaping. The museum holds a fine collection of relics from America's Brilliant Period — Tiffany glass, mechanical musical instruments, toys, furnishings and costumes. There are plenty of eye-catching exhibits for children, an Antique Mall shopping area and a museum shop.

Museum Theater

5 Cordova St., just down the street from the visitors' center.

(904) 824-0339

Open from 10 a.m. to 6:15 p.m. daily. Single movie tickets are $2, or see both movies for $3. Children less than 15 pay $1 for each film. Seating is limited to 100. Buy tickets in advance to be assured of seats.

Rainy days and Mondays in St. Augustine don't stop visitors from their appointed rounds, but this theater can give children a break from the gloom with two professionally produced historic films. Together they provide a full cinematic introduction to America's oldest city.

Oldest Store Museum

4 Artillery Lane.

(904) 829-9729

Open 9 a.m. to 5 p.m. Monday through Saturday, and noon to 5 p.m. Sunday. Admission: adults, around $3; children ages 6-12, $1; and 6 and younger admitted free. Free parking.

How did people shop during the B.M. (that's Before Malls) era? This turn-of-the-century store has shelves crammed with more than 100,000 items to help answer this question. During the 1800s, most of the city's social and political contacts were made within the walls of this store, making it more than just a place to buy corsets and flour.

Open 9 a.m. to 5 p.m. daily. Admission: adults, $1; children ages 6-12, 50 cents; and 6 and younger admitted free.

Everyone gets a diploma for the time spent in this 200-year-old cedar and cypress structure. "Students," dressed in period costumes, describe life during the era.

Oldest Wooden Schoolhouse

14 St. George Street, one block south of city gates.

(904) 824-0192

Open daily 9 a.m. to 5 p.m. Closed Christmas Day. Tickets are in $4 range, with children 6 to 12 years a little more than half price, children 5 and younger admitted free.

No center of history would be complete without a wax museum. Potter's Wax Museum lets you look Napoleon Bonaparte in the eye, as well as pose for pictures with him and more than 150 other figures from history. The figures are created in England and brought to the museum's recently redesigned halls in St. Augustine. Theater displays and video displays help round out your visit.

Potter's Wax Museum

17 King St.

(904) 829-9056

4

Open 9 a.m. to 5 p.m. daily. Guided tour costs $2.50 for adults, and $1.50 for students (ages 6 to 18). A family ticket is available and there is a senior citizen discount.

Guides in colonial dress will accompany you on your trip through this piece of the 18th Century. This carefully restored section of the city gives visitors a window on the old community and lives of Spanish soldiers, settlers and their families near the fort Castillo San Marcos. Many commercial shops occupy restored buildings along St. George Street. There's no charge to soak in the feeling of shopping in a European village. Motor vehicles have limited access to this area, adding to the courtyard atmosphere.

Restored Spanish Quarter

Enter at the Triay House, 29 St. George Street, near Old City Gate.

Ripley's Believe It Or Not! Collection

San Marco Avenue, across from the Visitors' Center.

(904) 824-1606

Open 9 a.m. to 5:30 p.m. daily. Tickets are in $5 range, less for children ages 5 to 12 and senior citizens. Children under 5 years admitted free.

This museum of Robert Ripley's collected oddities is by no means a must-see in a place like St. Augustine, unless you just want to say you've seen it. Most young children will be bored but older kids may find a few items of interest, like the dummy of the world's fattest man. The collection is rather down at the heels and could stand a good dusting, but there is an electronic game room where kids can amuse themselves while parents walk the three floors of believe it or nots. There is a snack bar and gift store in the museum building.

Zorayda Castle

Downtown St. Augustine, on the corner of King and Granada streets across from Flagler College.

(904) 824-3097

Open 9 a.m. to 5:30 p.m. daily, summer hours 9 a.m. to 9 p.m. Tickets are in $3 range; with children ages 6 to 15 half price, and under 5 years admitted free.

Another oddity, this Moorish palace, modeled on the famed Alhambra of Granada, Spain, is flavored with the mysteries of the East. View harem quarters, a mummy's foot, and walk the Court of Lions, which is tiled partially with mosaic tiles from an Egyptian mosque. Also on display, the sacred cat rug, taken from a tomb in the Valley of the Kings along Egypt's Nile River.

While you're in the area

Alligator Farm

Two miles south of the Bridge of Lions on State Road A1A.

(904) 824-3337

Open daily 9 a.m. to 5 p.m. Tickets are in $6 range for adults, $4 range for children ages 3 to 11, those under 3 admitted free.

Haven't had enough of the "firsts" or the "oldests" in America? Established in 1893, the Alligator Farm's claim to fame is that it is the world's original alligator attraction. Wildlife fills the grounds of the farm and there are daily shows.

An elevated nature walk puts you above a lagoon of gators, while the faint of heart can watch scores of heron, egrets and ibis return to their perches after a feeding. If it swims, flies, or crawls, it's probably somewhere at this attraction. And children can feed ducks, goats, deer and peacocks after their thrills with the jaws that made Florida famous.

Amelia Island

Historic Amelia Island is shared by the Amelia Island Plantation resort on the south end and the city of Fernandina Beach on the north. The resort features biking, jogging and horse trails, golf and some just-for-kids fishing holes. Fernandina Beach has restored about 30 blocks of its old town center and Fort Clinch, on the island's northern tip, provides a convenient side trip. For information on accommodations on the island, call the Fernandina Beach Chamber of Commerce at (904) 261-3248 or the Amelia Island Plantation at (904) 261-6161.

About 60 miles north of St. Augustine on State Road A1A.

4

Fort Matanzas National Monument

The monument is open daily from 8:30 a.m. to 5:30 p.m., closed Christmas Day. Free.

The coquina tower at Fort Matanzas was built by the Spanish in 1742 to guard the south entrance to St. Augustine. It consists only of a gun-deck and living quarters, but an adventure here includes a boat ride because the fort is only accessible by boat.

The fort is situated on Rattlesnake Island in the middle of the Matanzas River, which isn't a river today, but a salt water estuary leading northward from Matanzas Inlet. Ferries from Anastasia Island, where you'll find a visitors' center, run daily in summer and on weekends the rest of the year from 9 a.m. to 4:30 p.m.

The gun platform is solid fill, necessary to support its former six cannons. The two you see today were made around 1750 and are typical of those used at Castillo De San Marcos. At the rear of the gundeck is a water cistern, the only source of fresh water on the island during the 1700s.

The lower room was the living quarters for seven to 10 men who occupied the fort on a month's tour of duty. At the top of the stairs was the officer's quarters. A narrow ladder is the only access to the top of the tower, which provides a good view of the inlet to the south.

Soft coquina served Fort Matanzas well during historic times. Today, however, walking, sitting, or standing on these fragile walls does wear away the "shellstone."

Fourteen miles south of St. Augustine off State Road A1A on Anastasia Island.

(904) 829-6506

Marineland

Twelve miles south of St. Augustine on State Road A1A.

(904) 471-1111

Open daily 9 a.m. to 5:30 p.m. Tickets are in $10 range for adults and $5 range for children 3 to 11. Ages 2 and younger are admitted free.

Another "oldest" for the area, Marineland is billed as the original marine attraction. One thousand species of marine animals frolic here in aquariums, pools, on film and in continuous shows. The Dolphin Restaurant and Sandpiper Snack Bar provide food, and a gift shop and citrus shop offer souvenirs for you and the folks back home.

AROUND THE STATE

• • • • • •

Discovery Center

231 S.W. Second Ave., Fort Lauderdale. Take Interstate 95 to the Broward Boulevard exit. Go east to Southwest Second Avenue, which is just before the railroad track, and drive two blocks south to the end of the street.

(305) 462-4115

• *Open noon to 5 p.m. Tuesday through Friday; 10 a.m. to 5 p.m. Saturday, and noon to 5 p.m. Sunday. Hours may change during holiday seasons. Admission: $3, children 3 and younger are free.*

Discovery Center, the hands-on museum located near the center of downtown Fort Lauderdale, is an excellent place for children to see, hear and touch the wonders of the world of science and nature.

Younger children delight in hearing the sounds of hundreds of crickets in the Insect Zoo and watching live bees producing honey. The Florida Finds room takes them through a cave they can explore. In the Everglades room, children are able to feel the contrasting textures of different types of animal fur. School-age children can follow easy-to-read instructions to operate and understand exhibits in nearly 20 rooms on the museum's three floors.

Every room in the museum is worth visiting. No one would want to miss making their own music in the Sounds of Science, seeing the "chickee" (home) in the Seminole Village, exploring the world of colors in Rainbows End, planting a seed in the Backyard Workshop. Plan on at least a two-hour stay, though older children might like to spend the whole afternoon.

The Explore Store, the museum's gift shop, offers a variety of souvenirs, ranging in price from 25 cents for dinousaur stickers to $45 for a hologram watch. The shop also offers kits for scientific experiments, animal card games, board games and coloring books for younger children, and resource books for adults.

There are no snack bars on the premises, and parking might be a problem. A large restaurant parking lot located on S.W. Third Avenue may be used by museum patrons until about 4 p.m.

Recommended for age 4 and older.

Open weekdays and Saturdays from 9 a.m. to 4 p.m., and 12:30 to 4 p.m., Sundays. Closed Thanksgiving and Christmas. Admission: around $4 for adults, and $1 for children in grades K-12.

Edison Home and Museum

2350 McGregor Blvd., Fort Myers.

(813) 334-3614

I n 1886, after he was instructed by doctors to seek a warmer climate for health reasons, inventor Thomas Edison made Fort Myers his winter home. He was a winter resident there for 46 years. Today, his 14-acre estate consists of the Edison Winter Home, laboratory and museum and botanical gardens. The property was donated to the city by Edison's widow, Mina Miller Edison, and opened to the public in 1947.

The stately, yet modest Edison Winter Home, overlooking the Caloosahatchee River, was the nation's first prefabricated home. It is surrounded by the inventor's spectacular botanical gardens, a wonderland of more than 6,000 varieties of trees and plants he gathered from around the globe. Included are the state's largest banyan tree and several Moreton Bay fig trees.

In Edison's laboratory, an authentic collection of test tubes and apparatus rest in their proper places, just as he left them. Even the cot he used for 15-minute naps between experiments remains in a corner of his office.

The genius behind Edison's 1,097 patents, which include everything from the lightbulb, phonograph and motion picture camera to waxed paper and gum tape for bandages, is displayed in the museum. Several rare antique automobiles are among the other memorabilia preserved.

Recommended for age 8 and older.

Elliot Museum

825 N.E. Ocean Blvd., Stuart. From Stuart, follow State Road A1A across the causeway to Hutchinson Island. The museum is adjacent to the firehouse, where A1A first curves north along the ocean.

(407) 225-1961

Open 1 to 4 p.m. daily. Admission: adults, around $3; children 6-13, 50 cents; under 6, free.

The Elliot Museum is a whimsical private storehouse of Americana from 1865-1930 displayed in a sprawling five-winged building.

Tired of the mall? Check out the Elliot's reproductions of 14 shops from long ago, including a shoe store, an ice cream parlor and an apothecary. The Gracious Living wing displays elaborate Victorian decor in a fully appointed parlor, an Oriental room, the embroidery room, even the actual Elliot dining room, fully restored.

The Elliots were a family of inventors. One of their inventions is the kingpin, essential to automobile mechanics in the days before power steering. Most kids will thrill to the separate wing of fully-restored antique vehicles, with horse-drawn carriages, cars, bicycles, even motorcycles.

There's also a contemporary art wing, and the Martin County wing displays artifacts of Indian life, including the colorful Seminole tribe. One guaranteed hit with kids is the Elliot's display of antique savings banks. Bring a supply of pennies and dimes — kids love sliding coins into the slots, then watching the railroad engine run or the cart wheels turn.

The museum will take at least an hour, but you might as well make a day of it — the Elliot is right on Stuart Beach. A concession stand directly behind the museum sells food and drinks; it also rents boogie boards, basketballs and volleyballs for the courts nearby. Even if you've seen the museum and it's too cold to swim, you can shoot some hoops or build castles — and memories — in the sand.

Recommended for all ages.

Gilbert's Bar House of Refuge

Hutchinson Island, Stuart. From Stuart, follow State Road A1A across the causeway

Open from 1 to 4 p.m. Tuesday through Sunday; closed Mondays and holidays. Admission: adults, $1; children 6-13, 50 cents; under 6, free.

The House of Refuge was commissioned in 1875 as a life-saving station for those shipwrecked off Florida's east coast. It was used by the Coast Guard and the Navy through both World Wars until it was closed in 1945.

Gilbert's Bar will delight children interested in history. The boat house is full of early life-saving and maritime equipment, and the main house is furnished in the late Victorian style. A clinker-built surfboat waits outside the main house, and a wooden lighthouse towers over the restored buildings. (The lighthouse is closed to the public.)

Even a curious child might miss much of what's here, though, unless you point out how differently, and with how much difficulty, people once lived in Florida, from the kerosene lights for the lighthouse to the fabric netting for the mosquito screens, and the 200-year-old, well-worn washboard.

Until very recently the House of Refuge raised turtle hatchlings to release in the wild. Most of the tanks are empty now, as funding is no longer available for that project, but a 303-pound green turtle and a large hawksbill still swim in a large pool in front of the main house, and several aquaria display varieties of marine life downstairs.

The House of Refuge rests on a narrow strip of land between the Atlantic Ocean and the Indian River. A short pier leads out into the Indian River, and visitors can walk out on the rock-strewn, pink sandy beach on the ocean side. Spend some time here with your child, to consider the hardships of another kind of life or simply to enjoy the extraordinary beauty of this place. Going through Gilbert's Bar took less than an hour, but its presence haunted for days.

Recommended for age 3 and older.

to the Indian River Plantation resort. Follow the signs into the resort to the House of Refuge.

(407) 225-1875

4

Open from 11 a.m. to 4 p.m. Monday through Friday, and from 9 a.m. to 4 p.m. Saturday. Closed Sunday. Admission: 75 cents.

Indian folklore always has held a special fascination for most children, and at the Indian Temple Mound and Museum, they can get their fill of it.

More than just a collection of tomahawks reproductions and a few arrowheads, the museum takes the area's history quite seriously as it guides young curiosity seekers through the timetable of Indian life, from prehistoric times until the Europeans settled here.

Covered in these exhibits are the Paleo, Archaic, Woodland, and Mississippi cultures of mainly the Creek Indians, thought to be native to the Fort Walton area, as well as the Seminole and Choctaw

Indian Temple Mound Museum

On U.S. 98 in Fort Walton Beach just West of the Intracoastal Waterway Bridge.

(904) 243-6521

tribes. Their lifestyles are presented in interpretive displays and pieces of actual stone items, pottery, bones and shells crafted for daily use.

The Temple Mound, which has a thatched covering, was an Indian ceremonial center. It is one of many such mounds found throughout the southeast.

Children are encouraged to handle special tools that Indians used to start fires and drill holes. The Temple Mound and Museum are owned and operated by the City of Fort Walton Beach, and was the first museum in Florida to be owned by a municipality.

Recommended for age 4 and older.

Jacksonville Museum of Science and History

Take Interstate 4 east to Interstate 95 north. Take the Main Street Bridge (the last exit before the toll bridge on I-95), which will take you near Jacksonville Landing. Museum is at 1025 Gulf Life Drive, Jacksonville, by the Landing.

(904) 396-7061

Open 10 a.m. to 5 p.m. Monday through Thursday, 10 a.m. to 10 p.m. Friday and Saturday, noon to 5 p.m. Sunday. Admission is around $3 for adults and $2 for kids.

The news of extinction obviously hasn't reached the Museum of Science and History because dinosaurs abound there. But there's nothing primitive about this setting: The mysteries of physics, physiology, biology and technology unfold everywhere, much to the delight of scores of children.

The museum has three floors of surprises. The entry is what's called a creative play area and is rife with environmental exhibits and a dinosaur movie that hints of things to come. Children can learn about animal survival via well-labeled displays. Live and stuffed animals, including a couple of whopper pythons, provide a quick but fun nature lesson.

Screams from a string of imposing foamlike reptiles greet visitors to the second level. Beside the dinosaur exhibit, in a strange juxtapositioning, is a computerized learning center about the U.S. Constitution and history. Then the real fun begins — hands-on experiments similar to those at Orlando Science Center but more of them.

The museum tries to intersperse facts and fun while catering to kids' short attention span. The Seminole Indian display is very small, thank you, but it provides a needed repose. Next is a physics exhibit using balls (why they gain speed going downhill, why they do a loop-de-loop). Children are invited to find out why in a math lab.

Then it's time for another breather — this one in the form of a mini Egyptian mummy display — and then it's off to a play cityscape. Kids climb and jump and run en masse. This ultimate playground includes a bus, a phone booth and buildings.

The third floor is more sedate, and it's probably a good thing. Visitors are given a history of Jacksonville and a couple of diverse examples of home styles. The circuit ends on an up note for kids with a look at more wildlife and fossils.

The exhibit with perhaps the most overall appeal is the Alexander Brest Planetarium, a rather elaborate production where programs continually are offered. Call the museum for a program schedule.

The exit leads visitors down the garden path to the gift shop.

Allow two to three hours for a complete museum tour, not allowing time for the planetarium. Older children may require more time so they can read about the displays and ask questions.

Recommended for age 5 and up.

Open 9 a.m. to 4:30 p.m. Monday through Friday; 10 a.m. to 4:30 p.m. Saturday, and noon to 4:30 p.m. Sunday. Closed Christmas Day. Admission: free.

Museum of Florida History

500 S. Bronough St., downtown Tallahassee, in R.A. Gray Building.

(904) 488-1673

Florida history comes in easy dosages here with child-enhanced exhibits that don't talk down to adults.

Kids, and adults, can climb aboard a reconstructed steamboat and through photographs and a diorama savor commercial river travel as it was in the late 19th century. The diorama, synchronized with a recording, depicts landing at Silver Springs.

Kids will find it fun to check out the van used by tin-can tourists who traveled in a crude version of today's sleek motor homes. Actually, the motorized wagon was cleverly compact, albeit clumsy-looking, and took some of the edge off roughing it.

You can get a taste of how the citrus industry grew, how forts were built during the Seminole Indian wars, and explore a woodland area a 6-foot armadillo — yup, six feet long — calls home.

All of this is indoors at the Gray Building, where

there is a gift and souvenir shop with a good supply of books detailing the state's history.

If that isn't enough adventure, the museum system also offers the San Luis Archaeological and Historic Site on a hilltop west of downtown.

This was the location of an important Spanish and Apalachee Indian village in the 17th century. Here in the spring you can watch archaeologists digging into the past. Exhibits along the trails tell the story of the early inhabitants. This is reached by traveling north from the Gray Building to Tennessee Street and turning left.

Recommended for all ages.

Planet Ocean

3979 Rickenbacker Causeway, Virginia Key, Miami. Take Interstate 95 south to Key Biscayne exit, then take Rickenbacker Causeway.

(305) 361-9455

Open daily, 10 a.m. to 6 p.m. Admission: adults, around $8; children 6 to 12, around $4; under 6 admitted free.

Is there a child who has not asked how clouds are formed, why rain falls, how waves originate?

Planet Ocean, the museum of the International Oceanographic Foundation, is the place for children to understand the answers to these and many more questions related to marine science. Designed to be equally informative to school children and to adults, this museum offers more than a hundred exhibits and many multi-screen theaters featuring special effects.

At Planet Ocean children can feel the force of a hurricane, witness the birth of our planet, touch an iceberg, climb aboard a real submarine, man a periscope, walk through a drop of ocean water, and generate their own sea storm.

Though Planet Ocean is for the school-age child and adults, younger children who have had some exposure to the space program and Florida marine life will enjoy many of the exhibits and films. As they watch *The Unlikely Planet*, a wide-screen film, they will enthusiastically recognize Saturn's rings and Jupiter's red spot. They will be fascinated by the shark exhibit. They will enjoy Mr. Crab and Mr. Fish, featured in the *Underground Christmas Tree* movie.

Plan on at least a two and a half hour stay. Inquisitive children will probably need more time.

The unattended snack bar provides food and soft

drinks from vending machines only. If you plan to stay through lunch, it would be best to bring your own lunch and use the outside picnic tables.

The Gift and Book Shop provides a wide variety of souvenirs including key chains, stuffed sea animal toys, sea shells and jewelry. It also offers a very large selection of resource books on every aspect of marine life and ocean studies.

Recommended for age 5 and older.

Open 9 a.m. until 5 p.m. Tuesday through Saturday, 12:30 until 5 p.m. Sunday. Admission: around $4 for adults and $2 children ages 4-15.

From the moment you enter this museum there is something for a child to see or do. Start with giving the once-over to a 1919 Model-T four-door sedan. Or, visit the zoo or a late 1800s farm, complete with animals tame enough not to bolt at children's squeals.

To one side there are three historic buildings: Bellevue, the Tallahassee home from 1854 to 1867 of Princess Catherine Murat, a great-grandniece of George Washington; Bethlehem Missionary Baptist Church, built in 1937 near Tallahassee; and the Concord School, built about 1893 in the Miccosukee community east of Tallahassee.

Follow the six-tenths mile trail — a catwalk where you mostly look down — to the unique Natural Habitat Zoo. Search the trees in the aviary for hawks, owls, osprey and even a pair of bald eagles. Catch the beauty of the bobcat's coat, be quiet not to startle a family of white-tailed deer, admire the aloofness of a pair of red wolves, laugh at the otter family, whether its members are asleep or romping in the pool.

Check out the main buildings of the museum where there might be a hands-on lecture about birds or snakes going on, look for a display of children's art, or you may be lucky enough to catch a performance in the small outdoor theatre. There's even a "touch tank" of fish.

Wander on over to the Big Bend farm, representing primitive rural life in the 19th century. There are sheep, goats, a mule, cows, and, of course, chickens.

Plan to take a lunch, even if you have to stop at a

Tallahassee Junior Museum

4

Off U.S. Highway 19-27 south of town, take left on U.S. Highway 319 to dead end by Tallahassee Airport, right on State Road 371 to Museum Drive, turn right.

(904) 576-1636

fast-food place on the way, for there are no nearby restaurants. There is a picnic and playground area with vending machines and restrooms.

Recommended for all ages.

United States Naval Aviation Museum

Naval Air Station, Pensacola.

(800) 343-4321, Pensacola Visitor Information Center

Open daily from 9 a.m. to 5 p.m. Closed Thanksgiving, Christmas and New Year's. Free. Ramps and parking are available for the handicapped.

The United States Naval Museum is the only museum in the world devoted exclusively to naval aviation. There are more than 70 aircraft on display, including a Martin P5M Marlin, Grumman S2 Tracker, Douglas A4 Skyhawk, McDonnell F4 Phantom II, and a Skylab command module.

Additionally, there is an aircraft engine display, aircraft carrier exhibit and several oil paintings of Navy aircraft. Try your hands at the controls of a jet and see a visual history of American aviation.

Recommended for age 6 and older.

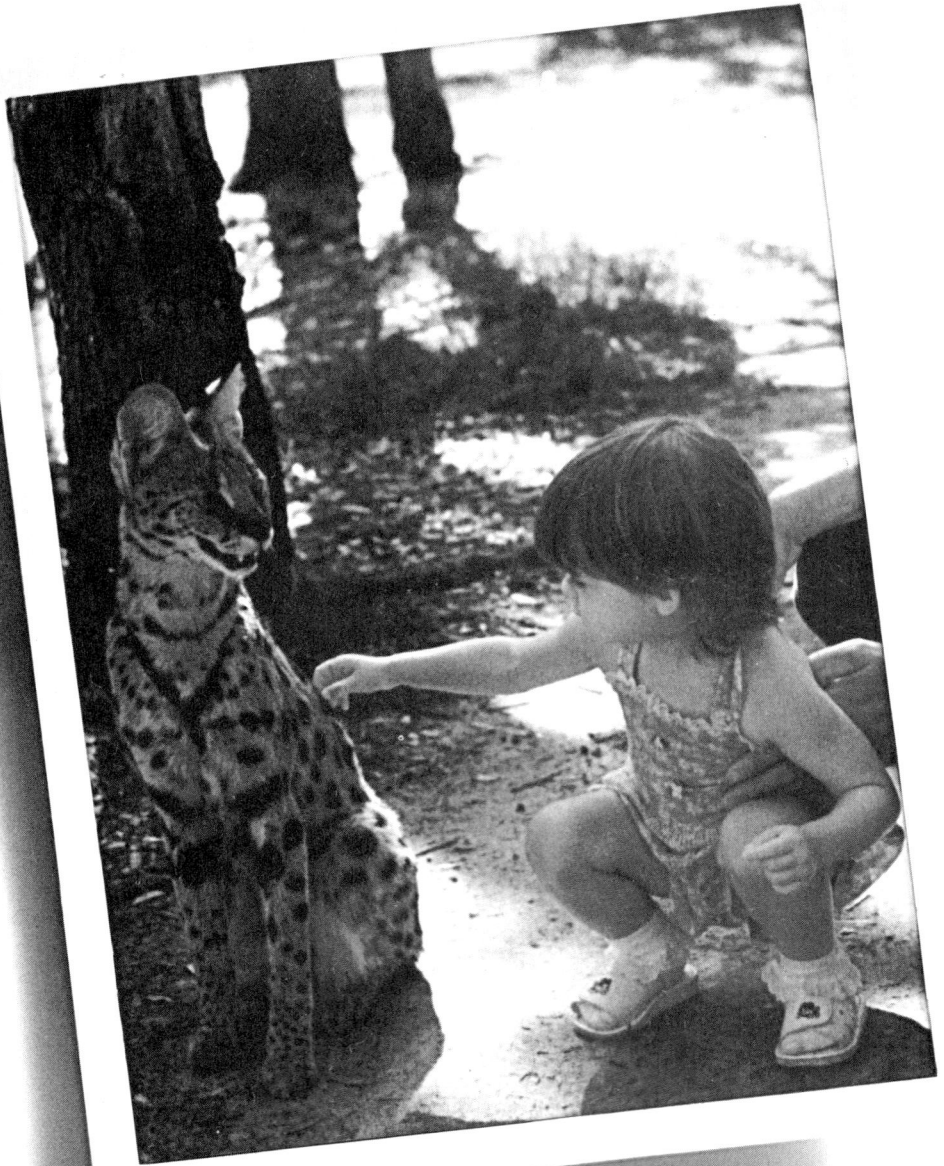

Chapter 5

• • • • • • •

SECRET GARDENS, FURRY FRIENDS

Nature is within easy reach in a state that blooms all year

Getting in touch with nature is easy for children in Florida — the state blooms all year and the abundant plant and animal life never takes a Northern vacation. Many of the animals are in theme parks, though care is taken in most to provide a natural habitat for the captive creatures. At other sites, animals can be safely viewed in the wild.

Kids can also learn about plants through a number of programs, pamphlets and tours for young people in the state's green spaces. Or, easiest of all, kids can see and learn about the state's greenery simply by spending time at one of the area's lush gardens.

• Laura D'Allessio pets a wild feline at Central Florida Zoo.

Aviary is open from 10 a.m. to 4 p.m. Tuesday through Saturday. The gift shop is open from 10 a.m. to 4 p.m. Monday through Friday, and 10 a.m. to 2 p.m. Saturday. Groups of 10 or more people are requested to make reservations for tours. Call well in advance because the center is usually very busy and schools often fill the schedule with tours. A $1 donation per person is requested, but the aviary is free.

More than 60 birds nest at the Audubon Center. The society is helping some injured birds on their flight to recovery. A great place to learn about the

Audubon Center for Birds of Prey

1101 Audubon Way, Maitland.

(407) 647-2615   109

society's work and feathered creatures of every sort. Off-site programs are available for a fee.

Recommended for age 6 and older.

Bok Tower Gardens

Three miles north of Lake Wales at County Road 17A and Tower Boulevard.

(813) 676-1408

Open 8 a.m. to 5:30 p.m. daily. Admission: adults, $2, children age 11 and younger are admitted free. Annual memberships are available.

About 130 acres of natural Florida for looking and listening. Music provided by a carillon, which plays short programs on the hour and the half-hour with a 45-minute mini-concert daily at 3 p.m.

Recommended for age 6 and older.

Brevard Zoological Park

One mile east of Interstate 95 on U.S. Highway 192 in Melbourne.

(407) 676-4266

Open 9 a.m. to 5:30 p.m. daily. Admission: around $2 for adults and children.

A good place to stop for an animal break if you're in the Melbourne area. Be sure to visit the state's only Kodiak bear who lives in this zoo. Also take a look at about 300 other animals including cougars, emus and that Florida favorite, the alligator.

Recommended for all ages.

Central Florida Zoological Park

U.S. Highway 17-92, one mile east of Interstate 4 near Sanford.

(407) 323-6471

Open 9 a.m. to 5 p.m. daily. Admission: around $5 for adults, and around $2 for children ages 3 to 12. Kids under 3 are admitted free.

Animals and kids share the stage at the Central Florida Zoological Park. Children can ride an elephant or a pony or pick out their favorite creatures along the elevated boardwalk. More than 500 exotic and wild animals prowl in this zoo, with the tamer varieties always ready for some attention at the petting zoo. The big guys here include hippos, bears, lions, leopards, tigers and gators, with monkeys and birds in attendance, too.

Birthday parties can be arranged by calling in advance. Also ask about Junior Zoologist classes.

Recommended for all ages.

Close encounters with a goat at Central Florida Zoo for H. Cielo Gaitan.

Open 9 a.m. until sundown daily, including holidays. Admission: $1 per car, paid by honor system.

Take your energy along on this trip. Wide wooden steps, 221 feet of them, lead down into the 120-foot deep sinkhole. Going down is fun, coming up is work and should it be a drizzly day beware — the steps can be slippery if they are wet. Children should be warned that the steps are not for running, and it might be best if those younger than 7 wait at the top with an adult. And mom and pop should be used to a lot of climbing before they attempt it with a child in a backpack.

Ecologically there is something to see every step of the way. Protected by the Florida Department of Natural Resources, Devil's Millhopper has been a place to visit since it was first advertised in national magazines in 1881.

The bowl-shaped cavity, which is 500 feet across from rim to rim, is a natural phenomenon. Its coolness and lush plant growth suggests the deep ravines of the Appalachian Mountains. In fact, some of the animals and plants found in the sink are not unlike that region.

Devil's Millhopper Geological Site

4732 N.W. 53rd Ave., (County Road 232) Gainesville, north of downtown and west of U.S. Highway 441.

(904) 336-2008

Exploration is only on the wooden path; no climbing up and down the walls of the sink, which would be destructive to the site.

From the top comes the sound of rushing water as streams trickle and tumble down the sides. At the bottom of the sink the water lazily makes its way into a cave before dropping into the aquifer, eventually winding up in the Suwannee River and flowing out to the Gulf of Mexico.

Researchers have found fossilized shark teeth and marine shells in the rock layers exposed within the sink. These finds indicate Florida was at one time under an extensive sea. The upper layers contain the fossilized remains of extinct land animals.

Local superstition gave the sink its name. Early pioneers thought that from the top it looked like a grist millhopper (the funnel-shaped container that grain was poured into), and when they found the bones of animals they were certain it was a place belonging to the devil.

Flora includes ferns and mosses and the various trees include dogwoods, scrub oaks, magnolias and pines.

A walk through with a ranger from the Division of Recreation and Parks is conducted at 10 a.m. every Saturday. Prearranged tours for five to 60 people also are conducted by rangers during the week.

Picnic facilities are available adjacent to the parking area. There are restrooms and a water fountain, but no other concessions at the small exhibit center.

Recommended for age 7 and older.

Florida's Sunken Gardens

1825 Fourth Street, St. Petersburg.

(813) 896-3186

Open daily from 9 a.m. to 5:30 p.m. Admission: in the $6 range. Children ages 3-11 are half price.

Lush Florida seems carpeted with lovely lawns and commercial gardens. It had to start somewhere and Sunken Gardens, established in 1924, was one of the first garden attractions in the state. Plants from every tropical region of the world have been brought together here, with 7,000 species putting down roots on these grounds. Additional entertainment is provided by hundreds of birds, which flit about the foliage. Touring takes about two hours. Strollers may be rented for a nominal charge. A cafe and gift shop are on the grounds for grazing and gazing.

Recommended for age 6 and older.

Open from 8 a.m. to 6:30 p.m. daily. Admission: around $5 for adults, and $4 for kids ages 3 to 11. Children 3 and younger are admitted free.

Gatorland Zoo

14501 S. Orange Blossom Trail, Orlando.

(407) 857-3845

Alligators are generally considered the official animal of Florida. They are showcased in parks like Gatorland that let visitors get an up-close but not too personal view of these aquatic beasties. Gatorland is a clean, well-planned park with an emphasis on creepy crawlers that visitors of all ages can enjoy.

During the Gator Jumperoo show, the trainer stresses that humans should never feed gators and should always exercise caution while touring the park. The show begins when the trainer rings a bell and the enormous alligators slowly make their way to the main pool.

The trainer fastens raw chickens onto a cable and moves them out over the waiting gators (and one crocodile). From then on, it's up to the gators as to whether they'll "jump" or not. The critters move slowly except when they feed, and then in a split second they can grab the chicken and swim away. The show is full of information and the alligators are among the largest you're likely to see anywhere.

Crocodiles and gators appear in their native habitats at Gatorland, with younger animals kept in the Baby

5

Fearless Jenny DeJean with a friendly alligator at Gatorland.

Alexa DeJean tortoise riding at Gatorland.

Gator Nursery or in tanks of their own. Many of the gators here are bred and sold for their meat and hides. Other animals in the walk-through zoo are zebra, pygmy goats, Yogi the Florida Black Bear, sheep and flamingoes. A miniature train steams through the greenery and also allows a view of the animals.

If kids like holding critters of a slimy persuasion, the best souvenir for them is found at the Reptile Photo Area. For under $5, children may pose holding a baby gator (one with its mouth taped shut) and/or draped with a snake (a safe species). Kids with tastes like Calvin of the Calvin and Hobbes comic strip will love this.

Recommended for all ages.

Other Gator Getaways

Alligator Safari Zoo: U.S. Highway 192 between Kissimmee and Walt Disney World, (407) 396-1012. Open 8 a.m. to dusk daily. Admission: about $5 for adults, and $4 for ages 4 -11. Another well-planned, well-attended gator garden.

Gator Jungle: 26205 E. State Road 50 in Christmas, (407) 568-2885. Open 9 a.m. to 6 p.m. Admission: about $6 for adults, and about $4 for ages 3 to 11.

Gator Jungle is also a gator farming operation and

you will see lots of big, fat gators here if that's your wish, but the "jungle cruise" is short and without expert commentary.

The zoo animals' environments are pretty barren. If you want a break from tinsel town, however, and come here, you can also see a Florida panther, crocodiles, baby gators, an Arctic fox and a skunk.

Green Meadows Children's Farm

Guided farm tours beginning at 10 a.m. daily. Admission: $7 per person (group rates available).

At one time or another, every kid dreams of growing up on a farm. But even though family farms are becoming a thing of the past, there is a place where kids can go to play out their farm fantasies.

Green Meadows Children's Farm offers all the charm and wonder a kid can conjure up. There are more than 200 resident animals, including pigs, cows, goats, sheep, chickens, rabbits, turkeys, ducks and geese. A two-hour guided tour gets children acquainted with their barnyard buddies. Afterward, kids are free to roam around to their hearts' content.

Pony rides, tractor-drawn hay rides and cow milking sessions highlight the day's activities. There's a picnic shelter for families who want to bring a lunch and make a day of it, and beverages and souvenirs are available.

Recommended for children of all ages.

Off U.S. Highway 192 on Poinciana Boulevard, Kissimmee.

(407) 846-0770

5

Genius Drive Peacocks

Open to the public Sundays only from noon to 6 p.m. Free.

More than 50 kaleidoscope-colored peacocks strut through this 150-acre preserve owned by the Winter Park Land Company. Spanish moss-draped oaks must provide the perfect environment for the exotic creatures who roam freely here.

Visitors drive their cars slowly down the bumpy dirt road and stop to photograph the outstretched plumage of the semiwild birds. A few peanuts or sunflower seeds offered by a human hand may prompt the reaction. Hikers and bikers see even more, since the area is home to mallards, owls, rabbits, raccoons and woodpeckers, too.

Recommended for all ages.

Genius Drive can be entered off Osceola Avenue through Henkle Circle or off Lakemont Avenue to Mizell Avenue in Winter Park.

Humane Societies

Orlando,
616 and 664 Barry St.,
Orlando.
(407) 298-2811,
(407) 293-6421

Seminole County,
2800 County Home
Road, Sanford.
(407) 323-8685

Call ahead for tours that show children how animals are handled and cared for at the shelters. Volunteers from the society will also go to schools for presentations on kindness to animals and their care. Adoption fees range from around $45 for dogs (all sizes) and $30 for cats. Fees include a certificate for spaying, neutering and some shots.

Lake Morton Ducks

Take U.S. Highway 98
exit off Interstate 4 to
Lakeland. Turn left on
Walnut Street, which
dead ends into the
lake.

Lake Morton is one of the premier bird-watching and feeding areas of landlocked Central Florida. Sea birds such as terns and snowy egerts stop off here between coasts, in addition to the usual mallards and teals. City officials estimate that some 45 swans, both black and white, reside at the lake.

Our feathery friends must have heard that the feeding is good around this lake where residents and visitors alike usually carry a bag of bread crumbs when they take an afternoon stroll. The large number of birds may scare some small children, but most are tame enough to eat out of their hands.

Lake Morton is a pleasant spot right in downtown, as are all the bodies of water from which the city gets its name. Take a few moments to enjoy the birds and spread out a picnic on a blanket.

Recommended for all ages.

Harry P. Leu Botanical Gardens

1730 N. Forest Ave.,
Orlando. Four blocks off
Mills Avenue at
Nebraska Street and
Forest Avenue.

Open 9 a.m. to 5 p.m. daily except Christmas Day, but closing times can vary. Admission: $3 for adults and $1 for children ages 3-11.

Visitors to Leu Gardens might expect to see a giant white rabbit in a vest looking nervously at his watch or a zany hatter sloshing tea all over his companions. The garden is a wonderland of flowers, trees, fountains and city history.

Inviting gazebos nestle among the trees, camellias blossom everywhere (in season) and there seems no end to the number and variety of exotic plants along the garden paths. The paved area, with its picture-perfect view of the giant floral clock, looks like it came from the imagination of an author of children's literature. And be sure to look carefully around the rose garden for an elf or two.

This urban botanical bouquet is a gift to Orlando from businessman Harry Leu and a tour of his former home is a high point of any day spent here. Kids can see some old toys and children's books in one of the superbly preserved rooms and also view a forerunner to the compact disc, a gramophone.

The park staff has given much thought to how youngsters might enjoy the 56-acre garden and grounds. "A Children's Guide to Leu Gardens," available at the visitors' center, is full of educational games and puzzles for kids to complete in the park or at home. There is a crossword puzzle, a dot-to-dot drawing to complete a Name That Flower game, word games and a maze. With pencil in hand, children can finish these teasers and learn as much about the garden's plants as grownups.

And this activity is just for daytrippers. More dedicated young botanists-in-the-making can take numerous classes offered by the park. Children can start their first garden in the Square-Foot Gardening class, learn about natural dyes for Easter eggs and much more in the eight classes offered each year. The park schedules the classes quarterly and space is limited so a call to the park's education coordinator is advised. Fees vary according to the materials required.

Recommended for ages 6-12 (or older for some programs).

Open from 10 a.m. to 6 p.m. daily. Admission: adults, around $3; children ages 3-12, $1.50; senior citizens, $2.

Lowry Park Zoo

A major renovation of Lowry Park Zoo several years ago has modernized the 1957 facility into one of the finest animal habitats in the state. The zoo is divided into three main areas: aviary, primate world and Asian domain.

The aviary is the free-flight home of approximately 70 species of subtropical birds. It includes an observation tower that enables people to climb into different areas of bird activity, providing an up-close look. The entire area is filled with dense vegetation and a variety of water exhibits, including lagoons, waterfalls and streams.

Primate world is home to eight species of

7530 North Blvd., Tampa. Take Sligh Avenue exit west off Interstate 275 until you come to North Boulevard.

(813) 935-8552

primates. All the exhibits here include water features and rockwork retainer systems at various levels, making the primates visible throughout the zoo. Nine species of native Asian mammals and two species of large birds live in environments that mirror their natural habitat in the Asian domain.

Adventuresome visitors can take a ride on an elephant or view their surroundings from atop a Bactrian camel from Mongolia for an extra $1.50. A petting farm is a recent addition to the zoo.

A visit to the zoo will take approximately half a day, so you may want to combine it with lunch at the neighboring picnic facilities along the Hillsborough River. Also right next to the zoo is Fairyland, where you can walk through life-size versions of the classic tales, Three Little Pigs, Cinderella, Little Miss Muffet, Humpty Dumpty and many more. The figures show signs of wear, but your child's imagination will probably not even notice it.

In addition, there is a small amusement park with kiddie rides, a ferris wheel, merry-go-round and small roller coaster behind Fairyland. Rides cost 60 cents each or six for $3.

Recommended for all ages, Fairyland for age 10 and younger.

Manatee Walk

West of Interstate 75; take Apollo Beach exit, which is Big Bend Road, and follow it west to Tampa Electric Company's Big Bend plant.

(813) 228-4111, ext. 34272

Open 9 a.m. until 4:30 p.m., Friday and Saturday; and 1 to 4:30 p.m. Sunday. Free.

Ah, give me a canal, where the manatee play and the water is warm all day.

That's what you will find about 15 miles south of Tampa in the discharge canal for Tampa Electric Company's coal-fired power plant.

When the bay water temperature drops to 68 degrees, the state-protected manatees, those friendly clowns, move into the warmer canal to play and live from mid-November through April.

A boardwalk extends about 300 yards out over the tidal flats where all kinds of water creatures — migratory birds, fish, crabs and all those things associated with tidal flats — can be observed. Adjacent to this is the Manatee Walk, a wooden platform that provides an excellent observation deck.

A 10-minute video in a trailer on the grounds discusses the area, and loudspeakers give additional information as you watch from the observation deck.

There are no facilities on the grounds, but there are fast-food restaurants on U.S. Highway 41, about one and a half miles east of the power plant in the Ruskin area.

Recommended for age 4 and older.

Caleb Keppeler makes friends with a horse.

5

Ocala Horse Farms

For information on specific farms that allow visitors, call the Florida Thoroughbred Breeder's Association at (904) 629-2160 or (904) 629-3526.

The Ocala area is noted for thoroughbred horses. Keep this in mind when your child is going through his or her *National Velvet* phase and says he will "die" without a horse.

Several of the farms allow visitors to watch horses being broken or trained. The rules are strickly against touching the animals at most farms, but children can watch these beautiful horses as they go through the rigorous regimen that, in some cases, makes them national champs.

In early October, Ocala Week marks the annual sale of some of the world's top racehorses with parties, a golf tournament and horse exhibitions. Call the breeders' association for details.

Recommended for age 6 and older.

Pet Shops

A visit to the neighborhood pet shop can be a fun, inexpensive adventure if you make it clear in advance that you are just visiting the animals, not taking them home.

You can introduce your child to many unusual animals from Amazon parrots to tarantulas. There are whole stores devoted to fish, and most have mice and hamsters. This is a good way for your child to become acquainted with the different breeds of dogs and cats so they can decide which one they might like to have for a pet.

Ravine State Gardens

Off State Road 20 in Palatka.

(904) 329-3721

Open daily from 8 a.m. to sunset for walking tours, 9 a.m. to 5 p.m. for driving tours. Free.

A three-mile rim drive passes more than 100,000 azalea plantings plus 200,000 tropical shrubs and plants in three deep ravines created from former sink holes during a Great Depression work project for the unemployed.

Sloping landscapes hide terraces, suspension bridges, tumbling streams and rock formations. Many paths lead to the floor of the sinks.

Today this is Florida's official state garden. Visitors can picnic here and enjoy nature free of charge. There is also an amphitheatre, civic center and outdoor Court of 50 States on the grounds.

Recommended for age 6 and older.

Reptile World

Four miles east of St. Cloud on U.S. Highway 441-192.

(407) 892-6905

Open from 9 a.m. to 5:30 p.m. Tuesday through Sunday. Closed Monday and the month of September. Admission: adults, around $4; students ages 6-17, around $3, and children ages 3-5, around $2.

If you have a budding herpetologist in your family, you won't want to miss Reptile World. Cobras, mambas, vipers, rattlesnakes and giant pythons are shown in clean, indoor displays.

A water monitor from Malaysia, a yellow anaconda and an albino Siamese cobra are among the most unusual specimens. Turtles and a Florida alligator are on display in outdoor enclosures.

Time your visit to be present during one of three daily venom programs at 11 a.m., 2 and 5 p.m. This show gives visitors an up-close yet safe viewing of the handling of cobras and vipers to obtain venom for research, the only such presentation in the state. Reptile World is primarily a research facility. It houses approximately 1,000 snakes for the production and distribution of venom.

The exhibits and show may be a bit low-key for children not really excited about snakes and reptiles. The gift shop has a good selection of books and unusual jewelry.

Recommended for age 8 and older.

Christopher Mullis rolls in the hay at Uncle Donald's Farm.

Open from 1 p.m. to 5 p.m. Sunday, 10 a.m. to 5 p.m. Tuesday through Saturday. Admission: around $3 for adults and slightly less for children.

Round up the kids for a day with barnyard animals and go for a hayride or a tour of the farm. Parents give this day in the country an A-plus. Supplies available at the country store on the grounds.

Recommended for age 3 and older.

Uncle Donald's Farm

North of Lady Lake on Griffin Avenue off County Road 25 in Lake County.

(904) 753-2882

Wilber's Farm

Located four miles west of Interstate 4, at 8100 W. State Road 46 in Sanford.

(407) 322-6870, 322-2898

Cory and Kevin Mulinare feeding the ibis at Sea World.

Open from 9 a.m. to 2 p.m. March through May for tours. Admission: around $1 for adults and students, reservations required.

The next time the task of planning a trip for a group of young children falls to you, call Delores and Richard Wilber and ask them how things are down on the farm. Each spring the Wilbers open their spread to youngsters for two-hour tours, ending with a hayride. A fenced play area gives groups room for games and picnics.

Encounters with the spring babies of farm animals including goats, pigs, chickens, cows and donkeys highlight a visit to the farm. The farm's staff encourages hands-on discovery about the young animals so kids can learn about their favorites up close. One of the Wilber's daughters, who is a teacher, has helped to shape the farm tours as a teaching tool as well as entertainment.

The Wilbers also work in cooperation with the Central Florida Zoo, taking in injured or overpopulated animals and giving them homes.

Recommended for pre-school and primary-grade children.

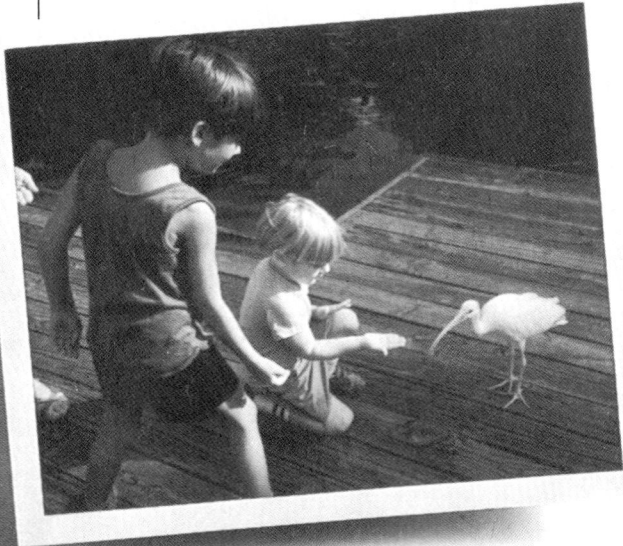

AROUND THE STATE

• • • • • • • •

Open 9 a.m. to 5 p.m. Thursday through Monday. Closed New Year's Day, Thanksgiving and Christmas. Admission: 50 cents, children under 6 and school groups free.

We may think it's a plastic world, but artificial hair products, chewing gum (yep, chewing gum) and shatterproof glass have a natural source — trees. At least 5,000 products are produced from the longleaf pine alone.

The forest industry has been a major source of income in Florida since the 1800s and today produces $3.7 billion annually. That makes it the third largest industry in the state.

But this spot is a charmer, not a place of dull facts. Inside the small museum there are dioramas of the turpentine industry, exhibits of products from trees, a map of the state made with a piece of wood from each county and — to the delight of youngsters — a talking tree. Push a button and Terry Tree talks about the life cycle of trees.

Here you can trace the history of the turpentine industry from the 1700s to the first attempt in 1900 to extract the turpentine without killing the tree. Exhibits bring you to present day mechanized production where only three people are needed to process 12,000 trees in a single day.

The geodesic dome that forms the center of the museum is made of cypress trusses and features the various woods of Florida: lignumitae, the hardest wood; black ironwood, the heaviest; and buttonwood, which burns the hottest with the least smoke.

If the kids grow a little weary absorbing all this knowledge, they can run it off by exploring the grounds around the museum. There is a picnic area with covered shelters and swings.

The park service also has reconstructed a Cracker homestead, neatly set off by a picket fence and furnished for family comfort in the mid-1800s. There are barns and other outbuildings to explore along with a grinding mill for cane.

Recommended for age 5 and older.

Forest Capital State Museum

West of U.S. Highway 19 at 204 Forest Park Drive, two miles south of Perry.

(904) 584-3227

5

Jacksonville Zoo

8605 Zoo Road, Jacksonville. About a half mile east of Interstate 95 off Heckscher Drive.

(904) 757-4466

Open from 9 a.m. to 4:45 p.m. daily. Admission: around $3 for ages 13-64; $1.50 for ages 4-12, and $1.25 for senior citizens. Children less than 4 and disabled people are admitted free. Parking is free, and there are picnic facilities.

The 61-acre Jacksonville Zoo features more than 700 animals from all over the world, including a herd of rare white rhinos in the new African Veldt exhibit. A chimpanzee exhibit just opened, plus an aviary featuring marabout storks, Pondicherry vultures and Patagonian buzzard eagles.

Recommended for all ages.

Miami Metro Zoo

12400 S.W. 152 St., Miami. Located just west of the Florida Turnpike Extension, 14 miles from downtown Miami.

(305) 251-0400

Open from 10 a.m. to 5:30 p.m. daily. Admission: adults, around $6; children older than 3, $3. Visitors who prefer riding over walking can take a monorail throughout the zoo grounds, including the aviary. A combination admission/monorail ticket is $8. A one-way ride back to the main entrance is $1.

Some advice for visitors to Miami's Metrozoo: Wear comfortable walking shoes.

Located on 290 acres, the zoo is home to 2,500 animals that live in areas resembling their natural habitats. That means no cages. It also means visitors have a lot of ground to cover — about three miles — it they want to see it all.

And there's plenty to see. Divided into three distinct geographic belts, the zoo has animals indigenous to Asia, Africa and Australia. There are the requisite lions and tigers and bears, but there are also animals few other zoos in the United States have. Among them: the white tiger and the koala.

Metrozoo, is, in fact, the only zoo outside of California that has a koala population. Three of the cuddly-looking, eucalyptus-munching marsupials arrived to open the Australian belt. They soon were joined by kangaroos.

The zoo also boasts one of the largest free-flight aviaries in the United States. Dozens of southeast Asian birds flit freely from tree to tree on one and a half lushly vegetated acres covered by a large, high net. Zoo visitors are free to walk through the aviary as well. Feeding times, at 11 a.m. and 3 p.m., are the best times to spot the most birds.

The zoo also has three elephant and wildlife shows each day, for which there is no extra charge.

Recommended for all ages.

Osceola National Forest

T his forest encompasses a state breeding ground for game, so your young naturalist may be able to view some of nature's youngsters at play. Young anglers can fish for bass, bream and perch under a parent's tutelage, but it should be kept in mind that hunting is also popular here, and many hunt camps are scattered throughout the forest.

The camping area has 50 sites at Ocean Pond, but no reservations are taken. Swimming, picnicking and boating are allowed at Olustee Beach in Olustee. Showers and grills are provided but no lifeguards.

Recommended for all ages.

East of Lake City on U.S. Highway 90. For information: Osceola Ranger District, Post Office Building, Lake City, Fla., 32055.

(904) 752-2577

5

The Zoo

Open daily 9 a.m. to 4 p.m. in the winter; 9 a.m. to 5 p.m. in the summer. Admission: adults, around $6, children ages 3-11, around $4, and under 3, admitted free.

T he Zoo, home for more than 500 animals, is a sure hit. Spread over 20 acres, The Zoo offers visitors a sense of intimacy with the animals, but provides lots of space for the animals, too.

Many will want to head straight for Colossus, the world's largest gorilla, who can be watched outdoors from two levels. But several trails meander through the park, so you can see African animals, cats, deer, primates and reptiles in whatever order you choose. The beautifully landscaped aviary is truly a delight. Fifteen species of brightly-colored birds from all over the world chatter and fly, unconcerned about guests — except, occasionally, to perch on someone's head!

The giraffe platform provides a rare treat: visitors can see these gentle beasts eye-to-eye, and even feed them. Here, as throughout the park, innovative graphics explain how the animal lives, what it eats, where it lives, and its current status in the wild. Kids will love the nearby petting zoo, provided you warn them — the animals lick back!

The Zoo plans several expansions, including the

5801 Gulf Breeze Parkway, Gulf Breeze. On U.S. Highway 98, eight miles east of Gulf Breeze and 15 miles east of Fort Walton Beach. From Interstate 10, take State Road 87 to Navarre, then west on U.S. 98.

(904) 932-2229

African plains and Florida swampland exhibits. It offers elephant rides on weekends and animal and puppet shows in the outdoor amphitheater from May through September.

Food and drinks are available at the restaurant. A playground and a fishing pier are nearby, so kids can stay busy while you watch lemurs and gibbons on an island in the nearby lake, also home to both native and exotic waterfowl.

Recommended for all ages.

• • • • • • • •

Chapter 6

DATES TO CELEBRATE

Mark your calendar for these events

Florida is a wonderful party state. Almost every weekend there's a festival, art show, parade or other celebration. But some bashes are planned just for children (or are especially kid-oriented) and this chapter describes a few of those, including holiday events. Newspapers and local chambers of commerce are the best bets for getting exact times for all events near you.

Held usually the first Sunday in April from 1 p.m. to 6 p.m. at Lake Eola.

Non-profit organizations and businesses that cater to parents get together each year to celebrate spring and kids with this very special event. The festival, sponsored by Community Coordinated Child Care of Central Florida, features activity tables where children can work in clay, fingerpainting and other crafts. Rides, such as ponies and a children's train, are available at a minimum charge. Live music, theater and puppet shows round out the entertainment.

Held usually the first weekend in November. Admission: around $3, children under age 10, $2.50.

The University of South Florida's College of Education has 10 years of experience in producing a children's festival. Plenty of hands-on activities are provided, from sand printing to a petting

• Kate Oberg portrays Mary in a Nativity play.

6

4C Children's Festival

Lake Eola Park, downtown Orlando.

(407) 894-8393

USF Children's Festival

129

University of South
Florida campus on
Fowler Avenue in
Tampa. Take Exit 54 off
Interstate 75. One mile
northeast of Busch
Gardens.

(813) 974-3350

Annual Antique Car Weekend

State Road A1A,
Ormond Beach.

**(904) 672-9947,
Ormond Beach
Jaycees**

Authors in the Park

Maitland Art Center and
Public Library, off U.S.

zoo. Kids produce rock videos and send postcards to their teachers through computer wizardy. There is a creative construction area where they do woodworking and even a graffiti wall where kids can legitimately express themselves.

Members of the USF basketball team are on hand with pointers for young hoopsters, and there may be parachute demonstrations overhead. In addition, there are karate, snake, and aerobics demonstrations, all in the interest of education. Every child leaves with a small souvenir, possibly a USF T-shirt.

The event is held annually beginning the Friday after Thanksgiving.

Children don't have to resort to watching Laurel and Hardy or reruns of old Keystone Kops movies to catch a glimpse of those skinny-tired automobiles from yesteryear. The Ormond Beach Jaycees and the city of Ormond Beach join forces on a yearly antique car show and parade that gives children an up-close view of those cars their grandparents and great-grandparents proudly cruised up and down Main Street. The parade has been held in the city known as "the birthplace of speed" for more than 30 years.

The antique cars stay around Ormond Beach for at least three days after the parade. Flea markets are held to display the cars at Ormond Beach Airport on Friday and Saturday following Thanksgiving, and various events and contests take place Sunday, such as putting cars through obstacle courses. The actual Gaslight Parade takes place Friday evening, with 200-400 cars traversing the scenic route.

"We always get a lot of kids because they enjoy looking at their past," said Barry Biss, an Ormond Beach crime prevention officer who helps coordinate the event. "You never know what cars will show up from year to year. It's always interesting."

Held the second Saturday in October.

Kids might not be impressed with meeting the well-known authors who advise aspiring writers during this annual event, but there are neat activities to keep them busy while slyly introducing them to the world of books.

A Storyteller's Corner brings words to life for young

130

listeners, and puppeteers give stories a lively new dimension. Children can also cut and bind their own volumes, and make bookmarks.

• EVENTS

Highway 17-92 between Packwood and Ventris avenues, Maitland.

(407) 740-0792, Orlando Public Library

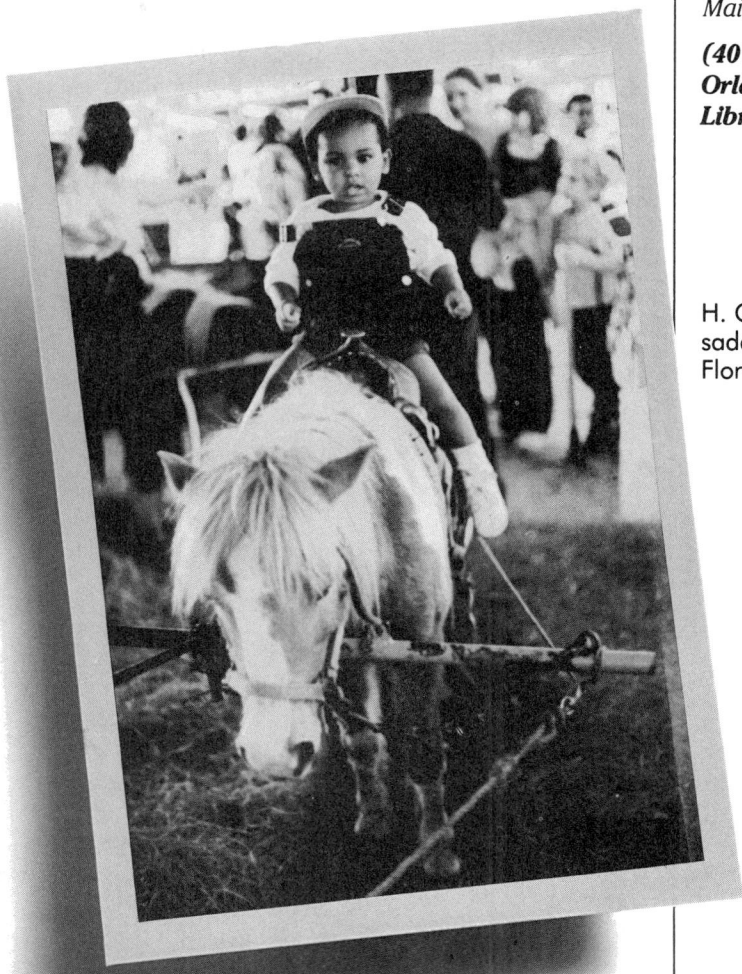

H. Cielo Gaitan in the saddle at the Central Florida Fair.

6

Usually held the last week of February through early March.

A great, big, old-fashioned fair is beyond compare as entertainment for children. This is one of the best and is a favorite among area families.

A lively midway, rides from the James E. Strates Show, community exhibits, livestock shows and big-name entertainers make this a real-live, really big show. Kids can't stay too long at this fair — there's just too much to see and do!

Central Florida Fair

West Colonial Drive and Fairvilla Road, Orlando.

(407) 295-3247

131

DeLand-St. Johns River Festival

*Fort Mellon Park,
Seminole Boulevard,
Sanford.*

**(904) 734-4331,
DeLand Chamber of
Commerce**

Held the third weekend in September.

Whatever a child's interest, there is sure to be something at this riverside festival to please. Hot-air balloon rides give kids the chance to experience adventure firsthand, while skydiving demonstrations, a horse show and boat races provide vicarious thrills.

River raft races are also fun to watch, and there's barbecue and Southern-fried fish when hunger pangs strike.

Don CeSar Sand Castle Contest

*Don CeSar Resort, 3400
Gulf Blvd., St.
Petersburg Beach.*

**(813) 360-1881,
ext. 519**

The Don CeSar Sand Castle Contest has been held on the beach behind the resort for the last nine years, usually at the end of June. Participants can register as early as 9 a.m. or as late as 1 p.m. the day of the competition. Judging is at 3 p.m.

The warm sun beats down upon your brow and the rolling Gulf of Mexico surf sneaks up behind you as you pack and wedge and mold and smooth countless tiny sand granules into the ultimate beach creation. This hardly can be termed stressful competition.

And so it goes as another sand castle contest gets under way at the bright pink Don CeSar Resort on tranquil St. Petersburg Beach. Two of the competition's five categories are designated for kids: one category for those ages 5-9, another for those 10-14.

Sure, there is some seriousness that goes into all this fun. Some participants show up on Friday night to pile sand near where they'll be working. There is some artistry involved, but it's mostly pure fun.

Recently, Christel Roever took home the first-place trophy for Best of Show. Her story may be one of great inspiration to young sand sculptors. Roever, you see, left a job teaching computer programming to become a professional sand sculptor at Sea World. Making sand castles for a living? Ahhhh. To a kid, that's heaven.

Held the first full weekend in November.

This annual event features more than 500 booths offering arts, crafts and ethnic foods. Kids can nibble egg rolls and be entertained by strolling musicians while parents contemplate purchasing an abstract painting or raku vase.

Pointing out various art works and talking about them will make it an educational experience as well as a fun day. When they're tuckered out from soaking up culture, youngsters can take a break by the lake and soak up a great view.

Held first Thursday through second Sunday of March.

Even though some youngsters balk at eating fruit, most love bite-sized, luscious strawberries. But booths offering everything from plain strawberries to strawberry shortcake are only part of the scene. There's also a midway with plenty of rides and games, as well as a livestock exhibit good for showing city kids that there are more — and bigger — animals than cats and dogs on the planet.

Young country music fans will get a big thrill seeing top Nashville stars such as The Judds, Barbara Mandrell and Tanya Tucker live on stage. Between shows, they can pan for gems in dirt from North Carolina mining country.

As a bonus, kids through high school age are admitted free until 4 p.m. on the festival's first Saturday.

Usually held the first week in February.

Florida kids get to see pirates as real as they come in this century in this "invasion" of the fair city of Tampa in February. Based on the legendary pirate Jose Gaspar who is said to have made his headquarters on the state's west coast, pirates (members of the Ye Mystic Krewe of Gasparilla) sail into Tampa Bay and take over the city for a day of merry-making, including a parade with bands from across the nation.

Booms from cannons mounted on pirate floats can be heard throughout the downtown. A favorite souvenir of the young crowd is spent shells from the pirates' revolvers as the grisly invaders fire blanks

Fiesta in the Park

Lake Eola Park, downtown Orlando.

(407) 422-7649

Florida Strawberry Festival

Plant City Fairgrounds, off U.S. Highway 92.

(813) 752-9194

6

Gasparilla Invasion and Parade

Downtown Tampa business district.

(813) 228-7338

133

while walking the streets. The pirates also throw trinkets from the floats. Some younger children may be frightened by the loud noises.

A visit may be combined with a stop at the Florida State Fair, which is held at the same time. This is the largest fair in Florida with participants from around the state. It includes a restored "Cracker Village" from the state's pioneer days.

Kite Festival

Loch Haven Park, 2416 Mills Ave., Orlando.

(407) 896-4231, Orlando Museum of Art

Usually held in mid-March for one day. Admission: free; $1 registration fee per kite per event.

A spring celebration that provides plenty of healthy activity for all ages, the annual Kite Festival holds contests in three age categories: 8 and younger; 9 to 14, and 15 to adult. You or your child could win a trophy for the highest flying kite, quickest-launching kite, or the smallest, largest or most unusual kite.

Even if you'd rather be a spectator, there are still fun things to do. Food such as hamburgers and ice cream are served, and you can picnic in the park. A plant sale and used book sale are also held.

Registration for all events takes place at the festival. Contests are open to every type of kite: homemade, modified kit, and kit (storebought).

Light Up Orlando

Downtown Orlando business district.

(407) 648-4010, Downtown Orlando Partnership

Held on second Saturday of November.

Giant street party in the downtown business district offers plenty of diversion for kids, who are allowed to walk in the middle of the street for a change without being punished.

The ever-amusing Queen Kumquat Sashay kicks off things. This parade parody features grown-ups in silly outfits acting like, well, kids. And there's a "kiddie run" foot race in addition to similar contests for adults.

Street theater by Sak Entertainment, a laser light show and fireworks also are sure to capture the interest of youngsters.

Because the event attracts between 125,000 and 150,000 revelers each year, small children who see nothing but adults' legs might get cranky or confused by all the activity. Bigger kids are more likely to enjoy the variety and excitement, but be sure to keep track of them.

Held the first weekend in December for two days.

Pet Fair and Carnival

Exhibits and a carnival with rides, games and food give this annual event a special twist for children. The point of it all, however, is animals, animals! Kids can enter their pets in one of several categories for judging. There's even a category for the best-dressed pet, so be sure Fido is wearing his Sunday finery.

Tickets are sold in advance at most schools for a reduced price, usually about $2. Admission fee gets you a hand stamp, which allows guests to ride the rides and play the games free.

*Orlando Science Center
810 Rollins St.*

(407) 896-7151

Patrick Smith with Charlie.

Held the weekend before Halloween.

Pioneer Days Folk Festival

The early days of Florida come alive during this two-day folk festival. Activities take place in three restored "Cracker" houses on the grounds of the art center.

Exhibits on folk life feature demonstrations of skills such as syrup making, blacksmithing, butter churning, quilting, meat smoking, calligraphy and sugar cane grinding.

Crafts, music and food from the old days are featured, with an emphasis on Central Florida. There is a special area for children with hay rides, a bonfire and small games.

Pine Castle Center for the Arts, 5903 Randolph St., Orlando.

(407) 855-7461

Silver Spurs Rodeo

Silver Spurs Arena, U.S. Highway 192 between Kissimmee and St. Cloud.

(407) 847-5000

Held the third weekend in February and Fourth of July weekend.

The stakes are high in this nationally known rodeo, with cowhands from the United States and Canada competing for thousands of dollars in prize money. This event lets families watch cowboys do some fancy roping and riding, and brings the flavor of the Old West to Central Florida.

The antics of the rodeo clowns are sure to be a favorite with the kids.

Winter Park Sidewalk Arts Festival

Central Park, Park Avenue, Winter Park.

(407) 644-8281, Winter Park Chamber of Commerce

Held the third weekend in March.

Kids can enter their artwork through their school. Tents of such work show the talent of area youngsters and are a pleasant place to take a break from the enormous crowd at this festival. There's usually a children's art table where youngsters can get "hands-on" art experience, too.

Zellwood Sweet Corn Festival

4253 Ponkan Road, Zellwood, two miles east off U.S. Highway 441.

(407) 886-0014

Held last weekend in May.

Kids who think that food comes from supermarkets instead of farms will learn the tasty truth at this festival that celebrates Zellwood's sweet corn crop.

Continuous servings of Southern-style meals — featuring corn-on-the-cob, of course — guarantee full tummies and satisfied taste buds. Adding to the fun are live country bands, an arts-and-crafts show and corn-eating contests in which table manners go out the window.

AROUND THE STATE

• • • • • • •

Held Memorial Day weekend.

A rare opportunity to show children what Florida looked like before subdivisions, interstate highways and malls covered the landscape. Held on the banks of the famed Suwannee River, the festival celebrates a rapidly vanishing way of rural life.

Storytellers spin tales handed down through generations, folk singers sing and craftspeople display authentic folk art. The area's natural beauty is an attraction in its own right, perfect for a little guided exploration.

Down-home food served at the festival includes black-eyed peas and collard greens, but hamburgers and hot dogs are also in plentiful supply.

• Florida Folk Festival

Stephen Foster Folk Culture Center, U.S. Highway 41, White Springs.

(904) 397-2932

Held the first week in March from 10 a.m. to 6 p.m. Thursday through Sunday. Admission: around $7 for adults, and $3 for children ages 5-12. Lower cost advance tickets and group sales are available by writing: Ringling Museum, 3505 Bayshore Road, Sarasota, Fla. 34243.

C ourt jesters roam the grounds of the former home of John Ringling, circus owner and art collector extraordinaire, once a year; and maidens in period costumes hawk flower garlands in olde English, of course.

His Royal Majesty, the king, and his queen open the festivities each day with a parade of the participants — street performers, archers, knights and ladies. Two not-to-be-missed events are the jousts and the human chess tournament.

Food is plentiful for medieval feasting between viewing the events and the arts festival that is held at the same time. Save time to visit the state-owned Ringling Art Museum and residence, Ca'd'Zan, that are open at no charge during the festival.

Medieval Fair

6

On the grounds of the John Ringling home and museum, U.S. Highway 41, Sarasota.

(813) 355-5101

Shayla Scott becomes
"Oscar" for
Halloween.

HOLIDAY HAPPENINGS

• • • • • •

Many departments of recreation, police departments and YMCAs sponsor supervised holiday activities just for children. For a more detailed schedule of events in your area, call local sponsoring organizations. (Also see chapter on resources.)

Star Spangled Spectacular

Walt Disney World Magic Kingdom. Exit U.S. Highway 192 from Interstate 4.

Held July 2-4.

Patriotic-theme marching bands, singers and dancers performing at various times throughout the Fourth of July weekend provide extra excitement for a youngster's Magic Kingdom visit. A truly spectacular fireworks display lights up the night.

138 *(407) 824-4531*

Held from mid-December to Jan. 1.

A Disney Christmas

Nobody can put on a party like the folks at Disney, and they don't skimp on the extras when it comes to the bash they play host to during the Christmas season. The thousands of lights that sparkle on a 70-foot holiday tree surely will put a gleam in your child's eye.

The festivities include the Christmas story told by a visiting celebrity and a thousand-voice choir procession down Main Street in the Magic Kingdom, and a live Nativity at Disney Village Marketplace at Lake Buena Vista.

Lake Buena Vista (exit State Road 535 off Interstate 4) and Walt Disney World Magic Kingdom.

(407) 824-4531

6

Larry Adderly checks his list with Santa.

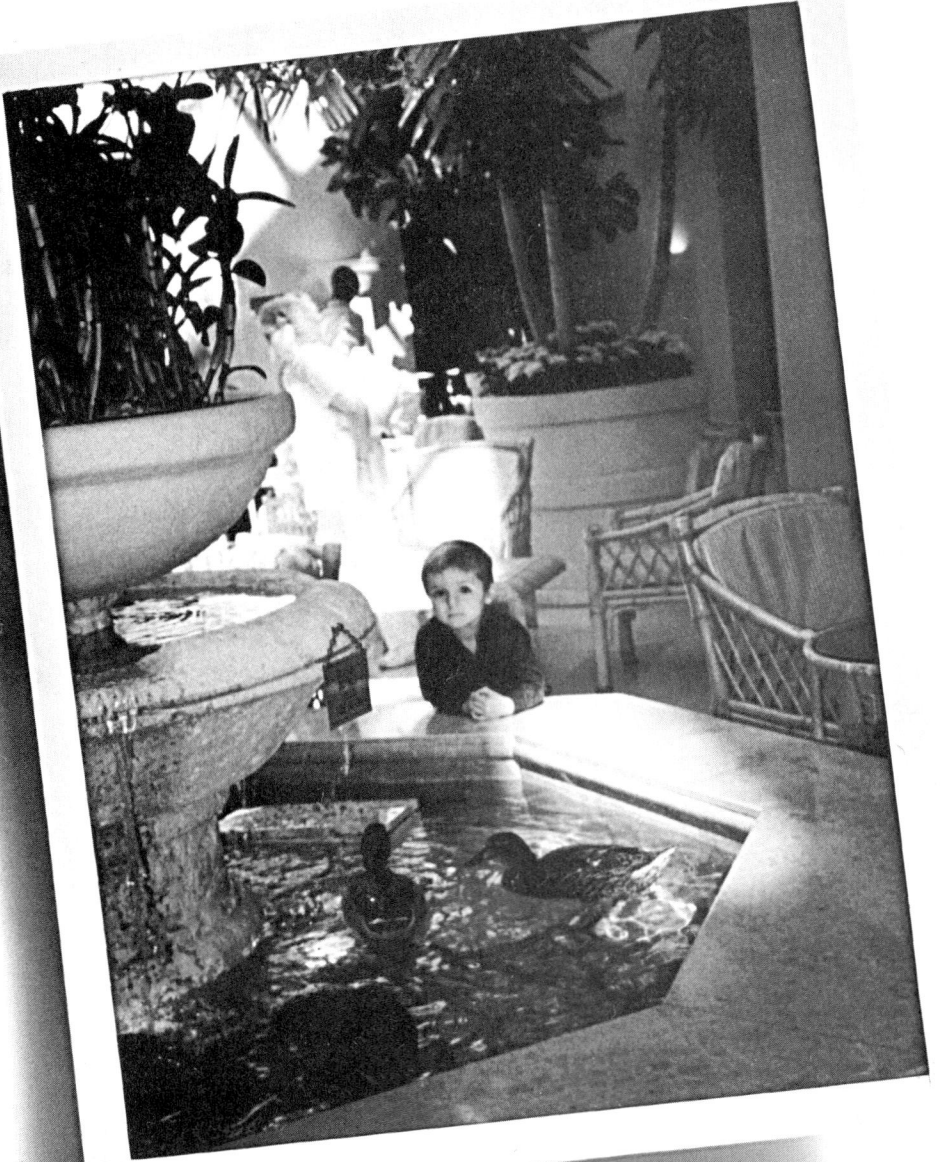

Chapter 7

SQUARE PEGS

Offbeat adventures offer something completely different

You know what to do when kids say they want to go see Mickey, or see some gators or go for a swim. But what about something completely different? What about train trips, marching ducks and marching sailors? It is difficult to put labels on some of the offbeat adventures to be found around Florida. The following activities can provide a change of pace for children when gator shows and swimming holes lose their allure.

- The Peabody ducks entertain Shelby Martin.

Pirate's Island Adventure Golf: 4330 W. Irlo Bronson Memorial Highway, Kissimmee, (407) 396-4660. Open from 9 a.m. to 11 p.m. daily. Green fees are in $5 range for 18 holes. No charge for duffers under 3 years of age.

Pirate's Cove Miniature Golf: 8601 International Drive, Orlando, and 2845 Florida Plaza Blvd., Kissimmee (behind Old Town), (407) 352-7378. Open from 9 a.m. to midnight daily. Admission is in $5 range, slightly less for ages 12 and younger. Kids 3 and younger get in free.

Adventure and Miniature Golf

7

Trains have a special place in children's literature and in their imaginations. Orlando kids can get a taste of the real thing in small enough doses to whet but not drown their curiousity.

Amtrak's one-way trip to Sanford doesn't cost much and doesn't take long, making it ideal for kids who get a little antsy on long trips. The train leaves Orlando at 2 p.m. and arrives in Sanford at 2:38 p.m. every day; another leaves at 9:23 p.m. and arrives at 10:03 p.m.

Amtrak Rail Adventures

Boarding is at 1400 Sligh Blvd. in

141

*downtown Orlando
and at 150 Morse Blvd.
behind Central Park in
Winter Park.*

(800) 872-7245

Tickets are around $5 for adults and almost $3 for kids 2 to 11.

In a 40-minute traffic-stopping trip, they will see a cross section of Florida. The route starts in downtown Orlando and passes Church Street Station, from which it briefly parallels Interstate 4 and goes past Lake Ivanhoe. Passengers then parallel Orange Avenue behind homes in Winter Park. The train then crosses Fairbanks Avenue on its way to Park Avenue, its first stop.

After the stop, the train picks up more speed than it had in its first stretch in preparation for its next stop in Sanford.

Scattered industrial areas and orange groves dot the path through Altamonte Springs, Longwood and Lake Mary. This segment of the ride for the most part offers a taste of pre-concrete Florida.

It may be wise to track the route with your child on an Orlando area map. Also, if your child is old enough, you could suggest he or she read up on Sanford's history.

Also, be sure to arrange for someone to meet you in Sanford because the trip only goes one way — unless you start from Sanford. Families should ask a friend or relative to meet them if they want to take the trip together.

Travelers looking for a round-trip ride can pay an extra $5.50 per adult and $2.75 per child to go all the way to DeLand. The train leaves DeLand for Orlando at 9:23 p.m. and arrives at 10:23 p.m.

Early risers may want to try the Kissimmee trip, which starts from Orlando at 7:44 a.m. and arrives at 8:05 a.m. The train leaves Kissimmee for Orlando at 1:15 p.m. and arrives at 1:45 p.m. Tickets are $4.50 per adult each way and $2.25 per child each way.

A daylong trip is available to and from Tampa. The train leaves Orlando at 1:15 p.m. and arrives in Tampa at 3:32 p.m. each day and leaves Tampa for Orlando at 7:38 p.m., arriving at 9:23 p.m. Adult fare is $15.50 each way; kids' fare is $7.75 each way.

Recommended for age 2 and older.

More rail adventures

Gold Coast Railroad Museum: Located at Metrozoo, 12450 S.W. 152nd St., Miami, (305) 253-0063. Open from 10 a.m. to 3 p.m. weekdays, 10 a.m. to 5

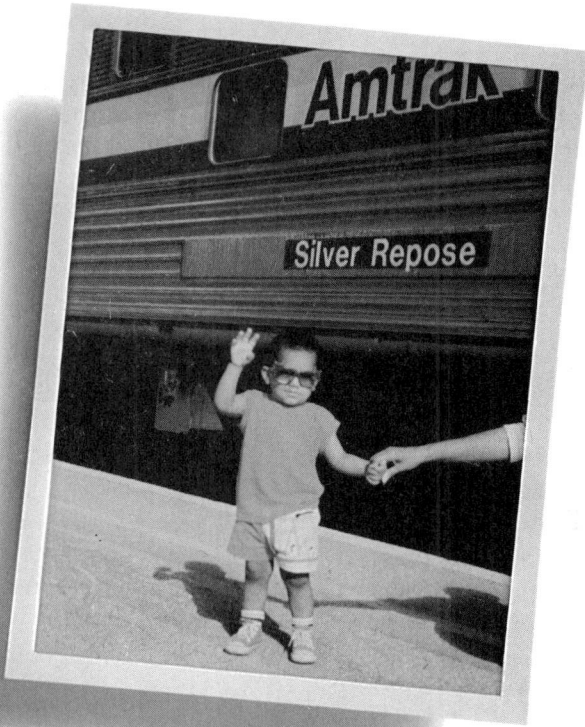

Jonathan Pittman
departs on an Amtrak
adventure.

p.m. Saturday and Sunday (and most holidays). Contains operating, full-size steam locomotive, U.S. Presidential Pullman, authentic antique passenger cars, cabooses and historic displays in museum car.

Lionel Train & Seashell Museum: On U.S. Highway 41, Sarasota, across from the Sarasota-Bradenton Airport, (813) 355-8184. Open from 9 a.m. to 5 p.m. daily. Operating toy trains on display plus a large array of trains on exhibit. Also, an extensive seashell, coral and sea life collection.

Railroad Museum: Located in former Tavares & Gulf Railroad Depot, 101 S. Boyd St., Winter Garden, (407) 644-6777. Open from 2-5 p.m. Sunday or by appointment. Free. Railroad artifacts and memorabilia with a particular emphasis on Central Florida.

Offers four- and eight-week camp sessions at a cost ranging from approximately $1,200 to $2,300.

C ircle F Dude Ranch has been providing children experience in outdoor living for 35 years. The rustic camp carries out a ranch theme on its 500 acres of valleys and hills along Florida's ridge area.

Circle F Dude Ranch Camp

Six and a half miles east of Lake Wales on State Road 60.

(813) 676-4113

Its primary emphasis is teaching proper horsemanship. Instruction on beginning through advanced levels is given, with opportunities for awards, horseshows and overnight trips. Jumping is part of the riding program for qualified riders. In addition, a well-rounded camp program of water sports, arts and crafts, tennis, nature lore, and evening activities is provided.

Open to children ages 6-16.

Elvis Presley Museum

5931 American Way, Orlando, across from Wet 'n Wild.

(407) 345-8860

Open daily from 9 a.m. to 10 p.m. Admission is in $4 range, with children ages 7 to 12 slightly less. There is no charge for ages 6 and younger.

The crisis in American education no doubt extends to children's grasp of history. If your kids have done their schoolwork, however, allow them a plunge into a bit of cultural history at the Elvis museum. Perhaps they'll understand that he was a singer, and they may even understand why he gets his own museum.

This place boasts more than 300 items from furniture and cars to more personal items like his belts, jewelry and his original birth record. Why all the fuss about The King? Maybe the kids can explain it to you.

Recommended for age 8 and older.

Falcon Helicopter Tours

8990 International Drive, Orlando.

(407) 352-1753

Open 9 a.m. to dusk daily. Cost: $15-$85 adults, $15-$43 children age 3-11, depending upon duration of flight.

An exciting, bird's-eye view of some of Central Florida's most popular attractions is available aboard one of Falcon's comfortable Jet Ranger Executive helicopters.

Chopper rides over Disney World, Epcot, Sea World, Wet 'n Wild, the Butler chain of lakes, Lake Buena Vista area, Universal and MGM movie studios and International Drive guarantee a spectacular view of the action without the long lines and parking hassles on the ground.

The helicopter maintains an altitude of 800 to 1,000 feet, making photographing and video-taping simple and convenient. Pilots also narrate the tours, pointing out specific highlights within the attractions.

Recommended for children age 4 and older.

Towers are manned from 8 a.m. to 5 p.m. Monday through Friday, and usually 1-5 p.m. on the weekend. Call for locations and to find out when a ranger will be available.

Fire Towers

Fire towers present a great challenge and opportunity for little people. The 100-foot structures are used by the Florida Division of Forestry for rangers to observe any fire activity and decide if it is a controlled fire or cause for alarm. Towers are usually located in rural or wooded areas, although suburbia almost surrounds some.

The towers offer children the chance for a view of the world not often available at their height, that is if they can get up the gumption to climb the 134 steps to the top, and convince an adult to go with them. Once there, they may unintentionally take in some safety information, and find out what a ranger does in today's urban setting.

Recommended for age 8 and older.

Numerous locations throughout the state. Check your local telephone directory under State of Florida, Division of Forestry.

(407) 632-1342, Brevard County

(407) 855-0621, Orange County

(407) 847-6330, Osceola County

(407) 339-1229, Seminole County

Open Friday, Saturday and Sunday from 8 a.m. to 5 p.m. rain or shine. Free admission and parking. Recommended for ages 5 years and up.

Flea World

Flea markets in America have attained the status of the Middle Eastern *souk*, with hundreds of merchants getting together to sell their wares and services. Food and entertainment are abundant and the atmosphere is a festive one at Flea World. Newcomers to the area may giggle at the name, but Flea World is one of the most popular "worlds" in Central Florida, with 1,200 dealer booths. How far the humble flea market has come in the fast-changing world of buying and selling.

And as if that isn't enough, Flea World has opened a zoo with two areas set aside for children to safely touch some of the more than 250 animals. There is a small admission fee to the zoo, but an annual membership cuts the price in half for adults, plus they receive a newsletter full of zooey tidbits.

Recommended for age 4 and older.

On U.S. Highway 17-92, near Sanford.

7

(407) 645-1792

Malibu Grand Prix Raceway and Castle

*5863 American Way off
International Drive,
Orlando.*

(407) 351-7093

*Open 11 a.m. to 11 p.m. Sunday through Thursday,
11 a.m. to midnight Friday, 10 a.m. to midnight
Saturday.*

If they pass the size requirement, youngsters are rewarded with an authentic looking driver's license to drive this multi-loop track. The game arcade, rides or miniature golf and batting cages next door at Malibu Castle will easily keep the smaller tykes entertained.

Drivers must be at least 4 feet, 6 inches tall to drive smaller cars, and must be 16 years old, have a valid driver's license and the signature of a legal guardian to use the larger cars.

Mystery Fun House

*5767 Major Blvd.,
Orlando. Take
Interstate 4 to State
Road 435 North,
Kirkman Road.*

(407) 351-3355

*Open 10 a.m. to 11 p.m. daily. Admission is in
$7 range, slightly less for children ages 4-12. Price
includes mini-golf.*

The Mystery Fun House might have been put under the attractions category, but it's too much of a mixed bag for that. Kids can get lost in a maze, look in distortion mirrors, walk through a spooky forest, try to climb a twisty ladder or play golf with a wizard. Other features include a gift shop, shooting gallery, arcade, kids' playroom and snack bar.

The Fun House runs a trolley that tours the Orlando tourist strip. There is also a hot air balloonist on the grounds to provide an uplifting experience during your visit.

Recommended for age 4 and older.

Naval Graduation Parade

*Orlando Naval Training
Center on General
Reese Road, enter off
Corrine Drive.*

(407) 859-0706

Each Friday at 9:45 a.m. Free.

The recruits parade left and right at weekly graduation ceremonies and the viewing is free. Small generals can watch their wooden soldiers come alive and march in straight lines.

Recommended for age 5 and older.

The parking garage provides amply close parking for $1 per 45 minutes. Park 'n Ride has an even cheaper rate. Don't miss the elevator with windows that takes you to the terminal level, or the rock fountain between the garage and the terminal.

Orlando International Airport

One Airport Blvd., Orlando. Take airport exit off East-West Expressway, or State Road 436 South.

(407) 826-2055

Combine watching airplanes take off and land with the hustle and bustle of a modern airport for an afternoon adventure at Orlando International Airport. It's a good idea to make it clear that you're just there to watch, since the child's natural inclination is to want to get on a plane.

Just getting to an airside terminal can be exciting — there are escalators and shuttles or monorails to ride. An explanation may be necessary about the difference between a sky cap and a policeman. An older child may be interested in the different time zones shown on airport clocks, or they may want to locate different destinations on a map. It might be fun to try to guess travelers' destinations or pick out which attraction the visitors attended, based on the hats and stuffed animals they are taking home.

When the youngsters tire of watching planes and all the preparations needed for take-off, it may be time for a snack or a look in the airport shops. Official Walt Disney and Sea World souvenir shops are located at the Orlando airport, perhaps a less expensive way to experience the attractions. Also, an Air and Space Center offers plane and rocket models and souvenir emblems of NASA flights back to the Apollo and Gemini programs.

7

Recommended for age 4 and older.

Outdoor Resorts' River Ranch

Dude Ranch and RV Resort

24700 State Road 60 East, Lakes Wales.

(800) 282-7935, (813) 692-1321

If rough camping, with just a sleeping bag under the stars, is a little too rough on you and the kids, don't be shy about going for a stay at this dude ranch. You can rough it or take it as easy as you like here.

You can pick your accommodations, from a recreational vehicle to a fully-equipped cottage on the 1,500-acre grounds of the ranch. If you prefer riding onto the spread in your own rig, the ranch has more than 1,200 RV sites in secluded settings.

River Ranch will put you on horseback or let you sink back in a sauna. Other activities include golf, swimming, archery, tennis, horseshoes, volleyball, badminton, hayrides, fishing, biking and a rodeo each Saturday.

Recommended for all ages.

147

Public Libraries

Check your local directory for the one nearest you.

(407) 639-9096, Brevard County

(407) 425-4694, Orange County

(407) 846-7870, Osceola County

(407) 339-4000, Seminole County

Orange County libraries are open from 9 a.m. to 9 p.m. Monday through Friday, 9 a.m. to 6 p.m. Saturday, and 1-5 p.m. Sunday. Seminole County libraries are open from 10 a.m. to 9 p.m. Monday through Thursday, and 10 a.m. to 5 p.m. Saturday and Sunday. Free to county residents.

Amid the excitement of mega attractions, tried and true activities such as trips to the library may be overlooked.

Libraries haven't stood still through the years, but have kept pace with the electronic age by lending children's videotapes and books on tape, in addition to hardcover books. Storytelling times also are offered in the evening to accommodate working parents.

Seminole County libraries have special-event nights, featuring jugglers to Florida panthers, and puppet play times. Orange County has a story time for parents — to teach them how to read to their children.

Most library children's sections have an open, appealing atmosphere, with comfortable child-size chairs. Some have wooden puzzles spread out on tables to occupy the very young child. Although the area may not be far from the adult area, a reasonable sound level is tolerated. In this atmosphere, far from the television, a child's appreciation for books can be nourished.

Recommended for age 3 and older.

Resort Hotels

Why leave the resort hotels to just the tourists to enjoy? The architecture of some Orlando resorts can be as exotic to a child as the Taj Mahal to an adult. All the hotels have restaurants, with one usually especially geared to families. If brunch prices are too steep, just stop in for an afternoon beverage and enjoy the surroundings. If children maintain the proper decorum, management will probably not mind you touring the lobby and grounds. The resorts do offer weekend package deals that might make a mini-vacation at home attractive.

Grand Cypress: One Grand Cypress Blvd., Orlando, (Lake Buena Vista exit off Interstate 4) (407) 239-1234. A child can be introduced to fine artwork by American, European and Oriental artists in this resort. A glass elevator travels to the top of the open lobby for those brave enough to try it. Ride the restored trolley to the nature area and Audubon walk with a one-mile boardwalk, and then return for a ice cream next to the lagoon pool with its grottos, tumbling waterfalls and rope bridge. The Grand Cypress Equestrian Center offers English or Western-style riding and instruction to local residents.

Marriott's Orlando World Center: World Center Drive, Orlando, off State Road 536, (407) 239-4200. Walt Disney World and MGM Studios are visible as the glass elevator climbs to the 20th floor of this resort. Pizza, snacks and ice cream are available next to the tropically-landscaped pool here. Golf and tennis packages are available.

The Peabody Orlando: 9801 International Drive, Orlando, (407) 352-4000. Sundays may never be the same once you've taken the kids to the Peabody for brunch and a duck march. Each day at 11 a.m. and 5 p.m. the famous web-footed friends of the hotel ride their own elevator down from their palatial home on high and march (as well as any ducks can) down a red carpet to the amusement and amazement of spectators and guests in the lobby. The stirring strains of John Philip Sousa's "King Cotton March" provide the background music for this ducky promenade. Their destination? A fountain in the lobby for a day of swimming and eating. This is a relaxing outing for families, and one that fits nicely into a weekend schedule. Brunch is served Sundays at the hotel's Capriccio restaurant on the lobby level from 11 a.m. to 2:30 p.m. Reservations are recommended.

Stouffer Orlando Resort: 6677 Harbor Drive, Orlando, (Directly across from Sea World.) (407) 351-5555. The Stouffer's 10-story atrium features a waterfall cascading down into a pool filled with Japanese Koi fish. Colorful flowers and tropical foliage bloom throughout, and exotic birds fly free in a Victorian-style aviary. Twin glass elevators climb the walls on both sides of the atrium.

Recommended for age 3 and older.

7

Open from 9:30 a.m. to 5 p.m. every day but Christmas Day. Free.

You've heard the saying, "Christmas comes but once a year." Well, at Rogers Christmas House and Village, it's Christmas all year round.

A cluster of five small cottages is filled with lavish

Rogers Christmas House and Village

103 Saxon Ave.,
Brooksville.

(904) 796-2415

Christmas decorations, gift ideas, toys, crafts, books, gourmet foods, furnishings, candles, china, linens, crystal, stocking stuffers, artificial trees and a host of other yuletide paraphernalia.

Each tiny house is decorated differently, but perhaps the favorite among children is Storybook Land. The cottage is filled with toys and stuffed animals, and mechanized animated scenes from favorite children's stories.

The sidewalk outside the 10-room main house bears the handprints and autographs of dozens of children, and on the front porch, a line of rocking chairs faces the garden.

Inside and out, Rogers Christmas House and Village is a festive and inviting way for children (and their parents) to get into the holiday spirit. Kids can pick out their own tree ornaments or help put together the animals for a Nativity scene. And, who knows, you might just spot some elves!

Recommended for children age 2 and older.

Shiloh Station

Toy Soldiers for the Collector

909 E. New Haven Ave.,
No. 7, Melbourne.

(407) 951-0515

Open 10 a.m. to 5 p.m. Monday through Saturday.

Don't let the name put you off. Owner Phil Bordan says that many of his customers are parents who bring in their children hoping to whet the kids' appetites for history and old-style toys. With most kids, the tactic works.

"And of course, parents hope the kids will pick up a book, too," he said.

Bordan is the commander of legions of fighting men — toy soldiers, that is — that include the British in their battle finery, brightly clad Sudanese, Egyptian pharaonic warriors, Italians, French. Many are set up in his tiny shop and Bordan can walk about and tell visitors the origin of each little fighter or member of the guard. The soldiers come from manufacturers all over the world, and some collectors pay top dollar for more rare figures.

Gone are the days when a child can go to Woolworth's and pick up an entire army for a dollar, Bordan says. What he calls real antique toy soldiers were not made after World War II. He has about 3,200 figures in his private collection and will track down missing figures for his customers.

Recommended for age 8 and older.

Reservations and information are handled at the original Space Camp in Huntsville, Ala. Parents may call toll-free (800) 633-7280, or write to U.S. Space Camp, P.O. Box 1680-A, Huntsville, Ala. 35807. Or call the Huntsville office direct at (205) 837-3400. Cost is $450 for a five-day mission in the spring, and $500 in the summer.

These days Peter Pan isn't the only one who can fly in a child's world. At Space Camp Florida, children float through zero-gravity exercises and perform a mock space shuttle mission. Science was never, never this much fun.

The camp, the second in the country, is right near the heart of the country's space program, NASA and Spaceport USA. This means kids can soak up a lot of atmosphere at real launch pads and see grounded rockets during their "mission" at the camp. Most of the children's training is done in teams of 12 in a 12,000-square-foot structure. Campers learn about the Gemini, Apollo and Mercury explorations, and about the role of the ground crew during each flight.

The emphasis is on learning by doing, not on lectures, so children can count on an action-packed experience at the camp. Instructors may also set up surprise "emergencies" for the mission team to allow them to use creatively all they have learned about space flight. At the end of their stay, kids graduate in a ceremony at Spaceport's Galaxy Theater and outstanding campers are recognized for their accomplishments.

Missions run from April through September. Call well in advance if you desire a special date. Tuition includes housing at a private wing of the Howard Johnson Motor Lodge near the space center, meals and all program materials.

Space Camp Florida is operated jointly by the Mercury 7 Foundation, which was established by NASA's original Mercury astronauts, and by the U.S. Space Camp Foundation. Both are non-profit educational foundations.

Open to fourth through seventh graders, ages 10-13.

Space Camp Florida

*6080 Grissom Parkway
in Gateway Center
Industrial Park,
Titusville.*

(407) 267-3184

7

Spook Hill

Take U.S. Highway 27 exit off Interstate 4. Turn east on Central Avenue in Lake Wales and north on Alternate 27 to North Avenue.

(813) 676-3445, Lake Wales Chamber of Commerce

Park car on white line at bottom of hill, release brakes and clutch, and watch your car roll uphill. Free.

Of course cars don't roll uphill, but they do on Spook Hill!

Pioneer mail carriers were among the first to discover that their horses were laboring downhill. Some years later when the citrus industry began to sprout in the area, workers driving their wagons around the lake were startled to find their mule teams struggling downhill with a load. Even though the road, North Avenue, is now paved, residents and visitors find that their cars still roll uphill by themselves.

Some link the Spook Hill mystery to a battle between an Indian chief and a huge bull alligator. Others say Spook Hill is an optical illusion. It isn't an incline; it's a decline. The illusion is possible because at the "bottom" of Spook Hill, another, larger hill — an incline — begins. The curve of the road, combined with the view of the larger hill, makes it seem like Spook Hill is an incline. If you come from the opposite direction, you can see it is not. It's a one-way street.

Experience it with your kids and see what you think — it's an eerie feeling!

Recommended for age 6 and older.

Tupperware Tour

Tupperware International Headquarters, five miles south of the Florida Turnpike on Orlando's South Orange Blossom Trail.

(407) 847-3111

Free tours are given from 9 a.m. to 4 p.m. Monday through Friday.

A tour of the beautifully landscaped grounds of Tupperware Headquarters is more like going to a park than going to an office complex. The headquarters, sitting on a 1,500-acre tract, was designed by architect Edward Durell Stone. He made sure the headquarters, with its gardens and lakes, blended well with the natural landscape surrounding the site.

An exhibit of food storage containers is the educational high point of a visit here, with a history lesson that dates back to ancient Egyptian times and spans the globe. Easy-to-follow pamphlets and maps provide a guide to the exhibit and the grounds.

Recommended for age 5 and older.

BOAT TOURS

Rates vary depending upon duration and destination.

Aboard the comfortable and modern Osprey II, passengers can get a rare glimpse of the real Florida. Alligators, waterfowl, bobcats, turtles, fish, birds of prey, monkeys, deer, raccoons and an occasional bear can be seen along the banks of the Oklawaha and Silver rivers, particularly during the winter when trees are bare.

River pilot Capt. Nancy Smith narrates the cruise as she steers the 32-passenger boat along the peaceful winding waterways. The entertaining and educational cruise also touches on the history of river boating in Central Florida in the late 1800s.

The daylong river cruise includes lunch and costs around $30 per person. Group rates are available. The Osprey II departs from Moss Bluff Lock and Dam in Oklawaha Tuesday, Wednesday and Thursday at 9 a.m., returning at approximately 4 p.m. Advance reservations are required.

Shorter excursions are available also. The Osprey II departs from Lakeside Inn in Mount Dora at 1 p.m. Friday, 9 a.m. and 1 p.m. Saturday and Sunday and 9 a.m. Monday for a two-hour cruise in upper Lake Dora and Lake Beauclair. Cost is about $8 per person.

One-way cruises from Moss Bluff to Mount Dora on Friday morning, and from Mount Dora to Moss Bluff on Monday afternoon cost $15 per person. Land transportation can be arranged.

Recommended for children age 3 and older.

Oklawaha and Silver Run River Boat Co.

P.O. Box 1301, Oklawaha.

(904) 288-2470

7

Tours at 10 a.m., 1 and 3 p.m. Monday-Saturday; approximately $7 per person.

The scenic and shady Dora Canal is thoroughly explored in this leisurely and informative cruise in a covered pontoon boat.

Passengers will be able to view water birds, fish, turtles and alligators during the cruise, which lasts approximately 1½ hours.

A closeup look at the abundant cypress knees is a delight for children who look for shapes and images in the gnarly wood.

Capt. Charlie's Dora Canal Guided Tours

Gator Inlet Marina,

153

north U.S. Highway 441, Tavares.

(904) 343-0200

Captain Charlie narrates, commenting on the history of the Dora Canal, and pointing out items of interest, including alligator nesting areas.

Recommended for children age 4 and older.

AROUND THE STATE

• • • • • •

Key West adventures

Key West Welcome Center,
3840 N. Roosevelt Blvd.

(305) 296-4444

• **F**or kids, Key West is a veritable treasure trove of activities. There are festivals nearly every month and plenty of year-round attractions.

Mel Fisher's Maritime Heritage Society: 200 Greene St., (305) 295-9936. This museum houses the millions of dollars worth of gold, silver, gems and artifacts the famous treasure salvager and his crew recovered from the Spanish galleon Nuestra Senora de Atocha.

Visitors can view the National Geographic video that tells the story of Fisher's tragic and triumphant adventures at sea; touch and lift a gold bar; and, would-be treasure hunters can even sign up for daytime salvaging trips with Fisher's crew.

Key West Aquarium: 1 Whitehead St., (305) 296-2051. Kids and adults get hands-on experience with some friendly creatures of the sea here.

At the reef pool, visitors can touch and pick up various live sea animals (starfish, conchs, sponges, etc.) and participate in an informative and educational discussion of marine life. Sharks, sea turtles, stingrays, colorful tropical fish and other animals are on display as well.

Key West Seaplane Service: 5603 Junior College Road, (305) 294-6978. Take a seaplane to the Dry Tortugas, where you can explore historic Fort Jefferson, snorkel in crystal clear waters, sunbathe or do some birdwatching. Half-day or full-day trips are available, and overnight camping trips can be arranged.

A must for Key West visitors is a trip on the Conch Train. The open-air trams circle the island, and drivers deliver information on history, scenic places and attractions. Interesting highlights include the Hemingway house, Wrecker's Museum, Mallory Square, Lighthouse and Military Museum, the southernmost house, shrimp boat docks and marina, and the Audubon House.

Scuba diving, snorkeling, sailing and fishing excursions can be arranged through a number of vendors in town. A good source of information and vacation planning assistance is the Key West Welcome Center.

Recommended for children age 6 and older.

Open from 9 a.m. to 5:30 p.m. daily. Admission: around $5 for adults and $3.50 for children. Airboat rides are available for an additional fee.

Miccosukee Indian Village

On Tamiami Trail, U.S. Highway 41, just west of Shark Valley, part of Everglades National Park.

(305) 223-8380

Visit the Miccosukee Indian Village to see how these indigenous Americans lived. The village isn't exactly a real Miccosukee village, at least not now. Indians don't live there anymore. They use it exclusively as a tourist attraction and museum.

Nonetheless, the village provides an inside glimpse of how traditional Miccosukees still live and hunt on the Big Cypress National Preserve. It is dotted with chickees, thatched roof cypress huts that the Miccosukees built as homes.

The museum traces the history and culture of the 500-member tribe and is filled with tribal artifacts, including canoes carved from cypress trees that most Miccosukees long ago traded for airboats.

Visitors can watch Indian women, wearing traditional colorful and intricately stitched skirts and blouses, weave baskets out of sawgrass. They can also see wood-carving, beadworking and dollmaking.

And, of course, there's alligator wrestling. While Miccosukees don't wrestle these fearsome reptiles for sport, they do catch them for their hides and meat. As visitors will see, there's a real art to trapping a gator.

For a culinary treat, visitors can eat at the Miccosukee restaurant where tribal delicacies, such as fried pumpkin bread and fresh frog legs, are served. Standard American fare is available, too.

Recommended for age 4 and older.

7

Chapter 8

ON THE TOWN

Kid-friendly establishments cater to young guests

Many parents groan at the thought of taking the young ones shopping or out to eat, but there are kid-friendly establishments in the area that cater to young guests. The key is diversion — while waiting for food, or between shops. Shopping centers with play areas or interesting landscape rank high on the list. Lush foliage and fountains provide a relaxing place for short rests.

Family restaurants (and the standard fast-food outposts) are in plentiful supply, but Central Florida is also high on pizazz. Several dining establishments put lavish shows and entertainment first on the menu. Many of these restaurants are fine amusements for kids and most feature children's menus and prices.

A sampling of ice cream parlors is included in this section, since that's one thing parents can always count on kids finishing.

- Jennifer and Laura Murchison enjoy Goofy service at a Disney Character Breakfast. (See page 26.)

SHOPPING

Open daily from 10 a.m. to 10 p.m. Free.

Disney Village can be almost like a visit to Disney World for the small child. All his friends, Mickey, Donald, and Goofy, are there in the character shop and throughout the Village. The Village can provide a quick and less expensive dose of Disney.

Mickey can be seen high atop the huge Christmas tree in the Christmas shop putting on a bulb. Every

Disney Village Marketplace

Take State Road 535, Lake Buena Vista exit off Interstate 4, Orlando.

(407) 824-4321

child is fascinated with Christmas, and the moving displays and unusual ornaments add to his excitement. If little hands want to touch, lead the child toward the toy shop where there are toys set out that he can play with. There are moveable wooden trains he can drive and an elaborate Playmobile scene under plexiglass.

The You and Me Kid shop has complete movie director, junior zoologist and herpetologist outfits. A pretend movie camera is included for the director, play binoculars for the zoologist, and a fake frog and snake for the herpetologist. The outfits also come at a steep price.

There's a surf shop for teens and Team Mickey for the sports fan.

The unusual playground at Disney Village is always a center of activity. This can provide a diversion for youngsters if Mom wants to peruse the more delicate glassware and fine jewelry shops. Maybe she can take turns watching the kids with someone else in her party. They never seem to get too much of the high wooden tower with several niches to explore.

An inexpensive alternative to the appealing food smells at the Village is a slice of pizza that is ample enough for lunch. Popcorn carts provide a filling snack that can be topped off later with a Disney character ice cream bar.

For those who have more time, a variety of boats are available for hourly rental to explore Bay Lake. They include pedal boats, canopy and float boats, and motorized water sprites.

Elegant dining is offered aboard the Empress Lilly, and Pleasure Island, directly in back of Disney Village, will offer a full range of nighttime activities when it is completed.

Florida Mall

8001 S. Orange Blossom Trail at Sunny Day and Florida Mall drives, Orlando.

(407) 851-6255

Open 10 a.m. to 9 p.m. daily, except noon to 6 p.m. Sunday.

Central Florida has been thoroughly "malled," as the developers say. There are malls of every size and design imaginable, but parents have given a thumbs up to Florida Mall as a place to take the kids.

The mall has the feel of a storybook, indoor city. You'll find lots of big plants, jolly archways and streets lined with mostly small stores. There is little of the claustrophobia associated with mall shopping. Families may finish shopping actually feeling refreshed.

Jonathan Ezra Pittman takes a ride at The Florida Mall.

The pastel facades and floor plan may seem familiar; they are reminiscent of Disney's Main Street area.

Kids will find the Florida Games arcade a fine spot to spend their extra quarters and smaller children may want to spend theirs at the kiddie ride pavilion. The pavilion, located outside Florida Games, has a pony (not a live one), a helicopter and car rides in sizes perfect for 2 to 5 year-olds.

As for shopping, older children will find a wealth of "teen kitsch" stores with hip-colored pens, buttons, T-shirts, sunglasses and all manner of youthful paraphernalia. Check it all out at The Barefoot Mailman, T-shirts Plus, Scribbles & Giggles, and rocs. If they're into computers, kids will want to stop at Babbage's, which carries the latest software, games and replacement joy sticks.

Toy shoppers have several alternatives at Florida Mall, including Kay-Bee Toy & Hobby, Circus World and The Early Learning Center (ELC).

The ELC lets kids from infants on up, under the supervision of their parents, try out toys in a large, open play area, and kids love it. The stock is divided into 12 categories including books, games, puzzles and categories such as first years, creative play, manipulative play (like Lincoln logs) and pretend play (play houses and dolls). Shelves are labeled with information about the toys, such as appropriate age group. Forms are available in the store to get on the catalog mailing list.

8

159

When miles of mall-crawling whets your appetite, the food court is an attraction in itself at Florida Mall. Outlets for good American grub and delights from other countries surround a central seating area. A quick trip around the perimeter will satisfy even picky eaters.

Harbour Island

In Tampa, take the Ashley-Tampa street exit off Interstate 275. Turn left on Whiting Street to Fort Brooks Parking Garage, or turn right on Franklin Street and go over the bridge to the island.

(813) 228-7807

Open from 10 a.m. to 10 p.m. Monday through Saturday, and noon to 8 p.m. Sunday. Free; people mover costs 25 cents each way, plus parking in the garage. First three hours of parking on the island are free.

Experience the future and ride the people mover to The Market on Harbour Island. The monorail takes 90 seconds to cross Tampa Bay to Harbour Island, a resort, condominium and shopping complex. Or, you can drive directly over and park under The Market.

When you arrive, stroll the waterwalk for a leisurely view of Tampa Bay. All sorts of boats are available for hire, including a Venetian gondolier. A hearty appetite can be satisfied on the food level of The Market, which offers pizza, barbecue, Philadelphia steak sandwiches, subs and natural smoothies. Tampa's famous Columbia Restaurant has a satellite location here, and an express outlet that offers Cuban sandwiches to go.

Retail shops range from those offering elegant resort wear and jewelry to an Everything's A $1 shop. Import shops carrying goods from other lands, and The Florida Shop sells the necessary souvenirs.

Mercado

8445 International Drive, Orlando.

(407) 345-9337

Open from 10 a.m. to 10 p.m. daily. Restaurants stay open later. Free.

Kids can listen to Mugsy's Merry Medley talking bird show every hour on the hour while Mom takes a break from shopping the more than 50 specialty shops at the Mercado, a Mediterranean-style shopping village. They may even be able to shake hands with Musgy Macaw, the Mercado's larger-than-life-size mascot.

A stroll through the red brick walkways can be educational. Mediterranean mosaics and frescoes on the Spanish-style buildings depict the landing of Hernando DeSoto in Florida and the subsequent development of the state. Fountains and lush foliage add to the Old-World atmosphere.

In The Marketplace with Mugsy is Gumball Alley Arcade and Sweet Sensations with frozen yogurt and pastries. All types of food, from pizza to chicken, is available in the food plaza, and various types of live entertainment are usually featured in the open-air courtyard.

While you're there

Mardi Gras Dinner Theater: (407) 351-5151, Two shows at 6 and 9 p.m. daily except Sunday and Monday, when it is at 8 p.m. This two-hour musical comedy extravaganza is especially recommended for children. It re-creates the tropical beat of the West Indies, the carnival atmosphere of Latin American and the rhythms of New Orleans Jazz. Unlimited beverages are served with a four-course Southern-style dinner.

Open 10 a.m. to 10 p.m. daily. Restaurants open earlier and stay open later. Free.

L ike many attractions in Central Florida, Old Town asks visitors to enjoy a trip back in time. This time, the trip is back to old Kissimmee, one of the models used in the Old Town construction.

This is a place where parents can pick and choose from 70 shops, several restaurants and a variety of amusements, many just for kids. Old Town's big plus is that it is one of the more manageable attractions near Orlando, and families can spend a day here without many of the strains associated with the mega-attractions. There may be crowds, but long lines are rare and the design and tone of Old Town seem to keep everyone in a Fourth of July frame of mind. And where else can you get a 5-cent Coke and watch a kite being made?

Highlights of a visit to Old Town include The Great Train Store and its exhibit, the Museum of Woodcarving, horse and carriage rides, "Big Eli" the 1928-built Ferris wheel, and the 1909-built carrousel with its 44 hand-carved animals and two chariots. Kids might also enjoy a look at Little Darlin's Rock and Roll Palace, though the entertainment here starts at night. However, the palace is open for viewing and eating from 8 a.m. to 2 p.m. daily.

Old Town

5770 W. Irlo Bronson Memorial Highway, Kissimmee, one mile east of Interstate 4.

(407) 396-4888

8

Beau Kelley on Old Town's carrousel.

Old Town also has special children's package tours at very reasonable prices for groups. The tours include lunch at one of three Old Town restaurants, a carousel ride carriage ride, the Back to The Future simulated roller coaster ride, samples of taffy at the Taffy Shop demonstration, a visit to the Candlelite Shop to watch candles being made and a sample of one of the 52 varieties of popcorn available at the Popcorn Shop. Call ahead to make arrangements for groups. Tour selections must be paid when the group arrives.

DINING

Show begins at 7:30 daily; reservations are recommended, as is arriving about 7 p.m. Dine and be entertained for around $25 per adult, less for children 3 to 11. Children 2 and younger are admitted free.

Arabian stallions, Lippizans and American quarter horses are the main attraction at this dinner showplace. The horses dance, fly and re-enact the chariot race from the movie *Ben Hur*. Dinner includes French onion soup, Cornish game hens and ribs.

Arabian Nights

Interstate 4 and U.S. Highway 192, about three miles east of the entrance to Walt Disney World.

(407) 351-5822

Open from 6 p.m. until. . . . six days a week. Closed Monday. Dinners of classic German favorites range in price from $7 to $12. Children are given a 50 percent discount on entrees. Lighter, late-night menu begins at 9 p.m.

The imported oom-pah-pah band entertainment is continuous. When family members aren't dancing, they can sit back and watch Orlando's own German dancers, The Alpine Schuhplattleres, in one of their three nightly shows.

Bavarian Bierhause

7430 Republic Drive, behind Wet 'n Wild.

(407) 351-0191

Open for lunch from 11:30 a.m. to 2:30 p.m. A lighter, late lunch is served from 2:30 to 5 p.m. Dinner continues until 10 p.m. Monday through Thursday, and until 11 p.m. on Friday and Saturday. Reservations are taken Sunday through Thursday. A children's menu is available.

It is impossible to describe the decor of The Bubble Room. Outrageous, Hollywood-eclectic comes close, but you really have to see it to believe it. While waiting for your table, the kids might enjoy a peek at the reclining pig that holds the piano in the piano bar. Get the picture?

The Bubble Room is a favorite for those celebrating birthdays. The waiters and waitresses, dubbed Bubble Scouts, gather round and sing the guest of honor a birthday "bubble tune" and all the diners generally applaud and join in the singing. And birthday kids usually get to wear one of the Scouts' wacky hats for the night.

Bubble Room

8

1351 S. Orlando Ave., Maitland.

(407) 628-3331

Portions at the restaurant are massive so ordering from the children's menu is a good idea and even then kids will have a tough time getting their badge from the Clean Plate Club. Plan on having the leftovers the next day for lunch. The food is fresh and innovative, and the desserts, like the decor, are beyond description.

Helena Belmonte in the Bubble Room garden.

Fort Liberty

5260 W. Irlo Bronson Memorial Highway, Kissimmee.

(407) 351-5151

Lunch is served from 11 a.m. to 2:30 p.m. for less than $2. The show, however, begins at 8:30, costing less than $25 for adults, and around $15 for children ages 3-11. Children 3 and younger are admitted free. Reservations for dinner are recommended.

Kissimmee is famous for its cowboys and Fort Liberty rounds up a herd of them for a wild west show at this attraction. Dinner with a Western flair features barbecued pork, fried chicken and apple pie.

Open for lunch from 11 a.m. to 2:30 p.m. Monday through Friday. Dinner is served from 5 to 10:30 p.m. Monday through Thursday; from 5 to 11 p.m. Friday and Saturday, and from 4:30 to 10 p.m. Sunday. Reservations are recommended, and a children's menu is available. The cabaret is open until 2 a.m. Friday and Saturday. A champagne brunch is served Sunday for around $13 for adults, and $6 for children age 12 and younger.

4th Fighter Group Restaurant

494 Rickenbacker Road, Orlando, off East State Road 50.

(407) 898-4251

The budding G.I. Joe and junior aviator will feel right at home at this bunker-converted-farmhouse overlooking Orlando's Executive Airport. From the moment you ride past the guardhouse into the parking lot, you seem to be in another era. Big Band music greets you as you walk past the military jeeps and trucks outside.

World War II memorabilia lines the walls, and portions of aircraft wings and unarmed bombs hang from the ceiling. The decor is built around the 4th Fighter Group, which was the first fighter group organized after the United States entered the war in 1942. The members of the group established themselves as the elite fighter pilots of the American forces.

What will certainly keep the kids amused before the food arrives are earphones tuned into the air traffic tower at the airport. There are eight pairs of earphones available, but there may be a slight wait for a table with them, even with reservations. Ample windows along the side of the airstrip also provide a good view of planes taking off and landing.

Since lunch is not served on Saturday, the champagne brunch might be a good time to take kids, or as a special treat during school vacation. The children's menu at night does include such favorites as cheeseburger, tortellini, ravioli and fried chicken.

8

Open 5:30 a.m. to midnight, Sunday through Thursday, and 24 hours, Friday and Saturday. The most expensive meal is less than $7.

Herbie K'S Diner

2080 N. Atlantic Blvd. Cocoa Beach. On the east side of State Road A1A, about three blocks

Herbie K's is truly "a blast from the past," as the menu proclaims. This old-time diner features the decor of a 1950s hangout, and a menu to match. Black formica tables, ice-blue vinyl seats in the booths, even hula hoops hung over the hatracks —

south of State Road 520.

(407) 783-6740

King Henry's Feast

8984 International Drive, Orlando.

(407) 351-5151

Lone Cabbage Fish Camp

State Road 520 at St. Johns River, three miles west of Interstate 95 in Cocoa.

166 **(407) 632-4199**

Herbie K's is designed for fun, as your gum-chewing bobbie-soxer waitress will demonstrate.

The juke box plays hits from the '50s and '60s, two plays for a quarter; the whole family can rock while you wait for your order. And it's worth the wait for real milk shakes and malts in fountain glasses, seconds in the stainless steel shaker, and hamburgers on homemade rolls, automatically "all the way."

This is a real diner menu, blue plate specials and all; onion rings, french fries, and mashed potatoes are genuine, and the desserts are homemade. The flamingos in the back room are definitely plastic, and so are the hula hoops, which you're welcome to try.

Kick back and relax — it's what Herbie K's is designed for. At last, a place you can take teen-agers — and have them think you're cool for thinking of it.

Two shows daily at 6 and 8:30 p.m. for less than $25 for adults, around $15 for children ages 3 to 11. Children under 3 are admitted free. Reservations are recommended.

Entertainment fit for a king, and the type probably performed for old Henry. The family-style chicken or ribs dinner would have satisfied the royal appetite, too.

The two-and-a-half-hour show includes a string of medieval entertainments: juggling, balancing acts, aerial shows and a swordfight between the Black Knight and the White Night. There's musical merry-making too with minstrels singing ballads and playing traditional instruments like the mandolin.

Airboat rides run from 10 a.m. to dusk daily, weather permitting; boat rentals and dining room from 7 a.m. to 9 p.m. daily. Airboat rides cost around $9 for adults and $6 for children 12 and younger. Canoes are rented by the hour, and boats are available for five hours or the day. Call for latest rental rates.

This is a great Florida adventure in eating and one children won't soon forget. What can keep kids from fidgeting in a restaurant? How about a thrilling 30-minute airboat ride along the St. Johns

River? The zippy boats speed passengers through cypress trees, offering a view of alligators and other wildlife in their natural habitats. If you desire a slower pace, rent a canoe or boat. Bait, tackle and a free fishing pier are available if you want to drop a line before dinner.

The family-style dining room is low on atmosphere and high on aquatic oddities like frogs' legs, catfish, alligator tail and (more conventional) raw and steamed oysters in season. Kids with more routine tastes can order burgers and fries, chicken, or shrimp. Parents can order beer and wine.

Two shows daily at 6 and 8:30 p.m. for around $25 for adults, and $17 for children age 12 and younger. Children under 3 are admitted free and senior citizens are given discounts.

Medieval Times is joust about the right thing to do for an entertaining knight, with a show strictly out of the Dark Ages. Chicken or ribs are the main event in the multicourse dinners, and kids like the fact that silverware is optional.

Medieval Times

4510 W. Vine St., Kissimmee.

(407) 239-0214 or 396-1518

Chef Elijah Morse at the Old Sugar Mill, DeLeon Springs. (See page 59.)

8

Skeeter's

*1212 Lee Road,
Orlando.*

(407) 298-7973

Open 24 hours, seven days a week. Breakfast is served anytime.

Skeeter's doesn't exactly have a show, but it is an entertaining, country-style place to eat. And you won't drop a lot of cash at dinner for the ample portions of beef, seafood, pork and chicken, or pancakes and other fixings at breakfast. The pantry is always well stocked and the style is heap your plate and don't stop 'til y'er bursting.

Wekiva Marina Restaurant

*1000 Miami Springs
Blvd., Longwood.*

(407) 862-9640

Open 11:30 a.m. to 9 p.m. Sunday through Thursday, and 11:30 a.m. to 10 p.m. Friday and Saturday.

Kids will feel right at home at the Wekiva Marina Restaurant. The food is family fare (catfish, cheese grits, shrimp, oysters, barbecued ribs, fried chicken, prime rib, steaks, seafood and a salad bar); the atmosphere is casual.

The restaurant is situated on the scenic Wekiva River and canoes can be rented next door for an after-lunch cruise on the shady waterway. Or, stroll along the deck and watch the boaters paddle by.

In the evening, Mother Nature puts on a floor show. Raccoon food is set out on a platform on the opposite bank and dinner guests can watch from tableside windows as the critters congregate for their evening meal.

Reservations are accepted only for large parties, so plan ahead or be prepared for a short wait on busy Friday and Saturday nights. Prices are inexpensive to moderate.

BIRTHDAY PARTIES
• • • • • •

A sure hit with kids is a birthday party at their favorite fast-food restaurant. These bashes are also a hit with parents whose only role during the party is that of spectator.

Menus, activities and prices vary from restaurant to restaurant, but prices are very reasonable and are set for groups of a particular size, with additional charges for each child above that number. A hostess supervises games and some restaurants have playgrounds that may also figure into party plans. Decorations and cake are provided and children receive prizes at some restaurants. The birthday child gets a special present.

The restaurants recommend reserving the party one to two weeks in advance. Some outlets are favorite party spots and may be booked when you need them, so reserve early.

El Torito

Open from 11 a.m. to 10 p.m. except for Sunday when the hours are 10 a.m. to 11 a.m.

Birthday kids get a birthday serenade and their pictures taken wearing sombreros at this Mexican eatery. The menu includes steaks and seafood as well as Mexican specialties, with children's portions available. For birthday parties of five people or more, the management recommends reservations.

275 W. State Road 436, Altamonte Springs.

(407) 869-5061

Larry's Ice Cream

Usually open from noon to 10 p.m. daily, except Sunday when it opens around 2 p.m.; and Friday and Saturday, when it stays open until 11 p.m.

Larry's offers economical birthday parties that include pizza, beverage and balloons. The key word here is natural. Nothing artificial is added to Larry's flavors. A specialty of the shop is Larry's Delite, a combination of vanilla, chocolate chips and peanuts.

This may be the place to introduce your kids to frozen yogurt, too. An array of flavors are offered, many made with fresh fruit.

Various locations around Central Florida. Check your local directory.

8

Orlando Science Center

Open 9 a.m. to 5 p.m. Monday through Thursday; 9 a.m. to 9 p.m. Fridays; noon to 9 p.m. Saturdays; noon to 5 p.m. Sundays.

Budding scientists can celebrate their birthdays at the Orlando Science Center. For $60, parents can request a chemistry or reptile demonstration. The center's staff also will provide the room and the cake and ice cream. Best of all, they clean up when it's over.

810 E. Rollins St., Orlando, in Loch Haven Park.

(407) 896-7151

Showbiz Pizza Place

541 W. State Road 436,
Altamonte Springs

(407) 788-0122

7419 International
Drive, Orlando

(407) 351-3368

Open from 10 a.m. to 11 p.m. except Sunday when hours are 11 a.m. to 10 p.m.

What could be a better combination for kids in a "dinner" theater than pizza and a show? This is the place for both. Parties get the royal treatment here, so it is advisable to book well in advance, especially for weekend dates.

Brett Adams having a ball at Show Biz Pizza.

SELECTED SWEET SUBJECTS

Open from 8 a.m. to 11 p.m. Monday through Thursday, 9 a.m. to 11 p.m. on Sunday, and 8 a.m. to after midnight Friday and Saturday.

The menu here includes sandwiches, soups, pastry and salads. But the main item for children at this trading company is ice cream. It's homemade and comes in a rainbow of flavors and styles (scoops, sundaes, shakes and malts, that is). A loft area provides space for private parties. The restaurant will provide the cake if you request one when you call to make a party reservation.

• East India Ice Cream Company

327 S. Park Ave., Winter Park.

(407) 628-2305

Open from 11 a.m. to 5:30 p.m. daily. Indoor and outdoor seating available.

The hot dogs are "imported" from Buffalo, N.Y., and the hamburger is ground fresh every day at this pleasant drive-in. The meats are grilled and the curly fries done just right for a meal a cut above usual fast food. The coolest treat at Fire and Ice is the homemade Italian ice. Four flavors are made daily from in-season fruit and chocolate. The texture and taste of these Italian treats would pass muster with the pickiest ice expert.

Fire and Ice Drive-In

709 E. Michigan St., Orlando.

(407) 648-2227

Open from 7 a.m. to 11 p.m. Sunday through Thursday, and until 1 a.m. Friday and Saturday.

When you have a giant craving for ice cream with all the trimmings, or are with a group of friends, head for Ronnie's. Its Mogambo Extravaganza with seven flavors of ice cream and sherbert atop a slice of pound cake will serve a gang. It includes five toppings, banana, whipped cream and a cherry, of course.

For those with a smaller appetite or smaller sense of adventure, there's The Gigantic, an ice cream soda for two. Ronnie's normal sodas and sundaes are rather large, so this boggles the imagination. Pastries of all kinds are available from the bakery next door, and a complete line of sandwiches and dinner entrees is served in a New York deli atmosphere.

Ronnie's Restaurant

8

2702 E. Colonial Drive, Orlando, in Colonial Plaza.

(407) 894-2943

171

Sweet Shoppe

1895 S. Patrick Drive, Indian Harbour Beach, about a mile north of the Eau Gallie Causeway on South Patrick Drive.

(407) 777-4982

Open 10 a.m. to 5 p.m. Monday through Friday; 10 a.m. to 7 p.m. Tuesday, and 10 a.m. to 4 p.m. Saturday.

T his small shop is chock-a-block with supplies for cake decorating and candy making, and will take special orders for cakes and novelty candies. But owner Della Smith wisely included a large, clean teaching area at the back of her shop, where she teaches classes in cake decorating and candy-making, primarily for adults. She welcomes older children into her classes, provided they're already comfortable in the kitchen, and their mothers believe they can handle an adult situation.

For younger kids, Della provides one-hour tours in the art of candy-making, including the opportunity to make their own. She describes her work to her goggle-eyed audience, including the wonders of ordering a thousand pounds of chocolate at a time. After she demonstrates different methods of candy-making, she guides each child in making a few pieces to take home. This includes melting the chocolate, as well as dipping and molding techniques. Della emphasizes clean, safe cooking habits, so a Sweet Shoppe tour teaches skills and fun. Tours can be scheduled for groups of 10 or more, including adults, and cost approximately $2 per person.

The Sweet Shoppe also schedules birthday parties. They'll provide the cake, ice cream and punch, and the children all get a helium balloon to take home with the chocolate favors they make themselves. Birthday parties cost $40 for 10 children, with a $4 charge for each additional child. Mom and Dad are free and the Sweet Shoppe even cleans up the mess.

Thomas Sweet

122 E. Morse Blvd., Winter Park.

(407) 647-6961

Main store at Church Street Station Depot, Orlando.

Open from 11 a.m. to 11 p.m. Sunday through Thursday, and until midnight Friday and Saturday.

W hile you're waiting for a cone here, be sure to ogle the homemade chocolates in shapes from cars to guitars. A chocolate leg goes for $35, but a chocolate bottle of champagne is a mere $30.

(407) 240-4907

Takara Jacquleen
indulges on a trip to
Sea World. (See page
19.)

8

Chapter 9

• • • • • • •

A DAY ON THE SPACE COAST

Technology and nature make an interesting blend in Brevard County

There's so much to do along Florida's aptly named Space Coast that it deserves a book of its own. For our purposes, we will outline some options for a day trip and include the Kennedy Space Center and the Merritt Island National Wildlife Refuge-Canaveral Seashore area, which can be made a full-day trip or be seen on their own in about a half day.

Beginning in Melbourne, take your pick of things to do from browsing and grazing along quaint New Haven Avenue to hitting the beach.

The best shots for beaches are nearby Indialantic or Melbourne Beach. There's room to stretch out here without having to worry about cars on the beach. This feature can make a day more relaxing for parents who don't have to feel as if kids are playing in traffic between dips in the ocean. There is plenty of parking, lifeguards in summer, and surfing is allowed.

If you feel like a walk after your swim, slip over to the Florida Institute of Technology and explore its botanical garden. (Take Babcock Street out of town, and the garden is on your right.) Parts of the park are a bit down at the heels, broken benches and the like, but the sight of the giant ferns set along a stream is still worth a look. The garden's 300 plant species can be seen free from dawn to dusk daily.

If the day isn't right for surf or turf, other activities are plentiful in Melbourne. The animals at the Brevard Zoological Park (1 mile east of Interstate 95 on U.S. Highway 192 in Melbourne, open 9 a.m. to 5:30 p.m. daily) are always happy to have visitors and you never know when the kids will get another

• Jonathan Trapani orchestrating the ocean at Satellite Beach.

9

chance to see a Kodiak bear. Zoo admission is $2.25 for adults and $1.75 for children ages 2-11. Telephone: (407) 676-4266.

Brevard County is home to many artists and craftsmen. It is easy to find their work at several shops in downtown Melbourne. If older children enjoy galleries and museums, there are several in and around Melbourne and Cocoa.

• Brevard Art Center and Museum, 1463 Highland Ave., Melbourne, (407) 254-7782.
• Brevard Community College-Cocoa Fine Arts Gallery, on the BCC campus, 1519 Clearlake Road, (407) 632-1111, ext. 4050.
• Brevard Community College-Melbourne Fine Arts Gallery, 3685 N. Wickham Road, Melbourne, (407) 254-0305, ext. 211.

If your journey takes you through Cocoa Beach and you are looking for a cool place to pause and refresh, The New Habit frozen yogurt shop is just the prescription. The shop offers yogurt cups, cones, shakes and sundaes with carob and fruit toppings available. These goodies are perfect for parents who are trying to raise a sugar-free child.

The shop also has a full menu of juices, soups, sandwiches, salads, bagels and quiches. There's no junk in this yogurt parlor so parents can feel good about letting kids pile the toppings on creations such as the enormous Pleasure Mountain (extra large yogurt with fruits, dates, carob and banana chips, peanuts and coconut).

The New Habit, 3 North Atlantic, Cocoa Beach, Fla., (407) 784-6646.

BCC Planetarium

1519 Clearlake Road, Cocoa. Between Interstate 95 and U.S. Highway 1, about one mile north of State Road 520, at the western edge of Brevard Community College's Cocoa campus.

176 *(407) 631-7889*

Tuesdays, Thursdays, and Saturdays at 8 p.m. Admission: around $3 for adults and $2 for senior citizens and kids.

Brevard Community College's Planetarium is an observatory, a museum and a theater all in one. Your visit begins in the lobby, Astronaut Memorial Hall, where displays include John Glenn's training capsule and a scale model of the Apollo space module. Besides this permanent tribute to the astronauts, other lobby exhibits change with the shows, so the family can browse while you wait.

Once inside the comfortable theater, visitors rock back in the cozy seats and watch the planetarium's programs as if actually sky-watching outdoors. More than 100 projectors immerse the audience in the mystery of the heavens, and the dome screen brings the stars all around and in close.

Programs change monthly and vary from December's favorite, "Story of the Star," which searches the ancient skies of Bethlehem for the star of the Magi, to "Lawnchair Astronomy," which examines the stars and constellations visible during that time of the year. After evening programs, visitors are invited upstairs to view stars and planets through the planetarium's large telescopes.

Not all programs are sell-outs, particularly matinees, but it's a good idea to make reservations. When you call, ask planetarium personnel about the appropriate ages for each show — not all the programs will interest young children.

One new program is specifically designed for younger children. Every Saturday at 11 a.m., "Max's Flying Saucer" takes pre-schoolers on an animated journey through the solar system. This is a terrific way for dads to spend time with their little ones. Some parents even credit this program with relieving their child's fear of the dark.

With its combination of science and adventure, the planetarium can easily become a favorite family outing.

Recommended for age 3 and older.

Open from 10 a.m. to 4 p.m. Tuesday - Saturday; 1 p.m. to 4 p.m. Sundays. Closed one month during the summer. Admission: adults around $4, students half price and children under 5 years are free. Children under 12 years must be accompanied by an adult.

Brevard Museum Of Natural Science And History

9

The Brevard Museum of History is dedicated to the preservation of life as it used to be in Florida. In one room is a comprehensive display of marine invertebrates, including a shell collection positioned low enough for small children to examine. One wall is stocked with mounted fish, intended to display the food chain; unfortunately many of the fish are so high that small children cannot see them. They **will** like the displays at their eye level, including one of a variety of bird nests.

Other rooms house displays of artifacts from earlier cultures: the Ais Indians, Spanish settlers and Florida pioneers. There is a Discovery Room, with a

2201 Michigan Ave., Cocoa. Michigan Avenue joins U.S. Highway 1 a mile or so north of State Road 520. Turn west off U.S. 1 and follow the signs on Michigan, about a mile.

(407) 632-1830   177

hands-on exhibit of bones, shells and fossils collected locally, including artifacts from an Indian shell-mound civilization.

The museum also hosts traveling exhibits, and in 1988 it staged its own exhibit of sunken treasure in Brevard. This fine collection included both historical records of wrecks and displays of "treasure" — most of it not gold or silver, but everyday examples of life aboard ship. On our visit, museum personnel did not encourage the relaxed approach that many children (and adults!) enjoy in museums. We were told where to start and how to move through the museum, and when we moved in a different direction, we were corrected. If older children balk at this, or roam through quickly, they can move outside to the nature trails, which travel through three Florida ecological systems — swampland, pine sandhills, and hammock.

Recommended for age 8 and older.

Canaveral National Seashore

Access to the National Seashore is via State Road 402 in North Titusville.

(407) 867-2805

A little advance planning might be needed to visit this east coast nature reserve since rocket launches and shuttle landings mean limited access and crowds. Don't forget we are on the Space Coast.

In this strange union of technology and nature, kids can see the nation's winged symbol, the bald eagle; the local favorite, the alligator, and the wonderful marine turtle. Some days, a pod of dolphins may visit offshore and provide a special show of their antics.

All the animals in the refuge are protected by law and thus interfering with them in any way means a fine or worse. The refuge offers the perfect chance to teach children the meaning of the words "endangered species" and about why it is important to protect the animals around us. Longer lessons in conservation can be had by camping in the area, which is available at Jetty Park.

The moonlight ritual of the marine turtle's egg laying in the sand can hold all the excitement of a Christmas morning for children. Families can conceal themselves among the dunes and watch the turtles come ashore at Playalinda Beach and deposit their eggs in the sand during June and July. The hatchlings then follow their ancient instincts and head straight for the ocean when they break free of their shells.

Reservations are required for the turtle watches and a ranger escort is mandatory.

Recommended for all ages.

Open 9 a.m. to 6 p.m. daily. Free.

Erna Nixon Park

This lovely 52-acre park preserves the plants and wildlife of two Florida hammocks. A half-mile boardwalk winds through low hammocks and pine flatwoods. A comprehensive guidebook, available for visitors' use at the ranger's office, describes individual plants as well as the overall ecology of the area.

Each plant or vista is lovingly described and beautifully drawn — even a newcomer to Florida will quickly learn the basics of native Florida plants.

There are plenty of benches for resting along the well-maintained boardwalk. Most parents will want to take the park in slowly and enjoy this rare experience of Florida as it was when the Ais Indians used these hammocks for hunting. Although traffic is restricted to the boardwalks, children can discover why the Indians called such places *hammaka* — island of trees. It's also okay to send your own Indians ahead on the trail to witness activity at the observation beehive. The bees' entrance is protected by screens, but the wooden cover of the beehive can be removed so kids (and adults!) can watch through plastic as these fascinating creatures work. The exhibit room near the ranger's office, with its display of feathers, shells and animal skulls found within the park, seems tailor-made for children in the primary grades.

There are picnic tables and bathrooms, but no snack machines, so a supply of cool drinks is almost a must. A picnic is a great idea, and in summer, a breakfast picnic will let you beat the heat **and** view animals in hiding most of the day. In fact, because Erna Nixon Park shows off Florida's seasonal changes, it's a wonderful place to bring your kids again and again.

Recommended for all ages.

Evans Road, Melbourne. Less than a mile from Melbourne Square Mall.

(407) 725-0511

Open 9 a.m. to 6 p.m. daily. Free.

This small outdoor showcase for tropical plants and trees is nestled at the heart of the Florida Institute of Technology campus, minutes from any shopping area in Melbourne. Unfortunately for budding naturalists, most plants are not identified, but this academic oversight seems not to bother children, who appreciate immediately their entry into "the jungle."

A tributary of nearby Crane Creek meanders through the gardens; several concrete paths and

9

F.I.T. Botanical Gardens

150 W. University Blvd., Melbourne. On the campus of Florida Institute of Technology one mile south of U.S.

*Highway 192 on either
Babcock Street or
Country Club Road.*

(407) 768-8000

bridges wander around and over its small bed. Always dark and cool and quiet, the gardens are a wonderful place to bring small children for a quick escape from the horrors of being housebound or following a rigorous shopping trip. The trails are delightfully serpentine — kids can pretend anything here. Benches are strategically set along the trails, so parents can sit and enjoy the silence while children explore.

Small children love the covered bridge not far away from the western entrance; the bridge leads to a parking lot on Babcock Street. Parking can be a problem at F.I.T., but visitors' spaces are usually available at the main entrance to the campus along Country Club Road.

F.I.T.'s student union is just a few yards west of the gardens. With its own post office, bookstore and food service, the Union fascinates kids old enough to consider what college is really like — they can sit in the square in front of the Union and watch the collegiate world go by. F.I.T.'s students seem to welcome young visitors.

The F.I.T. Gardens can become a small haven for families who live nearby. A few minutes here can restore harmony for parent and child. Even a short visit helps parents rediscover the reverence most children have for the natural world.

Recommended for toddlers through teens.

Jetty Park

*400 E. Jetty Road, Cape
Canaveral. Take State
Road A1A north out of
Cocoa Beach and
follow the signs to Port
Canaveral. Entry to the
park and port areas is
off George King
Boulevard.*

(407) 783-7222

Open 7 a.m. to 8:45 p.m.

Rock climbing on the jetty and fishing are the big draws at pretty little Jetty Park, at the South Dock area of Port Canaveral. Kids can cast a line here while they watch the big cruise ships come and go from the port area. A raised boardwalk affords a fine view of the boats and the dunes. An observation area atop the concession building is an even better vantage point, and also the best place to take pictures.

The park also has a volleyball net, full-time lifeguards from June to September; picnic tables, a campground, and playground equipment.

The North Dock area is a better site from which to see the ships come in. There is parking right near the water and many families just pull up here and fish while they watch the boats. Kids can also see a forest of yachts and cruisers on land at the many marinas and boat repair shops on the North Dock. If you plan to make a day of it at Port Canaveral, this is also the spot for restaurants (Oyster Island and Capt. Ed's) and picnic supplies.

Recommended for all ages.

Katrina and Brandon Nunes on a lunar exploration at Kennedy Space Center.

Open from 9 a.m. to 6 p.m. daily. Last tour bus departs at 3:30 p.m. Bus tour costs around $4 for adults and $2 for children. IMAX Theatre tickets are around $3 for adults and $2 for kids.

Kennedy Space Center

It's hard to find a kid these days who doesn't have at least one space-inspired toy or gadget in his toy box. But put away the laser guns and Space Invaders games for a day and show children what started it all at the Kennedy Space Center.

Smaller children might find the two-hour bus tour rather tedious, but the tour stops frequently for walks around some of the rockets and launch facilities. A simulated launch control room and fake launch near the start of the tour offers a valuable "you are there" learning experience for all ages.

Spaceport, the privately-run tourist area, is contained in a series of air-conditioned buildings for year-round sightseeing. The exhibit showing the history of space flight is especially instructive and the 70mm film *The Dream is Alive* at the IMAX Theater in

Take State Road 405 across the NASA Causeway to the space center.

(407) 452-2121

9

Galaxy Center is a thunderbolt of insight into flight crew training and launches.

If kids overdose on the grander sights here, take a walk through the quiet, cool art gallery in the theatre building. Artists from all over the world have contributed to this visual journey, inspired by American's reach for the stars.

Refueling stops are plentiful around Spaceport. The Orbit Cafeteria offers indoor seating; The Lunch Pad has barbecued ribs on its menu and several outdoor shops sell everything from beer and pizza for grownups to ice cream and soft drinks for all.

Film and souvenirs from laser photos to NASA hats are available in The Gift Gantry.

Ticket counters open at 9 a.m. so roll the kids out early to avoid the ever-increasing crowds at the space center. The trip can take a full day or a half day, depending on how long you linger over lunch and in the souvenir shop.

As day trips in Central Florida go, Spaceport can rightly boast that it is the best deal around. For launch information, call toll free in Florida only (800) 432-2153, from 9 a.m. to 8:30 p.m.

Recommended for age 5 and up.

Ron Jon's Surf Shop

4151 N. Atlantic Ave., Cocoa Beach.

(407) 799-8888

Open 9 a.m. to 11 p.m. daily.

Surfer kids have every reason to love Ron John's, Florida's most flamboyant surf shop. The whole family can shop here for the latest in beach apparel and equipment from swimsuits to beach unbrellas.

The neon-bright walls are lined with zillions of T-shirts, inflatable beach toys and floats, surf boards, skateboards, kites, stickers, jewelry, hats and sun tan lotions. The mirrored ceiling and zany murals give the store a beach party atmosphere, so it's just fun to shop here.

The good news for kids is that they have their own section of the store now, where they can shop for T-shirts and sweatshirts in their sizes (infant to pre-teen). Other children's clothing is found among the adult racks, but is clearly marked by size. A whimsical selection of toys in the kids' section includes Marine Band harmonicas, stuffed animals and water-toys like pink elephant water pistols.

Next to the centrally located fountain, a glass elevator awaits to take shoppers upstairs. Here you can find athletic shoes, women's wear, posters and restrooms. And, of course, more T-shirts with variations on the surf cruise/Ron Jon theme.

Many members of the sales staff are surfers and help youngsters choose the board that's right for them, according to height and weight. Ron Jon's scuba center, at the back of the store, offers equipment sales and rentals, and scuba lessons from beginner to dive master level. Children age 12 and older may take scuba lessons, if a parent takes the classes with them.

Recommended for age 8 and older.

Open 10 a.m. to 5 p.m. Tuesday through Friday; 10 a.m. to 4 p.m. Saturday. Admission: slightly more than $2 for adults, around $1.50 for children. Kids under age 3 are free. Members are admitted free.

Space Coast Science Center and Museum

1510 Highland Ave., Melbourne. One block east of U.S. Highway 1 and two blocks north of Eau Gallie Boulevard (State Road 518).

(407) 259-5572

The Science Center invites kids into learning. There's a lot of space here, and kids are welcome to roam and experiment with the equipment provided for their education in this free-spirited atmosphere. Among the permanent displays are a group of computers set up for math-type games, some simple enough for a pre-schooler to use. Other permanent exhibits include a room to demonstrate optical illusion and simple demonstrations of momentum and gravity.

Kids are encouraged to use their whole bodies in learning, even in the Nature Room, home for a number of living animals. These include snakes and, occasionally, turtle eggs maintained through the hatchling stage and then released into the wild.

Approximately every two months the Center sets up a new rotating exhibit, so successive visits continue to stimulate parents and children. These vary widely; an exhibit studying lasers and holography was recently followed by one about sharks. Temporary exhibits are hands-on, too.

Considering the free and easy atmosphere, the acoustics here are a marvel — the museum never seems noisy.

Exploration Station, the museum's first-rate gift shop, offers a wide range of games, posters, T-shirts, even high-tech gifts for adults. It also stocks a variety of books and supplies for science fair projects, a potential boon for desperate kids (or parents!).

For a nominal charge, the Center offers science

9

classes for elementary school kids on Saturday mornings and will provide theme birthday parties for the children of members.

No food is available, but the Center, in the heart of old Eau Gallie, is near several restaurants and across the street from Brevard Art Center and Museum. It's also less than two blocks to Pineapple Park, a lovely municipal playground right on the Indian River.

Recommended for age 3 and older.

Turkey Creek Sanctuary Park

1502 Port Malabar Blvd. N.E., Palm Bay. Adjacent to the Palm Bay Community Center, between U.S. Highway 1 and Babcock Street on Port Malabar Boulevard.

(407) 727-7100

Open daily, sunrise to sunset.

Turkey Creek Sanctuary Park preserves Central Florida in pristine serenity. A boardwalk begins just beyond the shaded picnic area and leads visitors past a sand pine forest and along the slow-moving creek. Wooden signs describe natural habitats along the way; smaller cards identify native plants.

At a fork in the boardwalk, kids can choose to walk out the Treehouse Trail, which ends up on a small platform as high as the nearby oaks. Here parents can share the sense of being "up a tree" with their kids. Point out the bromeliads attached to the trees, and listen together to birds and squirrels chatter in the shade.

The other trail winds through the mature hammock. Palms and hardwoods tower over a lush carpet of palmettoes, bracken and muscadine. When the creek widens out, kids enjoy getting close to the creek; there they watch fish, turtles, occasionally even manatee, warm themselves in the sunny pool. This is a great spot to rest with a cold drink. Bring your own — no snacks are available in the park.

For ambitious families, Turkey Creek has a wonderful canoe run. The park does not rent canoes, but if you can bring your own, this is the best way to explore the park. Canoeists can either portage in to the canoe deck from the main parking lot, or use the public launch at the Captain's House, 1300 Bianca Drive, Palm Bay. Distance is about a quarter mile to the launch ramp.

Recommended for all ages.

Chapter 10

• • • • • • •

THE JUNIOR SPORTY SET

Water sports, anything on wheels delight youngsters year-round

S ports, sports, sports are a year-round pursuit for Florida kids. The sunny climate here allows children to watch and do an unusual array of sports for all seasons.

Many sports activities listed are family affairs, with Mom and Dad taking children to see fast cars, fast boats or sky divers. But there's no shortage of participation in child-oriented programs in archery, water skiing and even deep-sea fishing. Parents are required to accompany young children at most activities and safety comes first, especially at racetracks and water sports.

As with any adventure, calling ahead can save time and ensure a good time for all. When calling about outdoor activities, ask about rain dates and covered picnic facilities in case there's an unpredicted shower.

• Karl Miller "gets air" at Orlando BMX track.

E njoy the thrill of the Olympics close to home. Sunshine State Games and Junior Olympics are held annually at this huge indoor pool. Group and private swimming and diving classes are offered for children of all ages and skill levels. Call for fees and schedule.

Recommended for age 8 and older.

10

Aquatic Center

8444 International Drive, Orlando.

(407) 345-0505

BMX Racing

BMX Lane off State Road 50 just west of the Central Florida Fairgrounds in Pine Hills.

Races are held each Saturday at 8 p.m., with practice beginning at 6 p.m. except during January, February and March when they are held at 2 p.m. with practice at noon. Additional practices are held Thursdays from 6 to 8:30 p.m. Beginner clinics are sometimes held on Sundays from 1 to 3:30 p.m.

Some 125 to 250 bike riders gather each Saturday at the Orlando BMX track to test their skills on its hills and curves.

The all-volunteer Orlando BMX Parents Council almost five years ago transformed a three-acre landfill into a clay track complete with bright lights and bleachers. The group is now constructing a mountain bike track right next door.

Although the majority of racers are boys and girls, there are some adults that regularly compete in the older category. Some racers are as young as 3.

All that's needed to race is a 20-inch BMX bicycle. Bikes must be inspected, and crossbars and handlebars must be padded, as well as the frame and gooseneck. If the bike has a kickstand, chain guard and reflectors or other gadgets, they must be removed. Riders must wear a helmet (available to rent at the track for $1), long sleeves or elbow pads, long pants, shoes and socks.

Beginners may race for a 30-day trial period, without paying the license fee of $25, to make sure they like racing. After they purchase the license, they start earning points toward participation in state and national races. Trophies and ribbons are awarded at each race, or riders can earn points toward a U.S. Savings Bond.

"There's no price you can put on keeping a child out of trouble," says track director Art Beeler, about what motivates him to devote much of his leisure time to the young riders. He says the goal of BMX is to teach competition and bike safety. For instance, "we try to teach them how to roll with a fall," he adds. Some 70,000 kids rode the track in one recent year and there was only one serious injury.

Recommended for age 3 and older.

Open 1 to 5 p.m. Tuesday-Saturday, except holidays. Admission is around $1 for adults and 50 cents for children under 12.

Birthplace Of Speed Museum

Since the early part of this century, man's quest for attaining high speeds has often brought him to the sands of Ormond and Daytona Beach. A fire gutted the famous Ormond Garage — the first "Gasoline Alley" — in 1976, and many of racing's early treasures were lost forever. The collection of memorabilia assembled at the Birthplace of Speed Museum is not vast by any means, but it nonetheless presents an interesting look at speed's early pioneers. The highlight of the small museum (which includes an adjacent library of racing literature) is a shiny red replica of the Stanley Rocket in which driver Fred Marriott broke the sand speed record in 1906, achieving speeds of 127 mph. A year later, in the same machine, Marriott was clocked in excess of 197 mph before a spectacular crash along the beach destroyed the vehicle, leaving only its boiler. Remarkably, Marriott survived.

160 E. Grenada Blvd., Ormond Beach, two blocks south of State Road A1A.

(904) 672-5657

Also on display are a 1920 Model T Ford; a 1928 Model A; and Dan Herman's Rocket Cart, a go-cart-like structure powered by a pair of rocket engines, capable of traveling 160 mph. The walls are dotted with pictures that chronicle various achievements in speed, including a photo of Glenn Curtiss' V-8 motorcycle that crossed the beach at 136.3 mph in 1904.

The museum can be thoroughly covered in less than an hour, and kids can get their photos taken in some of the machines. If taking the family to the famous Daytona 500 is on the agenda, the museum serves as a foundation that makes one appreciate speed's early daredevils, in the town "where it all began."

Recommended for age 6 and older.

Open from 10 a.m. to 8 p.m. Monday through Thursday; Friday and Saturday from 10 a.m. to 6 p.m.

Boots 'n' Bows Southeastern Archery

This is a great place to get your kids involved in a clean, indoor-outdoor sport. National competitors Manny Garcia and Laura Cale Van Wie welcome kids to learn the sport on their indoor range that can accommodate seven to eight archers at a time.

10

At the corner of Gatlin Avenue and South Orange Avenue in South Orlando.

(407) 851-4440

Also, they work with den mothers and scoutmasters on special rates. Garcia said they charge only $10 for a group of 10 youngsters. Some scoutmasters bring scouts there to earn their merit badges.

Furthermore, Van Wie, who competed nationally under the name of Laura Cale from Merritt Island, often goes and puts on archery demonstrations at schools and various functions for kids. "She's great with kids," said Garcia, who was a national competitor in Texas before moving to Orlando.

"It's great to have a job and get paid for something you love to do," said Garcia, who shows the kids how to hit targets and ballons at the indoor range. Garcia also is bow hunting advisor for Hoyt-Easton archery equipment manufacturers.

Youngsters and their parents may enjoy seeing some of the top archers in the nation compete on Tuesday and Thursday nights at the indoor range from 7 to 9 p.m.

This is the safe way to let children learn the fundamentals of the bow and arrow before venturing outdoors to participate in the sport. Learning from experts in the beginning can make all the difference.

Besides being a healthy and enjoyable sport, archery is probably the oldest sport around.

Recommended for age 8 and older.

Central Florida Race Tracks

Orlando Speed World, Orlando Speed World Dragway and Orange County Raceway are on State Road 50 near the State Road 520 intersection, about 15 miles east of State Road 436 in Orlando. New Smyrna Speedway is at the

Orlando Speed World Speedway holds races beginning at 8 p.m. Fridays throughout the year, while the affiliated New Smyrna Speedway schedules races beginning at 8 p.m. Saturdays throughout the year, and at 1:30 p.m. on some Sundays. Ticket prices for both tracks range from $8 to $15, and children 12 and younger are admitted free when accompanied by an adult.

Orlando Speed World Dragway holds races beginning at 4:30 p.m. Saturdays throughout the year, with testing and grudge racing beginning at 6 p.m. Wednesdays. Admission on Saturdays is $10; admission on Wednesdays is $7 for men and $5 for women. Children 12 and younger are admitted free when accompanied by a parent.

Orange County Raceway holds motorcycle and all-terrain vehicle races every Saturday, mixes in flat-track races the second and fourth Saturdays of each month and adds mud bogging and sand drags to the schedule on the third Saturday night of each month. Competition begins at 8 p.m. Admission is $7, and children 12 and younger are admitted free when accompanied by an adult.

In a motorsports world dominated by big-bucks cars and sponsorship, young racing fans may well wonder how a person gets started on the road to Daytona or Indianapolis. This eclectic bunch of race tracks, all located within a short distance of Orlando, helps provide an answer.

In the gritty, down-home atmosphere of Orlando Speed World and New Smyrna Speedway, where the cars can range from $1,000 salvage-yard refugees to $30,000 special-bodied Camaros, drivers and mechanics hone skills that can take a lucky few to the major leagues of racing.

Or leaping from a small asphalt oval to a big one may be less of a consideration than simply enjoying a moment of glory in front of friends and neighbors — especially when that moment may have been engineered through hard family teamwork.

Racing at Speed World and New Smyrna can be a family enterprise, as often is the case at the adjacent Orlando Speed World Dragway, where the object is to fly through the quarter-mile as swiftly as machinery can take you.

Being a fan at these small tracks can be as much of a family affair as the racing itself and offers an interesting and exciting alternative to more typical sports activities.

Even more exciting for youngsters interested in cars and racing is the opportunity, for only a few dollars more than grandstand admission, to actually go into the pits at the oval tracks and see closeup the machines that scream and grumble their way around the track.

At Orange County Raceway, which its management likens to a 50-acre sandbox, kids as young as 6 race mini-motorcycles on a flat dirt track, while entrants 10 or older race all-terrain vehicles. A number of father-son teams compete in the all-terrain competition. Beyond the cost of acquiring the requisite machinery and protective clothing, entering an event usually requires a $10 registration fee.

Soft drinks and snacks are available at these facilities, but taking along a small cooler of food and refreshments is a good idea. Because you will be in

intersection of State Road 44 and County Road 415, 12 miles east of Interstate 4 and six miles west of New Smyrna Beach.

Orlando Speed World,
(407) 568-1367;
Orlando Speed World Dragway,
(407) 568-5522;
Orange County Raceway,
(407) 568-2271; New Smyrna Speedway,
(904) 427-4129

10

the great outdoors, rain gear, sweaters or jackets are recommended during wet or cool months. Those with sensitive ears or who want to protect their children's hearing should bring earplugs.

Recommended for age 8 and up.

Daytona International Speedway

A mile east of Interstate 95 off U.S. Highway 92 at main Daytona Beach exit.

(904) 254-6767

Open on various race dates during the year. Ticket prices typically range from $20 to $40 for a grandstand seat, and from $15 to $40 for infield admission. Children 11 and younger are admitted to the infield free when accompanied by a paying adult. Car parking costs $10. Single-day recreational vehicle parking costs $30; two-day RV parking, $40.

Children's fascination with cars and speed can move from imagination to reality at the Daytona International Speedway, one of the nation's premier auto race tracks.

The speedway's heavyweight events are the Sun Bank 24-hour road race in early February, the Daytona 500 stock-car race in mid-February and the Firecracker 400 stock-car race in early July.

Youngsters from the general public are not admitted into the pit area; however, an extra $15 per ticket currently buys admittance to the paddock, a parking and viewing area adjacent to the pits and close to the steeply banked, curving front portion of the Daytona tri-oval.

Although refreshment stands are available, racegoers are urged to pack plenty of cold drinks, sandwiches and snacks, not to mention appropriate clothing for Daytona's broiling days and potentially chilly nights. Sunglasses and sun screen are highly recommended.

For the 24-hour race, parents are advised to break up viewing into blocks of a few hours each — at the beginning, in the night hours and at the finish — coupled with rest, in a van or recreational vehicle or at a nearby motel (make reservations early).

Also, on days when no races are scheduled, parents and kids can climb into a grandstand and view the track for free. The track is open from 9 a.m. to 4:30 p.m. You should ask in advance when racecar testing will be in progress, which will make your visit more exciting — or whether tours of the track by van are available. If they are, adult admission is $1, and children under 12 ride free.

Recommended for age 8 and up.

This event takes place around the first week in November each year on Saturday and Sunday. Tickets are around $10 at the gate for adults, but advance tickets are less expensive and two-day passes are available. Juniors, age 7-17, can get tickets in advance for around $5 or $7 at the gate. Children age 6 and under are admitted free.

Florida State Air Fair

At Kissimmee Municipal Airport, between Interstate 4 and U.S. Highway 92.

(407) 933-2173

This air fair has it all — from the Thunderbirds, the crack U.S. Air Force jet fighter aces, to the U.S. Army's aerobatic parachute team, the Golden Knights.

Sponsored by the Kissimmee Rotary Club, the show also includes such daredevil exhibitions as wing walking and precision flying formations. If your children have never seen the Thunderbirds or the Navy's Blue Angels, they're in for a real treat. (Some years the Thunderbirds perform and other years it's the Blue Angels.)

This show has enough aerial action to keep the kids from getting bored. One minute it's the Thunderbirds zooming over with dazzling precision performances; the next minute it's the Eagle's three bi plane team also executing precision flying with their slower aerobatics. Wing walking is another exciting event for kids and adults alike. Only the most daring acrobats would perform outside the craft during flight.

Other attractions include the Performing Warbirds Show; Jim Franklin and Johnny Kazian with their Waco Mystery Ship; Bob Hoover, Strike commander, and the Saber Liner Jet; and Bill Beardsley flying the Bud Light Jet. Beardsley is a former Navy Blue Angel pilot. Shows may vary from year to year.

Static displays that kids can take in at the air fair include Warbirds, antiques, experimental aircraft, home-built and military aircraft.

The show's format varies some from year to year, but it is always a spectacular air show with few delays between events. The gates open at 9 a.m. each day, but showtime begins at 1 p.m. This gives the kids and their parents time to check out the static displays.

10

Parking for the air fair is free. For more information, phone the number listed at the top of the article or write to the Kissimmee Rotary Club, P.O. Box 2185, Kissimmee, Fla. 32742-2185.

Recommended for age 4 and older.

Freedom Sports

*3000 21st St. N.W.,
Winter Haven*

(813) 299-8689

Sailplane rides and flying lessons are $37-$110, depending upon duration, altitude and content of flight.

For adventure, there's nothing like a flight in a sleek sailplane or glider. The planes float on rising columns of warm air, just like hawks, eagles and other birds, and the absence of a noisy engine truly makes sailplaning a "natural high."

At Freedom Sports, owners Steve and Vicki Coan share with passengers of all ages their love of flight. Kids as young as 5 have enjoyed the smooth, quiet rides, as have adults and senior citizens. And, because sailplanes don't have engines, youngsters who decide to learn to fly can solo at 14 and get their pilot's license at 16.

"It's a great motivator," said Vicki Coan. "It presents a challenge, and kids can really come away with good feelings of self-respect. Once they've flown, they feel that if they can fly a sailplane, they can do anything."

High school and college students can even earn credits through a local community college for flying.

A basic ride lasts 10 minutes and costs $37. An introductory ride (the most popular choice) is 30 minutes and lets the passenger get the feel of the plane and its capabilities. It costs around $50.

Aerobatic rides are available for the more adventurous and run $70 to $80 depending upon the difficulty of the maneuvers performed. And an hour-long cross-country ride costs $110.

Recommended for age 5 and older.

Open from 10 a.m. to 5 p.m. daily. Admission is around $6 for adults and $3 for children ages 3-12. Children under 3 years are admitted free.

Museum of Drag Racing

Off Interstate 75 at Exit 67, 10 miles south of Ocala.

(904) 245-8661

The thrill of seeing a long, lean bit of fiery fantasy thunder through the quarter-mile in a few, short seconds is an incomparable experience, especially for the young and impressionable. However, drag racing is such a quick business you might wish you could freeze the action sometimes to let kids absorb what, exactly, these land rockets are and do.

Thanks to Florida drag-racing ace "Big Daddy" Don Garlits, you can do better than that. You can take youngsters to Garlits' Museum of Drag Racing near Ocala and stand within inches of some of the exciting creations that took drag racing off the streets in the 1950s and turned it into today's high-dollar, high-technology sport.

As meticulous and gleaming as the more than 100 machines it houses, the museum that "Big Daddy" built brags that it is the only one dedicated to the all-American motorsport.

Even children who haven't the slightest interest in race cars should be awestruck by the long series of "Swamp Rat" dragsters that have carried Garlits to fame, and by the fleet machines of such drag-race heroes as Craig Breedlove, Shirley Muldowney, Tom McEwan, Don Prudhomme and Art Malone.

Garlits' eclectic collection also extends to lovingly restored classic and antique autos; and visitors can carry memories of the museum away with them in the form of photos, T-shirts, decals and videos, on sale in the souvenir shop. Those who want to construct their own dragsters can even buy models of the real machines.

Depending on personal preference and children's patience, you can spend as little as an hour or as long as all day. Pack a lunch or grab some hamburgers for eating en route. One note: The rule in "Big Daddy's" place is that "children under 3 must be hand held."

Recommended for all ages, but especially those 8 and older.

10

Ocean Pier Fishing

State Road A1A and Main Street, Daytona Beach.

(904) 253-1212

Open from 6 a.m. to midnight daily except Christmas Day. Admission: around $2 for adults and half price for children age 12 and younger.

Ocean pier fishing is a great way to spend a morning, afternoon or evening. The cost is minimal and when the kids get tired, you can reel in the lines and call it a day — or night.

Fishing is good year-round at Ocean Pier where anglers cast shrimp, cut bait, clams and sand fleas to an assortment of bottom fish, including sheepshead, drum, Spanish mackerel, sea trout, pompano, blues and other scrappers. These fish feed along the surface waters and along the ocean bottom and offer anglers excitement and fun.

Take a picnic lunch along and be sure to pick a day that isn't too hot or too cold. You don't want to burn the kids out on their first Atlantic outing. Also, don't keep them out too long on the first trip. Leave when they are ready to go and they will enjoy this wholesome sport for years to come.

If you don't have your own rods, reels and tackle, you can rent it all at the pier. For under $10, adults can rent all the gear. It's less for children and they even throw in a free cup of shrimp for each pole you rent. Too, you can leave and come back later in the day or evening if you like at no extra cost.

If the kids get tired of fishing and want some additional thrills, you can take them up on the Space Needle or the Sky Lift. For each ride, the admission is around $1, but if you want to enjoy both, a combination ticket is available. The Space Needle ascends to 160 feet into the sky. From there, youngsters can see all of Daytona Beach for miles around.

There are picnic tables at the pier and some covered areas, including the snack bar. There they sell sandwiches — including barbecue — and soft drinks and other snacks.

Be sure to take along some hats and sun screen if you're going to do your fishing in the daytime. Also, it's a good idea to call ahead of time to find out what's biting if you're really interested in catching fish. Even if you don't, the kids will still have a good time in the sun and surf.

Recommended for age 5 and older.

Arena box office hours are 10 a.m. to 6 p.m. Monday through Friday, and 10 a.m. to 6 p.m. Saturdays. Box office is closed Sunday, except when an event is scheduled that day. For tickets, write: P.O. Box 151, Orlando, Fla. 32802.

Orlando Arena

Part of the downtown Orlando Centroplex. Take Interstate 4 to State Road 50. Cross over to Huey Street and turn right when you see the entrance.

(407) 849-2020

O rlando's newest entertainment and sports facility offers an exciting schedule for adults and children alike. There is plenty for all tastes, too.

The 15,600-seat indoor arena is the site for ice shows, basketball games, rock and pop concerts, truck and tractor pulls, wrestling — and even the circus. The Orlando Magic will play here starting in October 1989. Single and season tickets are available.

Tickets for other events go on sale well before opening day and are available at the box office on the east side of the building. Tickets are also available by mail or at Ticketmaster locations throughout Central Florida.

The new facility is long on extras for patrons. Neon signs and colorful banners direct you to your destination. The concourse is lined with enough concession stands and souvenir booths to make any kid leap with glee. Inside the arena, you'll find some of the best seating anywhere in a similar entertainment complex. Soft, theatre-like chairs make it easy to enjoy a long event.

The building also is designed to put the seats closer to the action. There isn't a bad seat in the house, except, perhaps the sky boxes, but you need $45,000 a year for one of those anyway. Furthermore, there are more restrooms in this complex than in most such facilities. It's not likely you'll have to wait in line with a squirmy, uncomfortable youngster.

You're not allowed to bring your own food to the arena, so if you want to eat you'll have to buy food there. The prices are no higher than you'd find at a local attraction. Another touch: If Junior just has to have another order of french fries, you won't miss any of the action because you'll be able to watch any of the 28 color monitors installed near the concession stands.

It's a good idea to get there early. Arena doors will open 90 minutes before each event. Add extra time if you plan to park in one of the downtown lots and ride a shuttle bus. In any case, plan to arrive early enough to buy popcorn and sit back to watch the latecomers.

Recommended for all ages.

10

Orlando Ice Skating Palace

Parkwood Plaza, 3123 W. Colonial Drive, Orlando.

(407) 299-5440

Public skating is scheduled 2 to 5 p.m. and 7:30 to 10:30 Sunday, 2:30 to 4:30 p.m. and 7:30 to 10:30 p.m. Wednesday, 7:30 to 10:30 p.m. Thursday and Friday, 12:30 to 3:30 p.m., 4 to 7 p.m., 7:30 to 10:30 p.m. and 11 p.m. to 1 a.m. Saturday.

Admission is in $5 range, slightly less for 12 and younger. Skate rental is additional.

Ice skating classes start each September and are open to children age 5 and older. Classes are held Wednesday and Thursday from 5:15 to 5:45 p.m. and Saturday from 12 to 12:30 p.m. The fee is around $70 for the 10-week class and includes the half-hour weekly lesson, 10 half-hour practice sessions, and two free passes for regular rink skating. Skate rental for students is additional. A second family member joining a class receives a 10 percent discount. Children should dress warmly for the sessions.

Recommended for age 5 and older.

Orlando Jaycees' Junior Fishing Tournament

At Lake Eola in downtown Orlando at Rosalind and Robinson.

(407) 896-0474, Orlando Jaycees office, or 894-5404, Tim's Tackle Box.

This event usually is held the first week in December beginning with registration from 7:45 to 8:45 a.m. Tournament hours are from 9 a.m. to noon, at which time the prizes are awarded. Registration is $1 per child. Only kids 12 and younger may participate.

The Jaycees fishing tournament, co-sponsored by the city of Orlando, is a great place to get your kids hooked on freshwater fishing. Furthermore, they may even win a prize during the competition where every kid's catch of bream, catfish and bass is a prize within itself.

Show the kids how to bait a wiggly worm on their hook, or bait it for them if they're too squeamish. Chances are, they won't be, though. Lake Eola provides a scenic backdrop for this annual event that features other extras along with the angling.

Clowns, balloons and even tae kwon-do demonstrations are all part of the show. Not to mention prizes, trophies and a Bassmasters show that goes along with the entertainment.

There are three age groups with prizes awarded to the youngster in each age group who catches the biggest fish. Also, there are top prizes in each age group for the most fish caught.

Furthermore, a grand prize, (sometimes it's a remote control car) is awarded the kid who catches the heaviest fish. A sleek Schwinn Phantom bike usually goes to the youngster who catches the most fish during the morning tournament.

Some of the rules include registering by 8:45 a.m. on the day of the tournament; children 6 and under under must be accompanied by a parent or guardian; participants must wear shoes and fish from the grassy bank around Lake Eola.

Also, anglers must fish with cane poles (rods can be used if reels are removed). Each participant must furnish his own pole, tackle and bait (no artificial lures may be used) and each kid may use one pole only and it must not be left unattended.

Parents may not aid in baiting or removing fish from the line except in the 7 and under age group. Nets and chumming up fish are not allowed during the contest. Kids must immediately turn fish in at the weighing station for counting and weighing at the end of the contest.

Recommended for ages 3-12.

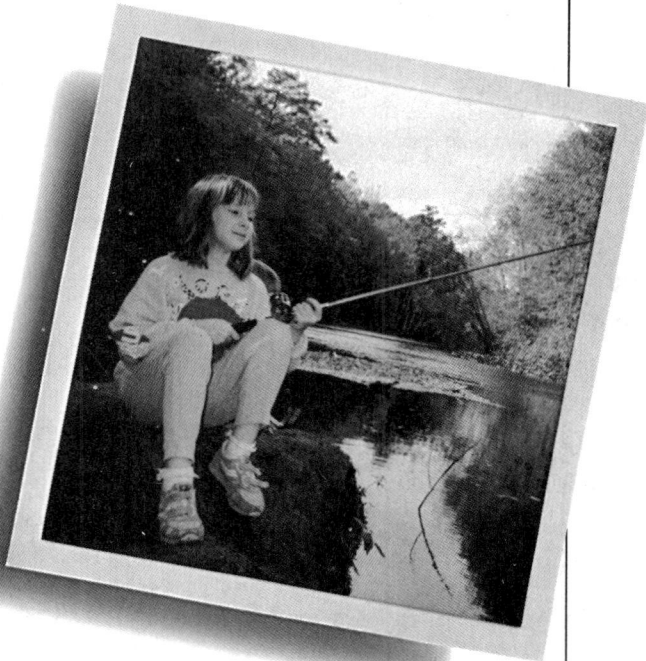

10

Alisha Hannah Bates gone fishing on the Oklawaha River.

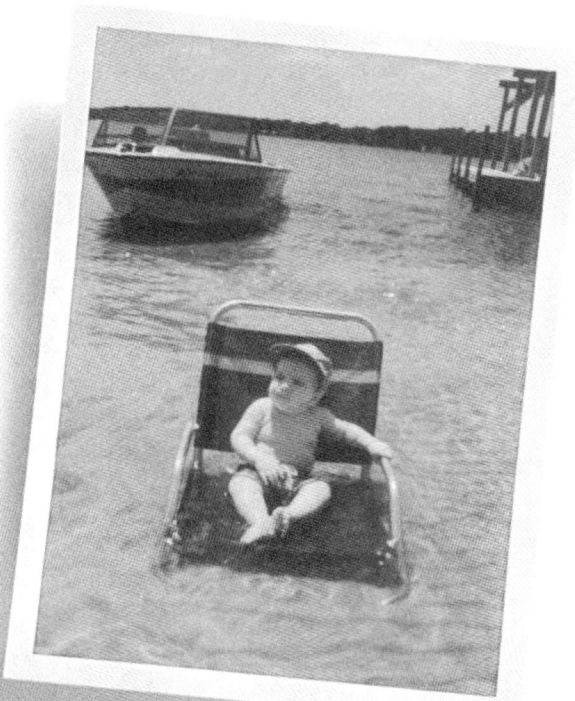

Austin Hoover cools off in Lake Conway.

Silver Dollar Regatta

Starke Lake, Ocoee. Lakefront next to Ocoee Community Center.

(407) 656-7796, Ocoee Fire Department

The two-day race is conducted the last of February or first of March each year. Admission is free.

Watching powerboats and hydroplanes zoom noisily around Ocoee's Starke Lake is an exciting spectator sport for youngsters. These boat racing aficionados come from all over the United States to compete at breakneck speeds while negotiating sharp turns and turbulent waves at speeds up to 100 mph.

Sponsored by the Greater Miami Power Boat Association, the Silver Dollar is one of the main races in a series of races throughout Florida called the Grapefruit Circuit. There is no admission to see these runabout boats and hydroplanes race for two consecutive days. The first races begin Saturday morning and continue throughout the day. On Sunday, however, the races do not launch until noon.

Youngsters and adults can see and talk to some of the drivers as they tune up their engines along the lakefront between races. Many of the drivers have family members crewing for them. One member of the Orlando Yacht Club who is a nationally-ranked sailor gave up sailing to be in the pit crew with his son, an avid hydroplane racing driver who later became a national champion.

Numerous champion drivers compete in the Silver Dollar Regatta and throughout the Grapefruit Circuit, which includes such cities as Jacksonville, Lakeland, Auburndale and Miami.

The Ocoee Fire Department provides free parking for spectators. The fire department also sells concessions at the races, including hot dogs and soft drinks.

Recommended for age 10 and up.

Open daily from 10 a.m. to sunset. For water-skiing instruction, Jet Ski, Jet Boat, or Waverunner rentals, the fee is the same for all: approximately $50 per hour; $30 per half-hour and $15 per quarter hour.

Ski Holidays

Near Interstate 4 and State Road 535 at Lake Buena Vista. Take exit 27 off I-4 and go south on S.R. 535 to private dirt road, Ski Holidays Drive.

(407) 239-4444

If your kids never have water skied, this is the way to go. Within 15 minutes, your youngsters should be up and skiing. Mike James, owner-operator of Ski Holidays, has a 95 percent success rate and has taught tots as young as 18 months to ski.

He starts the kids off with a ski boom attached to the boat. Then, once they've gained confidence, he starts them by holding onto the ski rope behind the boat. About 15 minutes is usually long enough for the kids. By then, their arms and wrists are tired from holding onto the rope.

For youngsters 14 years and older, Ski Holidays has Jet Ski, Jet Boat and Waverunner craft for rent. He recommends them all for fun water sporting, especially the Waverunner, which is easy to ride and takes very little skill to handle because of its unique engineering features.

The Jet Ski is fun, too, but it takes more skill and is more of a challenge. To get up on the craft, you must get it moving first while hanging out behind it. Next, you must get up on your knees. Once you've gained confidence, then you can try your hand at standing up and zipping across the water simultaneously.

All youngsters must wear life preservers while riding the watercraft or water skiing.

Ski Holidays teaches adults how to ski, also. You may want to learn how to ski or operate a Jet Ski or Waverunner alongside your kids.

10

Water skiing is recommended for 3 years old and older. The law requires that you be at least 14 years old to operate a Jet Ski or Waverunner.

Sky Dive DeLand

Just outside DeLand on U.S. Highway 92 at the east end of the DeLand Airport.

(904) 738-3539

The best months to watch sky diving are all months except June, July and August. Jump times are daily from 8 a.m. until sunset.

S ky diving is a sport that kids can enjoy without taking the plunge. At Sky Dive DeLand, where free fallers come from throughout the world to perfect their diving skills, youngsters can watch these daredevils of the sky leap from a plane at 13,500 feet and plunge to 2,500 feet above the Earth before pulling their rip cords.

"It's the closest thing to flying that one can experience," said Steve Branyon, an Orlando lawyer who gets his thrills by sky diving on the weekends at this popular jump site. "You actually fly through the air while controlling your movement and rate of descent," said Branyon.

Formation jumping is always fun to watch, especially when up to 40 sky divers plunge from the DC-3 that shuttles then up to the clouds. On a clear day, youngsters can see the men and women from the moment they leap from the plane until they flutter down on the landing strip just a few yards beyond the spectators.

Also, kids can watch the divers pack their own chutes before each jump. Some sky divers will jump four or five times on a clear day. Youngsters should bring a lawn chair along to rest between jumps. It takes the planes approximately 15 minutes to reach the altitude from which the jumps are made.

Bob Hallett, who owns Sky Dive DeLand, is such an adventurer that he shuts down the operation during the summer months and heads for the Grand Canyon where he is a white water rafting guide on the Colorado River. He has been sky diving for the past 16 years.

Parents who want to visit the sky diving site at peak times may give Hallett a phone call and he will arrange for groups to observe some of the teams that come from throughout the world to practice here. Among those are the U.S. Army's Golden Knights, the pararescue team for the Space

Shuttle, The U.S. Air Force Academy Team and government-sponsored teams from throughout Europe.

Hallett's wife, Jennifer, came over from Denmark five years ago to learn how to sky dive. That's how they met and today they sky dive together.

Any day that kids come to watch sky diving, Catherine Hocking, jump coordinator and a very congenial person, will give them a briefing and show them how to spot the divers as they leave the planes.

Several of the sky divers from Sky Dive DeLand participated in the sky diving festivities that opened the Olympics in Seoul, Korea. Also, the World Sky Diving Championships were held at Sky Dive DeLand in 1982.

Between jumps, kids may step across the street and watch soccer and football teams playing. Sky Dive DeLand sponsors YMCA teams in both sports who play next door to the jump site on weekends.

Recommended for age 5 and older.

Spring Training

Spring training time in Florida is the best time for young baseball fans to see and maybe even meet some of their favorite players. By mid-February, 18 of the 26 major-league teams are in Florida to work out under sunny skies as they prepare for the regular season.

For most fans, the "short season" in Florida is just as important as any pennant chase. Here is a chance to get close to the players, a time when almost everyone — players and fans — is relaxed. A time to sit and watch baseball come alive again after winter has been swept away and forgotten.

Florida has been a spring training home of major-league teams for 100 years now. The first team to train in the Sunshine State was the Washington Statesmen, who invaded Jacksonville in 1888. They ended up at a boarding house on the poorer side of town, paying $1 a night to a generous woman who gave them breakfast each morning.

One of the Statesmen was lanky Connie Mack, a second-string catcher who eventually entered baseball's Hall of Fame.

Hardly wanted for many of those early years, baseball teams are now well appreciated by the

10

towns that are fortunate enough to have a team each spring. Florida cities and counties actually wage war to get or keep a team.

Lee County and Fort Myers have been trying for the past year to lure the Minnesota Twins away from Orlando, where they have trained for more than 50 years.

Orlando's Tinker Field is one of the friendliest places to see the major-league players in the springtime. There are plenty of autograph opportunities for youngsters from Twins players and occasionally from the visiting teams.

When the Orlando Twins begin their Southern League season at Tinker Field, two players actually come to an autograph booth under the grandstand to sign autographs. Some teams — including the Minnesota Twins — may someday have a similar setup during training camp.

Another great place for youngsters to get autographs is Dodgertown in Vero Beach, spring home of the world champion Los Angeles Dodgers. The Dodgers are very friendly to fans. Dodgertown is a delight as fans actually can rub elbows with old Dodger heroes like Sandy Koufax and Roy Campanella and see the new stars like Orel Hershiser and Kirk Gibson.

A trip to Winter Haven can be an unforgettable memory to youngsters who can watch Ted Williams work on a side field with Red Sox minor-leaguers or catch Wade Boggs, Mike Greenwell and Dwight Evans in the cozy Chain O' Lakes Park.

The Kansas City Royals train in Haines City in a camp that is adjacent to the Boardwalk and Baseball amusement park. Where else could a boy or girl see George Brett and Kevin Seitzer play ball and then go for a bumper car or roller coaster ride?

The Houston Astros have their training camp in Kissimmee, and the players frequently take time to come to the stands to sign autographs and pose for pictures. Hall of Famer Yogi Berra, an Astros coach, usually has a silly grin for photo buffs and signs autographs generously.

The Cincinnati Reds train in Plant City, and the Detroit Tigers train in Lakeland. Pete Rose of the Reds is considered a tough autograph to get, but Sparky Anderson hardly ever lets anyone down in the Tigers camp.

If fans are polite, most players will respond in kind. Youngsters are encouraged to bring along an

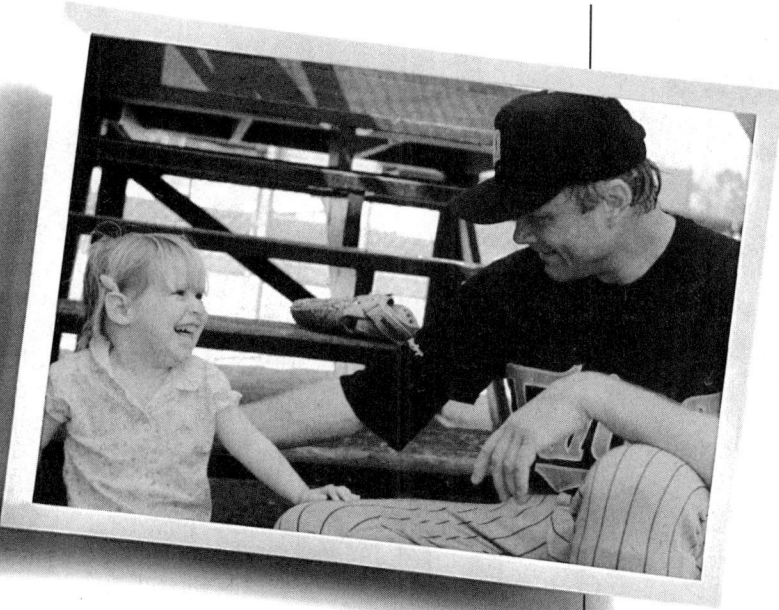

Anna Johnson in conference with Joe Niekro at spring training.

autograph book, baseball cards or pictures and to have a pen. The best pen for autographs is a Sharpie that can be found in most stationery or even drugstores. Don't ask for second or third autographs when there are others who haven't had their item signed.

Most of all, have fun and enjoy baseball in the spring.

Recommended for age 5 and older.

Open from 3 to 9 p.m. Wednesday through Monday. Admission: $5.50.

Thrasher's of Ocala

Thrasher's skate park has some 300 square feet of legal concrete that loops and dips and curves into waves and moguls. This is a refuge for skate boarders who are being chased from many cities' streets and sidewalks.

There is a freestyle area for younger skaters and a couple of half-pipes for the more advanced ones. Skaters are required to wear helmets, elbow and knee pads. The park has them available to rent.

An adult accompanying the youngsters is required to sign a waiver releasing the park from any liability before they are allowed to skate.

Recommended for age 8 and older.

3631 36th Ave. N.E., Ocala.

(904) 368-5088

10

Water Ski Museum

*799 Overlook Drive,
Winter Haven. Going
south on U.S. Highway
27, turn right at State
Road 550 then right at
Overlook Drive.*

(813) 324-2472

*Open 10 a.m. to 5 p.m. Monday through Friday.
Free.*

Central Florida has been dubbed by many as the "water skiing capital of the world." Thus, it's not surprising that the American Water Ski Association's Water Ski Museum and Hall of Fame is located in Winter Haven.

Here you'll see the father of water-skiing Ralph Samuelson's first skis, a video dedication to Cypress Gardens impressario Dick Pope, and numerous other exhibits detailing the history of the sport. Also featured are pictorial displays and trophies of U.S. national teams who've never lost at the World Championships, which have been staged every two years since 1949.

The hall of fame features oil paintings of inductees. Adjacent to this section is a video viewing room where visitors can watch tapes of exciting barefoot and trick skiing competitions.

Recommended for age 10 and older.

Wee Links Golf Course

*Enter at Magic Kingdom
main parking gate and
follow signs to the golf
resort.*

(407) 824-2270

*Open daily. Parking is $3. Greens fees for adults
are $13; children, $9 (includes clubs and up to 12
holes). Call the master starter to arrange a tee
time.*

The Wee Links, home of the International Pee Wee Championships, offers a course small enough, but challenging enough to keep the interest of young golfers. The course, which also plays host to a seven-week YMCA golf camp during the summer, recently was extended to nine holes, and the once-artificial greens were replaced with plush grass. Parents are welcome to play along with their kids but also can play Disney's other courses while the kids do their best imitations of Jack Nicklaus and Nancy Lopez.

Recommended for age 6 and older.

Open daily from 8 a.m. to sunset. Fee for the park is $1 per car, plus 50 cents per passenger 6 years old and older. Canoe rentals are $12 per day or a minimum of $6 for two hours. Required are a $12 deposit and a driver's license, which is held until the canoe is returned.

Wekiva River Canoeing

Wekiva Springs, five miles southeast of Apopka on Wekiva Springs Road, off State Roads 434 and 436.

(407) 889-3140

This is a great place for the kids to take a dip in the springs before adventuring on a canoe trip along the scenic Wekiva River — or, after your return trip. The springs' sparkling crystal and blue offer a refreshing swim.

Below the springs is the beginning of the picturesque Wekiva River. Here fish and wildlife abound, and, on occasion one may spot a black bear or a dear. Also, squirrels, rabbits, bobcats, deer, raccoons and other animals find refuge along the Wekiva.

You can make this trip as short or long as you desire. However, remember that paddling back against the current is much harder than going with the flow. If you prefer to paddle with the current and then return to the springs, it is advisable to paddle just a couple of miles and then paddle back.

However, if you prefer paddling with the current all the way, you can make arrangements to leave the canoe at Wekiwa Marina. To make this trip, though, you need to start your trip at Kings Landing near Rock Springs. This is an eight-mile run from Kings Landing to Wekiwa Marina. On this trip you will see lots of waterfowl, including herons, coots, ibises and water turkeys (anhingas).

Take along a picnic lunch for a relaxing outing. Also, include some bug spray in case the biting flies or mosquitoes happen to be hungry, too. Also, make sure there is a life preserver for every person on board, and that the non-swimmers wear theirs.

Recommended for age 5 and older.

10

DEEP-SEA FISHING

• • • • • • • •

Space Coast Sportsfishing Charters

Offshore charter boat trolling off Port Canaveral

(407) 291-9484

• **O**ffshore trolling in the blue waters of the Atlantic in your own plush sportsfishing boat for the day is a real turn-on for youngsters. Adding to the excitement is not knowing what kind of fish may strike at your bait next. It could be a blue or white marlin, a sailfish, wahoo, dolphin, king mackerel or one of many other fighters of the deep that attack your lure.

Parents can charter their own trolling boat for a day or share the expense and take several kids out fishing for the day. Most charter trolling boats will accommodate up to six anglers.

Be sure to take a long-sleeve shirt and a hat for your youngsters to ward off the bright sun's rays. Also, take along some 15 strength sun screen. Bonine is one of the better seasick preventives on the market. Be sure to read the instructions and have the youngster take the pill before leaving home.

Captain Dick Kelly of Orlando operates a 42-foot Hatteras sportsfishing boat out of Port Canaveral and welcomes kids aboard his fancy fishing rig. Also, he has an excellent record for catching marlin, sailfish, tuna, wahoo, kings, dolphin and other sportfish.

On weekends his wife, Gail, serves as mate on the boat. "She's great with kids," said the amiable Kelly. "She shows them everything from how to fight a fish to how to set the drag on the reel." The boat is complete with fighting chairs, air conditioning and the whole works. They will even videotape your trip upon request.

Cost for a full day of fishing off Port Canaveral with Kelly is $495 for up to six people. He furnishes everything, though, except for food and drink, including a mate to help boat the fish, rods, reels and lures.

Recommended for age 8 and older.

Sea Love Marina

If you decide to take the kids for a day or half-day of deep-sea bottom fishing aboard a party or "head" boat (they charge by the person or head), Daytona Beach is a good bet for fun and fish alike. These head boats can accommodate up to 40 or 50 persons per trip to the party grounds off Ponce Inlet.

Captain Frank Timmons has been fishing the waters off Daytona Beach and New Smyrna Beach since he was a lad. His boats venture out of Sea Love Marina at Ponce Inlet for a day or half day of fishing for red, mangrove, vermillion snapper, grouper, sea bass, triggerfish, sharks and assorted other fish that live along the bottom of the Atlantic.

His boats have the very latest in fish-finding and other electronic equipment. Catching fish is fun, but just being out on the water for a day is an adventure within itself. Non-fishing passengers can go along on a full day trip for half the price of a fisherman. Also, kids 6 and under can go free.

Cost for a full day on the water (from 8 a.m. to 4 p.m.) is $40 per person, which includes rods, reels, bait and tackle. For children 14 and under, the cost is $25.

For younger children, you may want to take the half-day trip for $25 for adults and $15 for children. Non-anglers can go for $10.

Take along sun screen, hats and long-sleeve shirts. Also, don't forget the sunglasses. Polarized are best because they allow you to see things under the water more clearly.

Recommended for age 6 and older for half-day trips and 8 and older for full day trips.

Offshore party boat bottom fishing off Daytona Beach-New Smyrna Beach.

(407) 293-2050 in Orlando or (904) 767-3406 in Daytona Beach

10

Chapter 11

• • • • • • • •

EXTRA! EXTRA!

Resources, travel tips and games for adventuring parents

• Books

Are We Almost There? By Valerie Levy, Perigee Books. Car games for the whole family.

BabyTravel: By Shaie Selzer, Patricia Burgess and Anne-Lucie Norton, Hippocrene Books Inc. An annual compilation of resources and hints on traveling with children.

How to Take Great Trips With Your Kids: By Sanford and Joan Portnoy, The Harvard Common Press. Covers preparations and tips for longer trips with children.

Kids' Games: By Phil Wiswell, Doubleday. A collection of great traditional indoor and outdoor games for children. The price is a little high for a plastic-binder book but it is money well spent if you have trouble coming up with rainy-day or backyard activities.

Kids in Orlando: By Mary Bold, Creative Printing. The bible of home-grown programs and activities for children in the area.

The Unofficial Guide to Walt Disney World & Epcot: Prentice Hall Press. Exhaustively researched insider's tool to help visitors get the most out of the Magic Kingdom and Epcot. The book includes children's opinions on rides and shows.

Jonathan Dean Johnston shops at Wal-Mart in Kissimmee.

11

Bookstores

Many bookstores have excellent children's departments. WaldenBooks, B. Dalton, Book Stop chains and many independent stores devote a sizeable part of their sales areas to this growing market. Ask for recommendations from the book buyer as to new classics and selections for the appropriate age and interest group. The sales staff may unearth some little-known literary treasures for you. Below are a selection of bookstores just for children.

Just for Kids: 966 W. State Road 434, Longwood, (407) 831-9885. For all ages from the toddler to the young scientist. Lots of accessories here, too, from jazzy book covers to the latest in stationery. Reference books for parents and inspirational reading for youngsters.

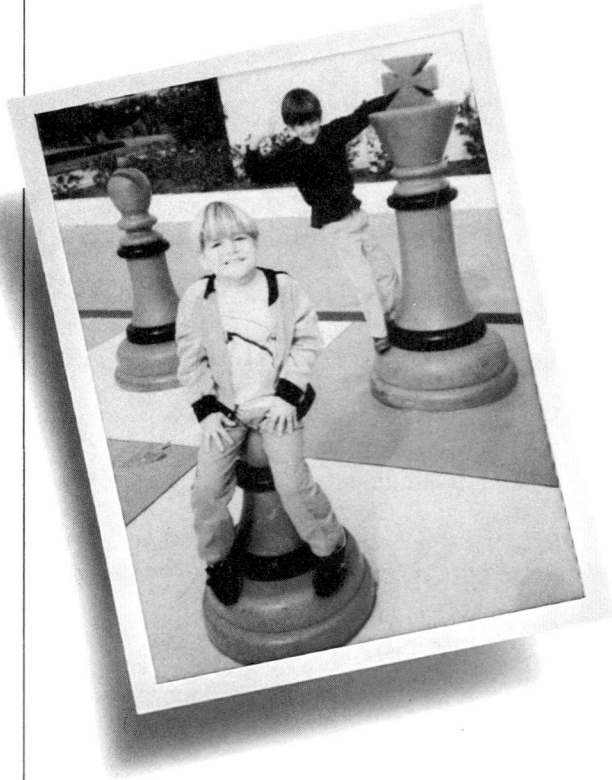

Cory and Kevin Mulinare at Places of Learning.

The Parent Store at Places of Learning: 6825 Academic Drive, Orlando, (407) 345-1038. Claims to stock the largest selection of children's books in North

America. This store for parents also features a children's plaza with a life-size chess game, giant maps and other types of learning recreations. A favorite with children is the guided tours of a giant map of the United States, complete with "real" lakes.

Pooh's Corner, Books for Children: 324 N. Park Ave., Winter Park (in the Hidden Gardens), (407) 628-8336. The collection of books for very young children is excellent here.

Parent Resources

Community Coordinated Child Care for Central Florida Inc. (4C): 1612 E. Colonial Drive, Orlando, (407) 894-8393. Offers advice on what to look for in a child care center, complete list of licensed and approved child care providers, and some subsidized day care for those who meet the financial requirements.

The Grove Counseling Center, Inc.: P.O. Box 4035, Winter Springs, (407) 327-1765. Nonprofit organization serving Seminole County, with its largest program being day treatment for chemically dependent teens, ages 12 to 20 years. Public awareness and education services also available to schools, church groups and civic organizations.

Jelly Bean Players: Dorothy Carlie, (407) 365-9301. Groups of 30 or more can request presentations on recognizing behaviors that can lead to child abuse. Reserve about two months ahead.

Jewish Community Center of Central Florida: 851 N. Maitland Ave., Maitland, (407) 645-5933. Has single-parent family services and teen seminars.

Parent Resource Center: 42 E. Jackson St., Orlando, (407) 425-3663. Mailing address: Valencia Community College, P.O. Box 3028, Orlando, Fla., 32802; or Seminole Community Colllege, Weldon Boulevard, Sanford, at the same phone number. Publishes a marvelous children's activity calendar with day-by-day schedule of crafts, recipes etc., and a newsletter, Parent Post. Center also sponsors support groups, education programs and outreach services. The center is a rich resource for anyone who loves children and is involved in raising them.

11

213

Chance Taylor Corbeil at the Baby Wellness Center.

Baby Wellness Program: Winter Park Memorial Hospital, 200 N. Lakemont Ave., Winter Park, (407) 646-7443. Call to reserve a place. The four-week classes are continuous, cost $35 each and include speakers and an outside activity. One class covers infant stimulation (from 6 weeks to crawling) while moms get back into shape after birth. Then development classes take babies through crawling and walking.

Florida Hospital Parent Education: 601 E. Rollins St., Orlando, (407) 897-1518; Florida Hospital Altamonte, 601 E. Altamonte Drive, Altamonte Springs, (407) 830-4321; Florida Hospital Apopka, 201 N. Park Ave., Apopka, (407) 889-1000. Call for fees and class schedules.

The Orlando hospital offers a range of Lamaze and exercise classes, breastfeeding and Caesarean classes. For families, the program includes a sibling class in which children ages 2-13 can learn about the birthing process, how to handle newborns, diapering and feeding, and see the obstetrics ward where mom will have their new brother or sister. Classes for first-time grandparents help grandpa and grandma learn about modern birthing procedures and what their sons and daughters will need as they become parents themselves.

Lamaze and Infant Care: Orlando Regional Medical Center, 1414 Kuhl Ave., Orlando, (407) 841-5111; Sand Lake Hospital, 9400 Turkey Lake Road, Orlando, (407) 351-8500; St. Cloud Hospital, 1500 Budinger Blvd., St. Cloud, (407) 892-2135.

ORMC offers first-time and refresher courses in Lamaze as well as basic infant care and Caesarean procedure. The Big Brother, Big Sister program for siblings is open to children ages 3-8. Grandparents, babysitters, family and friends are encouraged to join classes whenever possible. Call ORMC to register for Lamaze classes no later than the fourth month of pregnancy because classes fill quickly and are scheduled according to due date and whether or not it is the family's first baby.

Bike Trip Information: Florida Department of Transportation, Dan Burden, State Bicycle Coordinator, 605 Suwannee St., M.S. 19, Tallahassee, Fla., 32399-0450, (904) 488-4640. Don't leave home for a bike trip without calling Dan Burden's office. He can send biking families information about trails for every skill level all over the state. Burden is also the man to ask about bicycle safety programs in your area. His office is an excellent resource for the family that bikes together.

Children's Fitness Center: Live Oaks Boulevard, Casselberry, (407) 331-8123. The center specializes in noncompetitive gymnastics and development of motor skills and coordination through fitness instruction. Parents help out during workouts for the youngest children. Classes are held in half-hour sessions for children ages 1-3 and in 45-minute sessions for children ages 4-10, from 8:45 a.m. to 7 p.m. Monday through Saturday. Fees are $22 per month for half-hour sessions and $28 per month for 45-minute sessions one time per week. There is also a one-time registration fee of $10 per family. Fees increase if a child attends two or more classes per week. Call to reserve a place in the classes at least one month ahead.

Area **YMCAs** offer a wide variety of programs year-round for children and families. Parents are not required to be Y members for their children to participate in most programs. Some schedules include after-

11

school activities in which a Y bus picks children up after school so that parents can pick up kids at the Y after work. Ask your local Y about Home Swims, where a lifeguard or swimming instructor teaches a class at a home pool or apartment complex pool. Year-round recreation programs include swimming (starting with 6-month-old babies), soccer, basketball, track and gymnastics. Summer is camp time and Ys put on a full season of day camps and trips for all ages. Call for fees and information.

Downtown Branch: 433 N. Mills Ave., Orlando, (407) 896-6901.

Dr. Phillips Branch: 7000 Dr. Phillips Blvd., (407) 351-9417.

South Branch: 814 W. Oak Ridge Road, (407) 855-2430.

Tangelo Park Branch: 7101 Nectar Drive, (407) 351-3584.

West Orange Branch: 100 Windermere Road, Winter Garden, (407) 656-6430.

Winter Park Family Branch: 1201 N. Lakemont Ave., Winter Park, (407) 644-1509.

Eastbrook Program Center: 3510 Tourney Drive, Winter Park, (407) 679-9622.

Seminole Branch: 665 Lake Mary Road, Lake Mary, (407) 321-8944.

Golden Triangle Branch: 320 S. Grove St., Eustis, (904) 357-9500.

South Lake County Branch: 630 W. DeSoto St., Clermont, (904) 394-7243.

Osceola Branch: 2117 W. Mabbette St., Kissimmee, (407) 847-7413.

West Volusia Branch: 716 International Speedway Blvd., DeLand, (904) 736-6000.

YMCA Camps Office 433 N. Mills Ave., Orlando, (407) 896-9220.

Kids Arts and Classes

Civic Theater: 1001 E. Princeton St., Orlando, (407) 896-7365. A schedule of plays for young people is performed each season in the Loch Haven complex. Civic Theater also runs a series of workshops for different ages and skill levels.

Crealde School of Art: 600 St. Andrews Blvd. Winter Park, (407) 671-1886. Has classes for children and young adults. Call for fees and schedule.

DeLand Art Museum: 449 E. New York, DeLand, (904) 734-4371. A six-week series of art workshops is offered on Saturdays for children ages 6-12. A discount off the nominal fee is given to museum members.

James Best Theater: State Road 434 in Longwood's Watson Center, one mile east of Interstate 4. (407) 260-2020. Film and acting classes are offered for age 5 and older. Call for audition appointments, fees and schedule for workshops.

Jewish Community Center of Central Florida: 851 N. Maitland Ave., Maitland, (407) 645-5933. Summer camp with a broad range of "electives," including theater, music and art, runs for eight weeks. Children's attendance may be tailored to their schedule. A similar eight-week program runs after school during the winter.

Joan Wahl Puppet Theater: (407) 323-6349. Quarterly classes feature all facets of puppetry with guest puppeteers from all over the world. Ms. Wahl is currently head of the Central Florida Puppet Guild. Call for class rates, recommended ages and a schedule of shows.

Maitland Art Center: 231 W. Packwood Ave., Maitland, (407) 645-2181. Offers classes for children and young adults. Call for fees and schedule.

Mount Dora Center for the Arts: 138 E. Fifth Ave., Mount Dora, (904) 383-0880. Children's classes in ceramics, tie-dying and painting are offered periodically in conjunction with the city, usually for a four-week period.

Orlando Art Museum: 2416 N. Mills Ave., Orlando, (407) 896-4231. Classes in painting, pottery and sculpture are offered for kids ages 6-12. Call for schedule and fees.

Osceola Center for the Arts: 2411 E. Irlo Bronson Memorial Highway, Kissimmee, (407) 846-6257. Mailing address P.O. Box 1195 Kissimmee, Fla., 32742. Center holds two 2-week classes including instruction in art, music and drama for children ages 5 to 12. Classes are held from 9 a.m. to 12 p.m. Monday through Friday during the sessions, which begin in mid-June. Class sizes are limited to 50 children. Discounts are given to arts center patrons at the Century level and above.

Pine Castle Center of the Arts: 6015 Randolph St., Pine Castle, (407) 855-7463. Painting, pottery and

11

sculpture classes are offered for children ages 6-12. Call for information on times and fees.

Polk Art Museum: 800 E. Palmetto St., Lakeland, (813) 688-7743. Eight-week sessions in Introduction to Drawing and Painting and Adventures in Clay are offered four times yearly for elementary-age children. Discounts are given to museum members and summer art classes also are given.

Rollins College non-credit division: Winter Park, (407) 646-2632. A summer day camp, pre-first grade, junior high, high school and music programs are offered.

Young People's Theater: In the Ruth Henegar Center, New Haven Avenue, Melbourne, (407) 723-6935. Under the guidance of the Melbourne Civic Theater, YPT presents two major productions each year and special entertainments for community groups. Classes in acting, mime, make-up and improvisation are held for 6-12 year olds, usually in the summer.

Travel Tips

We don't know why, but Avon's Skin So Soft bath oil rubbed into the skin works to keep away noseeums. These invisible critters lurk in every corner of the state and many people, especially tender-skinned youngsters, can have severe reactions to them. For other bugs, bring along the bug repellant that works best for you.

If you plan to be on the road for a lengthy drive, give children notebooks, crayons and tape to keep their very own travel log. They can tape-in postcards and instant photos and "draw" their own conclusions about their trip with Mom and Dad.

Don't forget the sun screen when planning a day in the Florida sun. The higher the SPF (sun protection factor) the better for kids who burn easily.

Keep children (and yourself) fueled up by packing a cooler of juices and snacks (and don't forget the wet wipes) to take on your trip. If the family will be hiking, put lightweight munchies and foil-pack juice containers into your backpack. Granola, granola bars, fruit, nuts and raisins are all good touring snacks since they don't require refrigeration. Non-carbonated beverages travel well in plastic bottles. Try the type that bicyclers use.

Be sure kids are wearing comfortable knock-around clothes and shoes for day tripping. It's not a good idea to ruin new clothes or try to break in new shoes during an adventure.

New parents should make a nylon belt to attach to the bottom of their infant back carrier. Tie the belt around your waist to redistribute the baby's weight. You can find the nylon strips at sporting goods stores that cater to hikers.

Pack a traveling first-aid kit with items to care for routine injuries. Bandages, disinfectant, petroleum jelly for chapped lips, aspirin (for kids and adults) and first-aid cream are all musts. No need to let a scraped knee spoil a youngster's day.

Road Games

Clap Game: One person claps out the rhythm of a familiar song (Old McDonald) and others try to guess the name of the song. Winning guesser gets to clap next.

Count Up: See who can count the most of something (red cars or big trucks) in a specified time or by the end of the trip. Younger kids might like to draw their "somethings" while looking for them.

Don't Say It: One player is chosen, in turn, as the leader. The leader picks a word and forbids everyone from saying that word (like yes.) Then the leader asks the players questions designed to get them to say the word. Players must not say the forbidden word. First player to use the word is out.

Florida Places: One player says the name of a place; the next player has to name a place beginning with the last letter of the previous name. Example: Miami — Indialantic. If you're stumped, you're out. Last remaining player wins. (Younger kids can substitute animal names.)

Play Phone: The first player relays a message to the next player. Each person whispers the message to his neighbor without repeating it and the last player must say the message out loud. How close does the final version come to the original?

Storytellers: One person begins a story, continuing up to an exciting point; the next person picks up the tale and adds to it, and so on. Even small children can create characters and add to the plot in this game.

11

What Is It?: Draw a numeral or letter of the alphabet on a piece of a paper and let a child make a picture, animal or scene out of it.

What It May Be: One person names or draws an ordinary object and players try to come up with other uses for that object. For example a plate might also be a steering wheel on a toy car.

What's My Rhyme?: One player thinks of a word, then says, "Guess my word. It rhymes with (fill in the blank)". Number of guesses can be limited or unlimited. Word choices can be tailored to children or adults.

When I Go: First player says, "I'm going on a trip and I'm going to take a (fill in the blank)." Next player says the same thing and adds an item. Players must repeat items in order and add one of their own. Forget one or mix up the order and you're out.

Word Search: One person picks the name of a famous person (say, Abe Lincoln). Each player writes down the name and sees how many other real words they can make out of the letters in a limited period of time. Player with the most words wins.

Word Switch: A player picks two words with different letters, but the same number of letters. No proper names. The other players must change the first word into the second word a letter at a time, each change must form a real word. Example: from hit to pan would be hit-pit-pat-pan. A pencil and paper game for older children and adults.

Bryan and Ginger
Beckner wait for the big
one at Turkey Lake
Park.

Index

. . . . .

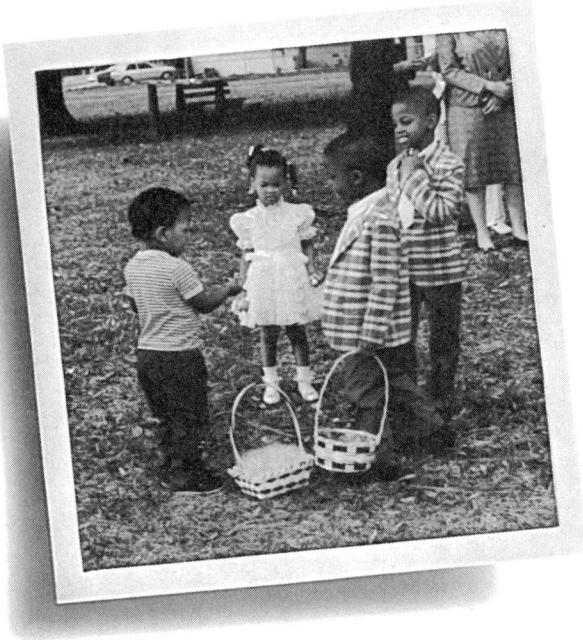

Michail Briggs, Ryan Briggs and Shonda Smith hunt for Easter eggs.

Laura Geier on the
dock at Lake Ivanhoe.